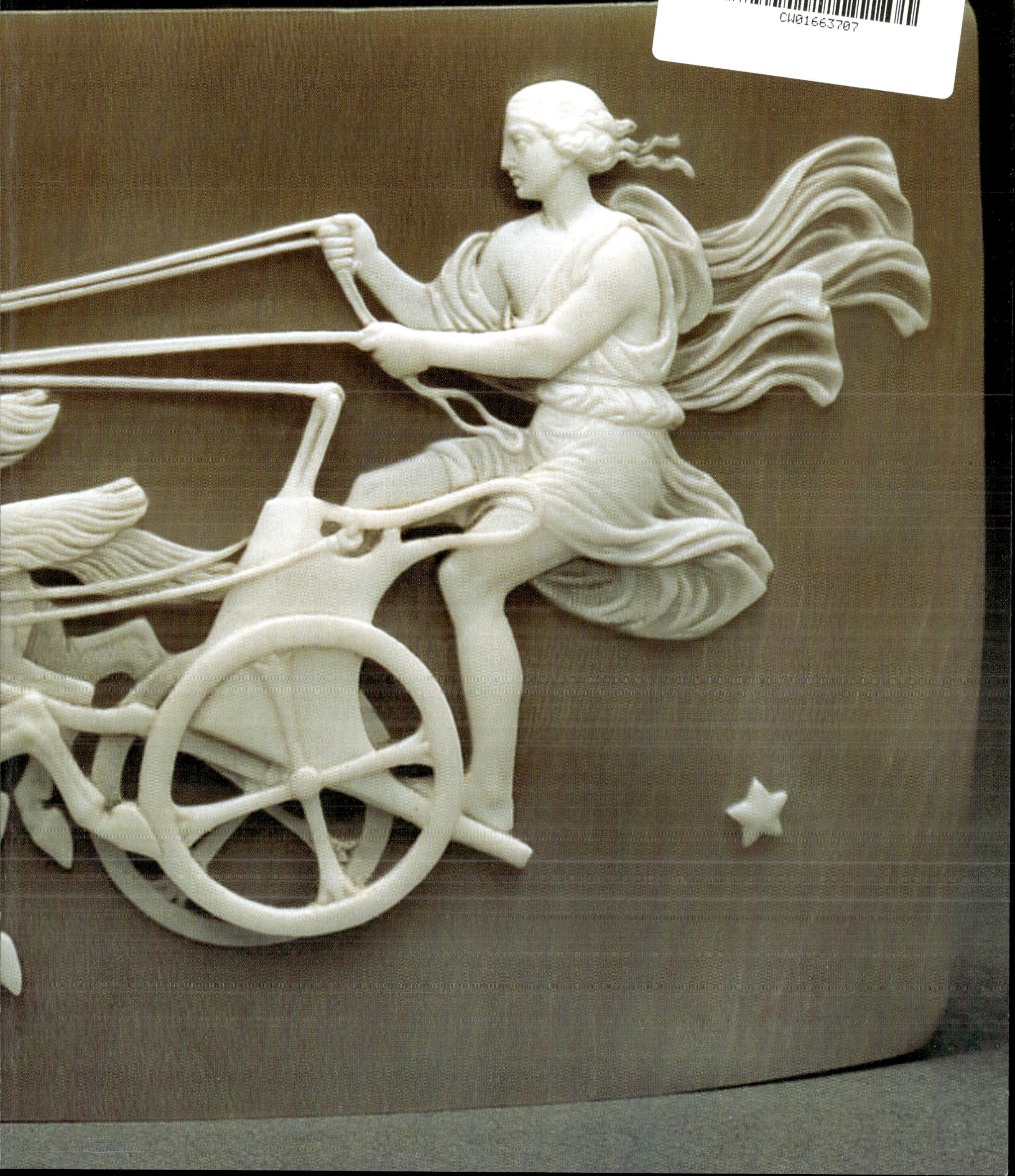

Nineteenth Century Cameos

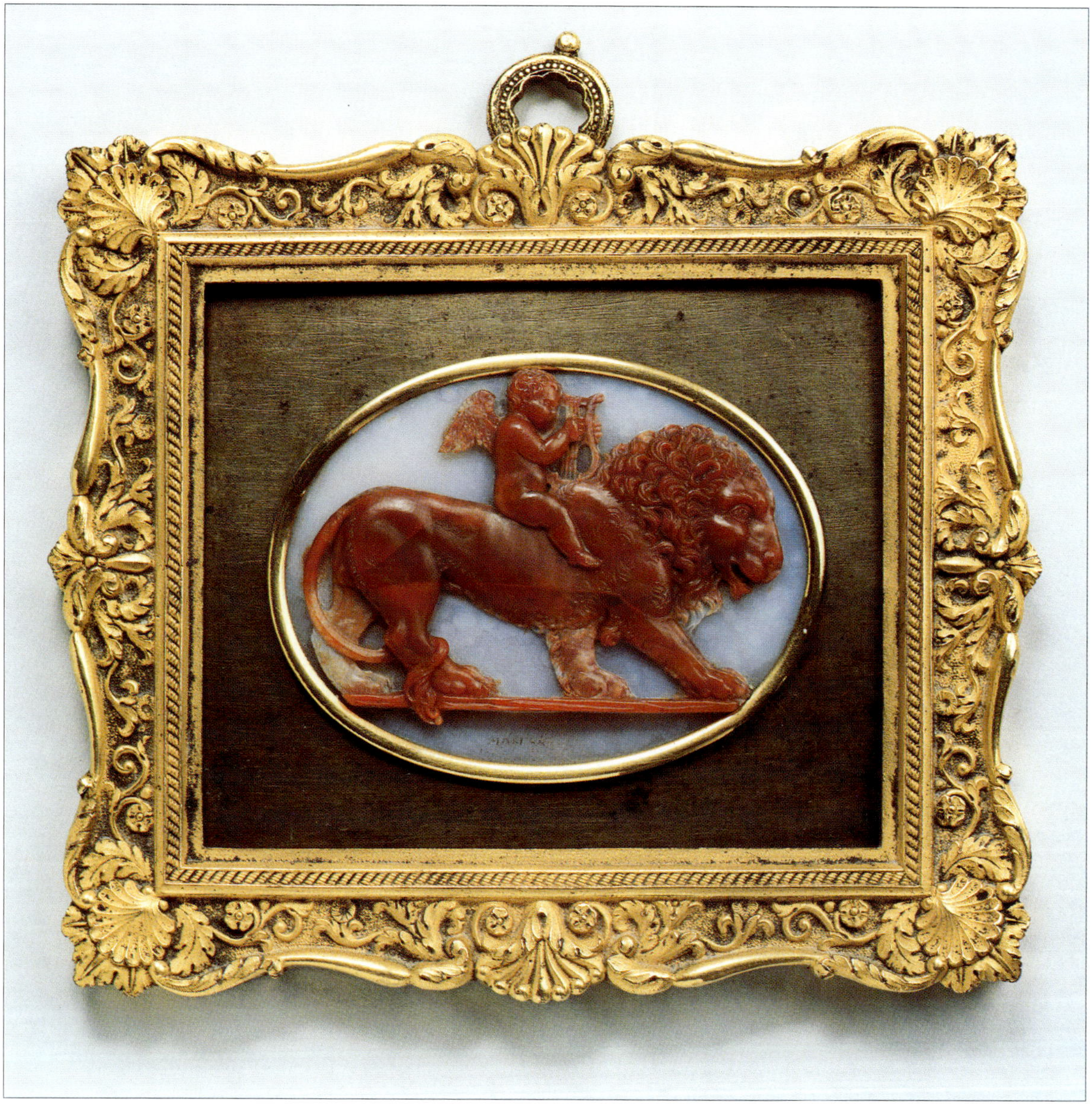

Sard cameo in ornate ormolu frame, circa 1800, 4½in. (11.5cm) long x 5¼in. (13cm) wide. Signed 'Morelli' for Nicolo Morelli, the celebrated gem-engraver who carved gems for Napoleon I. The subject is 'Amor Leonem Domans', after an ancient engraved gem signed 'Plotarchos', now in the Napoli Archaeological Museum. See Plate LIII in Stosch's Gemmae Antiquae Caelatae. *Cupid (Love) rides on a lion (Strength) and plays a lyre. Cupid has tamed the fierce creature, which willingly obeys him.* PRIVATE COLLECTION

Nineteenth Century Cameos

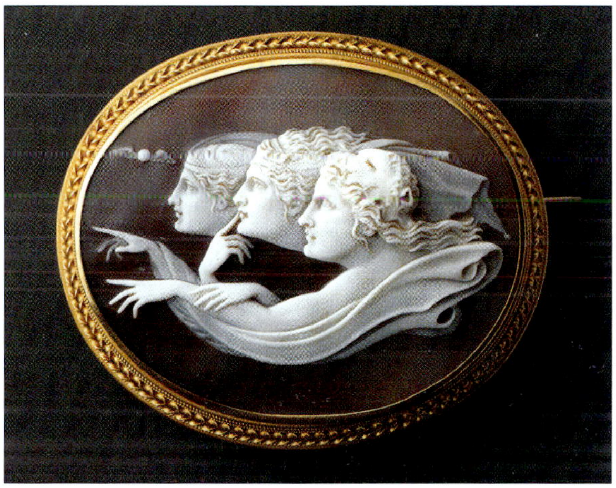

MICHELE ROWAN

Antique Collectors' Club

ISBN 1 85149 393 X

British Library Cataloguing-in-Publication Data
A catalogue record for this book is available from the British Library

Printed in England
by the Antique Collectors' Club Ltd., Woodbridge, Suffolk

CONTENTS

FOREWORD

Michele Rowan's book comes as a welcome addition to the cameo literature available today. It provides a straightforward guide to the fascinating world of Greek mythology portrayed on nineteenth century cameos. These dramatic tales are succinctly conveyed and well illustrated, bringing the ancient world into sharp focus. The book also includes information about materials and carving techniques and sensible advice on purchasing and caring for cameos. *Nineteenth Century Cameos* will be a treat for the antique jewellery enthusiast as an invaluable aid to interpreting the myths on cameos in museum collections as well as those available to the private collector.

Robert Raymond, FGA
London, 2004

AUTHOR'S NOTE

The subject of 'engraved gems' is certainly an expert's area and many eminent and scholarly works exist, documenting both the history of gem-engraving and important collections; yet I required a simple guide, a 'who's who' to identify the personalities from Greek mythology frequently appearing on nineteenth century cameos. Subsequently, I have endeavoured to present an accessible reference work to help interpret the vivid myths depicted on cameos.

In writing a book on engraved gems, the author realises she lays herself open to criticism by art historians, jewellery historians, scholars in the field of engraved gems, gemmologists and experts in the antique trade. Therefore, any corrections, amendments and additions will be gratefully received and noted in future editions.

NOTE ON PHOTOGRAPHS

The cameos illustrated are intended to cover a range, from superb museum pieces to affordable examples, available from antique dealers today. Where prices are quoted, they represent the vendor's retail price at the date of publication.

ACKNOWLEDGEMENTS

To the shops, museums and collectors who graciously allowed me to photograph their cameos to illustrate this book.

To Robert Raymond, Michael Bell, Peter Szuhay and Christopher Cavey for unstintingly sharing their knowledge and expertise.

To Sabine Genth-Zotz and Alexia Amato for translation of German and Italian texts.

To Lynn Miller of the Wedgwood Museum Trust for her help and advice.

To Vernon Layton and Nick Alloway for photography.

To Olivia Collings and Julie Fox for their support.

Most of all, to Sian Harlowe, my talented research assistant – without her input, advice and editing, this book would never have been completed.

THANK YOU

Michele Rowan

INTRODUCTION

All jewellery is personal adornment, designed to be worn. Yet the cameo, perhaps more than any other form of 'jewel', has long been appreciated as a work of art, an object of virtue, worthy of a place in a cabinet collection. For centuries engraved gems have been the subject of both scholarly research and avaricious desire. At various times in history, notably during the Renaissance and Neo-classical periods, a 'cameo fever' has obsessed members of royalty and many eminent collectors and patrons of the arts.

Cameos, being carvings in relief, in effect miniature sculptures, were ideal conduits for the revival of classical themes. Emulating the work of gem-engravers from the past, artisans in the nineteenth century carved their chosen materials to create figures or scenes which stood proud of their background. The striations in a stone or layers of a shell were exploited to enhance the prominence of subjects and were often used to effect a range of tones and markings. During the first decades of the nineteenth century cameos remained the province of erudite collectors, yet thereafter a transition occurred and they became fashionable items of jewellery available to a much wider audience.

The Neo-classical cameo revival in Britain occurred during the long reign of George III (1760-1820). The arts were pervaded with a taste for all things classical; painting, sculpture, architecture and fashion cast off the ornate Rococo decoration of the first half of the eighteenth century, and expressed the more formal and classical 'Empire' style. The study of ancient Greek and Latin, especially the work of Homer, combined with the 'Grand Tour' of ancient European cities, formed the basis of the young aesthete's classical education. The excavation of ancient ruins in Italy (Herculaneum from 1738, Pompeii from 1748) and Asia Minor inspired further interest in all aspects of civilisations which were idealised in British culture. Cameo carving provided the perfect expression of the Neo-classical mood and flourished as an art form. Gem-engravers from all over Europe flocked to Rome, 'Mistress of the Fine Arts', to practise their trade.

During this period serious connoisseurs avidly collected engraved gems (intaglios and cameos) of the ancient periods, along with copies by the most skilled engravers of the time. P. Stosch's *Gemmae Antiquae Caelatae* (1724) popularised ancient signed gems and provided carvers with ancient models. The Raspe Tassie catalogue, published in 1791, was another major reference work and etchings from *L'Antichita di Ercolana I* (1757) and *Pitture Antiche D'Ercolano* (1762) were copied extensively in cameo (see 'Satyr and Maenad', Plate 60, 'Vendor of Cupids', Plate 32). The work of eminent sculptors in Rome provided contemporary models for the cameo carver. Collecting reached its zenith by 1800 and the cabinets of Europe became widely known through illustrated journals. Through their collections, noted travellers and 'dilettanti' could confirm their elevated social status and display intellectual refinement and elegant taste. Sometimes false signatures were engraved on cameos, not so much in homage to carvers from antiquity, but in order to deceive prospective purchasers. Expert copies duped even the most knowledgeable collectors. The Polish Prince Poniatowski's famous collection of ancient engraved gems was rumoured, after his death, to exist largely of copies. The gem-engraver Anton Pichler (1697-1779) introduced the custom that contemporary carvers should sign their works, not only to establish their reputation and immortalise themselves, but also to prevent dishonest dealers cheating collectors. The celebrated engraver, Benedetto Pistrucci, described how this did not stop the unscrupulous:

> 'I must mention that the cameo-dealers began to practise deceptions with my works, which did not please me at all. Scarcely had they received from me those which I had executed for them, when they effaced my name, and wrote that of some old artist of much renown...or sold it as antique without any name at all.'
>
> Autobiography Of Pistrucci (1784-1855) from Archibald Billing, *The Science Of Gems, Jewels, Coins, And Medals*, 1867, page 147

A Scottish visitor to Rome in 1817-18 described the importance of this trade:

> 'hundreds of artists find support at Rome in making casts, sulphurs &., from ancient gems and medals, and in fabricating antiques, a most important and lucrative trade.'
>
> Charlotte A. Eaton, *Rome in the Nineteenth Century* Vol.II, 5th Edition, 1860, page 312

The Neo-classical spirit had germinated in France where Emperor Napoleon I championed the glyptic arts. At his coronation in December 1804 he chose to decorate his crown with cameos, and a school of gem-engraving was established in Paris. His Empress Josephine had great influence on the styles worn not only in French society, but throughout Europe. Cameos were often mounted 'en parure': double-drop earrings, festooned necklaces with multiple chains, belt-clasps (to be worn at the 'Empire line'), diadems and combs, all set in a delicate filigree goldwork known as 'cannetille' (see suite, Plate 30).

By the time of Queen Victoria's ascendancy to the throne in 1837, the Romantic and Gothic Movements, with their emphasis on the 'Imagination' and the dramatic, were becoming the prevailing themes in art, architecture, fashion and jewellery, superseding the more restrained feelings of Neo-classicism. The cameo lost ground amongst connoisseurs and became popular as a purely decorative item of jewellery within a changing social scene. The First Reform Act of 1832 had admitted a different social group to enfranchisement and the growth of industrialisation created a newly affluent social class eager to display its wealth. Amongst the 'nouveaux riches', women assumed the role of status symbols, their jewellery reflecting their husbands' economic success and also their social aspirations. The Victorians, visiting the Great Exhibition Of The Industry Of All Nations in 1851, marvelled at the attainments of their age – one characterised by innovation, technological advance, determination for supremacy and the desire for 'making it big'. Jewellery, correspondingly, became heavier, bolder and more ostentatious. Cameos too became larger and at times reached quite unwieldly proportions.

By the second half of the century the cameo had become essentially an item of feminine adornment. The Victorians were rather less concerned with mythological accuracy, instead requiring their cameos to follow the new aesthetic of Romanticism. Classical mythology was reinterpreted in the rosy language of Victorian sentimentalism. The maenads (bacchantes), for example, remained a favourite subject throughout the nineteeth century, but where they had been the wild, abandoned followers of Dionysus, now they were softened to resemble docile young maidens with vine leaves threaded charmingly through their hair. The coy images of mythological lovers, the ubiquitous cherubs, flowers and doves, all typified the Victorian passion for sentimental symbolism (typical examples Plates 35, 36, 39).

The demand for 'Grand Tour' souvenirs increased the desire for cameos and introduced the use of 'lava'. Coral, ivory and tortoiseshell offered yet further possibilities for the cameo carver. The renowned work of celebrated contemporary sculptors, such as Bertel Thorvaldsen, Antonio Canova, John Gibson and John Flaxman was another area fully exploited in cameo. Carvings after the works of Thorvaldsen and Canova are represented on Plates 10, 12, 21, 22, 25, 47, 91.

The cameo at its best is an art form of sculptural precision, great ingenuity and superlative craftsmanship. In the nineteenth century, probably more than any other form of jewellery, these gems closely reflected the changing influences and attitudes of the age.

Cameo Carving Tools

58 Lathe with pulley
59 Rotine
60 Strong lens (no. 70 magnified)
61 Plate
62-71 Various small tools which were alternated according to the carver's needs
72 Circular saw
73 Glazier's diamond (splinters of corundum or emery set in metal)
74 as **73**
75 Drill
76 Iron or copper tube with diamond powder and oil on the end

From Archibald Billing, *The Science of Gems, Jewels, Coins and Medals*, 1867 (illustration facing page 92)
COURTESY OF THE BRITISH LIBRARY

CAMEO TOOLS

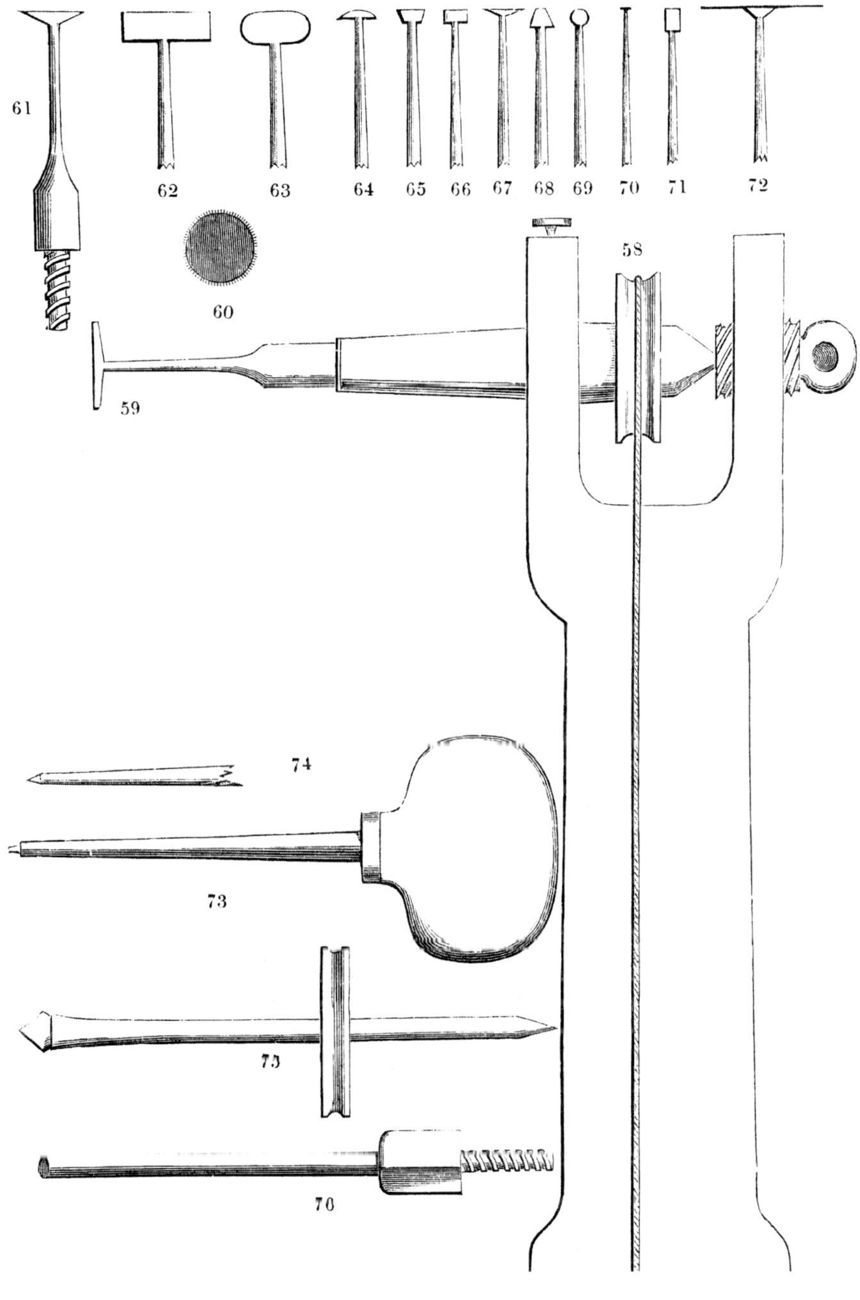

A BACKGROUND TO GREEK MYTHOLOGY

Many nineteenth century cameos were based on stories from Greek mythology, familiar to the classically-educated late Georgians and Victorians. In ancient Greece, *mythos* meant simply a 'word' or 'tale'. A myth was an entertaining story, a dramatic and exciting narrative, sung or recited to an audience by a poet, accompanied by music. These stories were about the lives and deeds of the gods and depicted the themes that preoccupy all societies – love, loss, death and redemption. Myths helped people define themselves and the world around them, articulating their fears and giving meaning to the otherwise unexplainable. They provided the Greeks with a sense of order and stability, confirming that ultimately the gods controlled all aspects of their lives:

> 'Pray to the gods. Theirs' is the power. Without the gods
> neither good fortune comes to men nor bad.'
>
> Anonymous, *Theognidea*, Greek, circa 6th century BC

Greek myths are believed to have been first recorded (as opposed to being handed down in the oral tradition) by the epic poets Hesiod and Homer in the late eighth century BC. Hesiod is thought to have named the gods and written their histories from the beginning of the world to the ascendancy of the Olympian gods in 'Theogony'. Homer recorded the roles and deeds of the gods in the *Iliad*. The question of whether either work was written by a single author remains a subject of debate. (As time passed, other poets embellished their stories, so multiple and often contradictory versions exist.)

The Greeks believed that the gods possessed supernatural powers, yet paradoxically they exhibited human fallibility and foibles. It is this that makes their myths both relevant and entertaining. Many gods had more than one role, discussed in more detail under their individual entries. The Olympians were only part of the family of gods. Other deities, also forces of nature, were believed to inhabit the land, rivers and oceans.

The twelve most important Greek gods are listed opposite. The Romans took many of the gods as their own and gave them Latin names. In this book, for the most part, subjects will be referred to by their Greek names. Where many interpretations of a particular myth exist, here the version predominantly portrayed on nineteenth century cameos has been used.

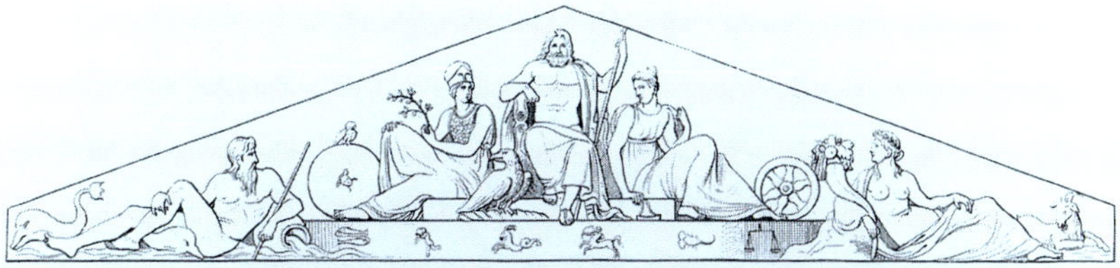

A sketch by Bertel Thorvaldsen, 1808.

THE GREEK PANTHEON

Greek Name	Roman Name	Role
Zeus	Jupiter	King of the gods
Hera	Juno	Queen of the gods
Aphrodite	Venus	Goddess of Love
Apollo	Apollo	God of the Arts
Ares	Mars	God of War
Artemis	Diana	Goddess of the Hunt
Athena	Minerva	Goddess of War/Wisdom
Demeter	Ceres	Goddess of Agriculture
Dionysus	Bacchus	God of Wine
Hermes	Mercury	Messenger of the gods
Hephaestus	Vulcan	Smith god/God of Fire
Poseidon	Neptune	God of Seas and Oceans

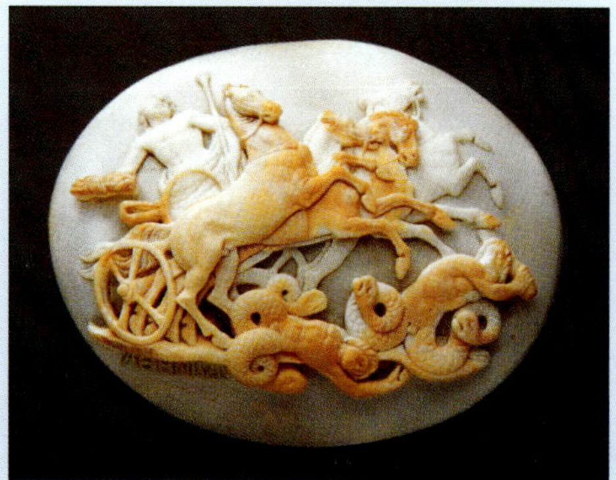

TALES FROM OLYMPUS

The Titans and the Olympian gods

Zeus, King of the gods

Hera, Queen of the gods

Hermes, Zeus's messenger

Hebe, Cupbearer to the gods

Hephaestus, the Smith god

– CHAPTER 1 –

TALES FROM OLYMPUS

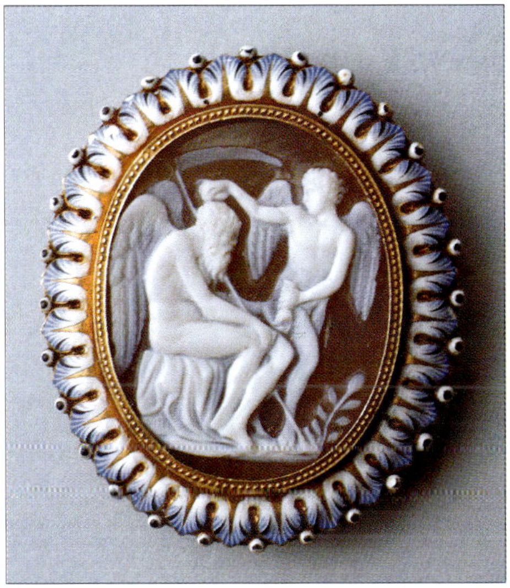

Plate 1. *Onyx cameo, gold, enamelled acanthus mount. Cameo in the late 17th century style, but 19th century. 2⅝in. (6cm) x 2in. (5cm) wide. A dozing Cronus with an hourglass and a scythe, symbolising his connection with Chronos (time) and the harvest. Eros pours water over Cronus and attempts to steal his hourglass (perhaps to 'steal time' for the pursuit of love and pleasure).*

S. J. PHILLIPS LTD., NEW BOND STREET, LONDON

Myths about the ascendancy of the Olympian gods over the Titans, the supremacy of Zeus and related stories. They are turbulent, passionate and dramatic tales, describing life on Mount Olympus. In many respects, they are the original versions of modern soap operas. Cameos featuring Zeus, and Zeus with Hebe, were very popular during the nineteenth century. The Titans and Hephaestus were rarer subjects.

THE BEGINNING AND THE TITANS

According to Hesiod, in the beginning there was only 'the Chasm' (Chaos) – a shapeless mass. Then Gaea (Earth) emerged and produced a son, Uranus (Sky). The union of Earth and Sky produced the Titans, a race of pre-Olympian gods, powers of nature. Cronus, ruler of the Titans, to prevent his children from overthrowing him, swallowed them at birth. Zeus, hidden by his mother, escaped this fate and was raised by nymphs. Later, Zeus rose against Cronus, who was forced to regurgitate his children. A violent struggle ensued between the two generations, resulting in the defeat of the Titans and the ascendancy of the Olympian gods. Zeus became King of the Gods, Poseidon became Ruler of Seas and Oceans, and Hades, Ruler of the Underworld.

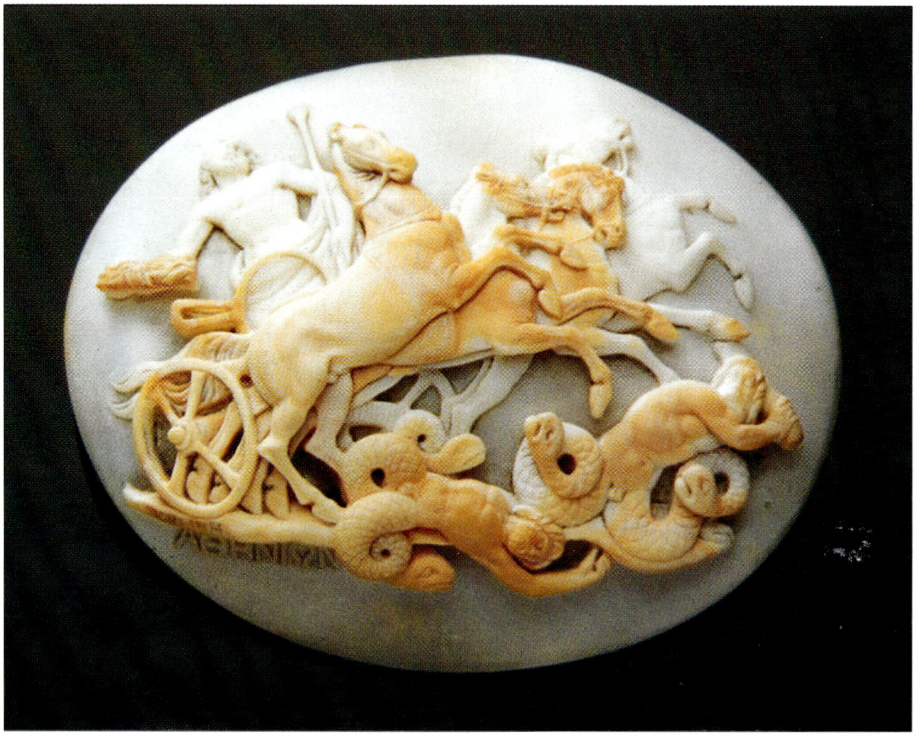

'Jove Darts Lightning at the Titans'

Plate 2. *Shell carving by Luigi Saulini (1819-1883), a prominent Roman gem-engraver. After an ancient gem signed 'Athenion', which is considered to be one of the first among signed gems (Naples National Archaeological Museum). Zeus (Jupiter/Jove) in his quadriga hurls bolts of lightning at the Titans. Saulini's carving vividly portrays Hesiod's description of this theme:*

> *'Now Zeus held in his strength no longer. Straightway his lungs were filled with fury, and he began to display his full might. From heaven and from Olympus together he came, with continuous lightning flashes, and the bolts flew thick and fast from his stalwart hand amid thunder and lightning, trailing supernatural flames.'*
>
> *Hesiod,* Theogony, *circa 8th century BC (page 23, West translation)*

COURTESY OF THE AKIBA MUSEUM OF ANTIQUE JEWELLERY, JAPAN

The Titans as Cameo Subjects

Rhea (Cybele), Titan Queen, a majestic figure wearing a crown of turrets and accompanied by a lion or lions.

Cronus (Saturn), the Titan King portrayed as an old man with a scythe and an hourglass, due to his association with both the harvest and Chronos (time). See Plate 1.

Zeus in a chariot darts lightning at the Titans, see Plate 2.

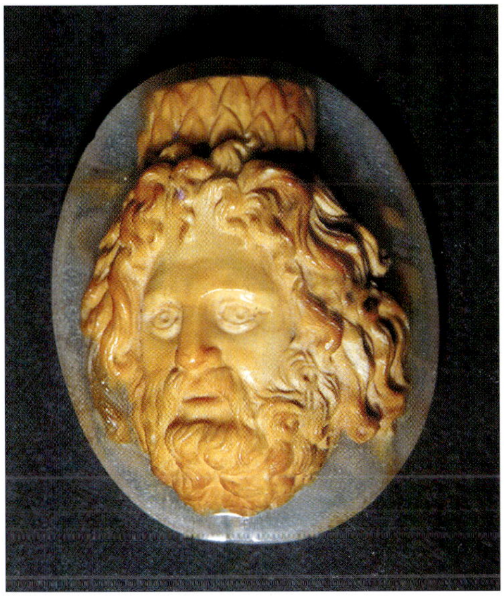

Plate 3. *Unmounted sardonyx, early 19th century. Zeus depicted as 'Jupiter-Sarapis' wearing a kalothos (a basket or corn measure), a fertility symbol, on his head. For similar, see Catalogue Entry 324 in* Geschnittene Steine des 18. bis 20 Jahrhunderts *by Ingrid S. Weber. 1³⁄₁₆in. (3cm) x ¾in. (2cm).*

S. J. PHILLIPS LTD., NEW BOND STREET, LONDON

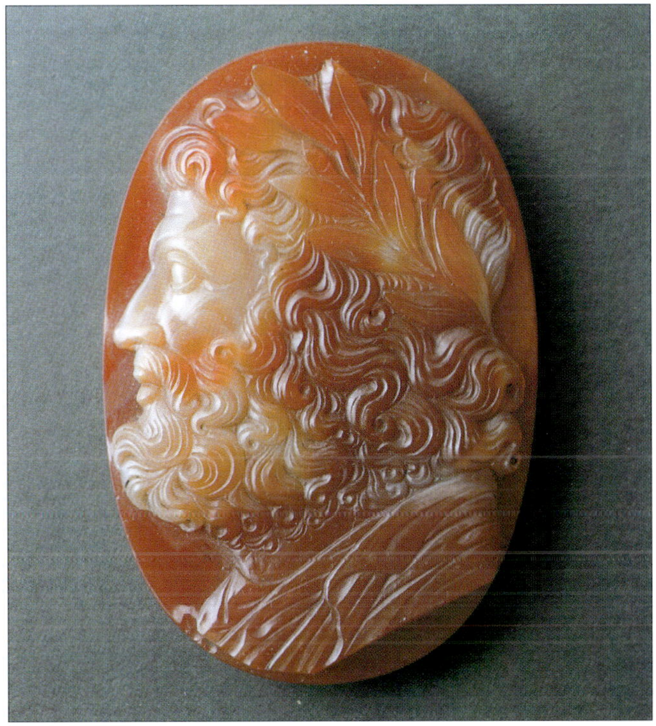

Plate 4. *Cornelian, early 19th century. Zeus in profile, crowned by a laurel wreath. 3⅛in. (8cm) x 2⅜in. (6cm).*

J. PHILLIPS LTD., NEW BOND STREET, LONDON

ZEUS (Greek)**, King of Olympus**
JUPITER (Roman)
Cameo Key: Regal male, olive wreath, eagle

> 'Zeus supervises every outcome.'
>
> Solon, *Political Poems*. Athens, circa 6th century BC

ZEUS was the supreme god in the Greek pantheon and all were subject to his will. Closely associated with political life, his authority justified royal power and the established social order. Zeus was also god of the sky and of weather, living in a palace above Mount Olympus, the highest mountain in Greece. There, he presided over all the affairs of gods and men:

> 'So the lord gods took their seats in the marble council chamber, and their lord sat, throned high above them, leaning on his ivory sceptre. Three times, four times, he shook those awe-inspiring locks and with them moved the earth, the sea, the stars.'
>
> Ovid, *Metamorphoses*, I (page 34, Innes translation)

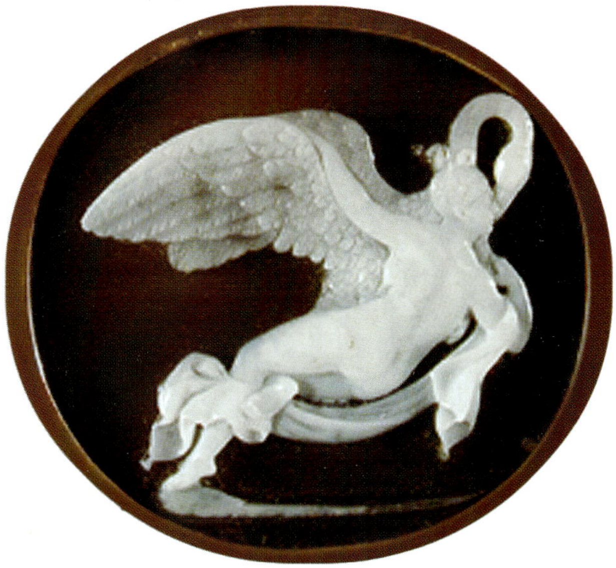

Leda and the Swan

Plate 5. *Onyx, gold mount, early 19th century, of the Spartan Queen Leda lying with Zeus (in the guise of a swan). 2⅜in. (6cm) x 2¾in. (7cm). Signed 'Girometti' for Guiseppe Girometti (1779-1851), the celebrated Roman gem-engraver, sculptor and medallist who worked in Rome, known for his cameos based on classical subjects, or his son Pietro (1811-1859) who used the same signature. 'Reclining Leda' after a 4th century BC Greek model. For similar see plate 728 in* Greek Gems and Finger Rings *by John Boardman (2001 edition).*

S. J. Phillips Ltd., New Bond Street, London

The son of the Titans, Cronus and Rhea, Zeus was the force responsible for the ascendancy of the Olympian gods. Cronus had swallowed Zeus's siblings so they could not overthrow him. Zeus escaped this fate, rescued his brothers and sisters and led them in a rebellion against the Titans, becoming supreme ruler of gods and mortals.

His symbol was the eagle, representing his power and

majesty. The oak tree was his sacred tree and it was said that Zeus manifested himself through it – when the oak leaves rustled, Zeus was speaking. Jupiter, his Roman equivalent, was also the supreme god. The Capitol in Rome was sacred to him and victors always made their first sacrifices to Jupiter to ensure his blessing.

Zeus's Love Affairs

> 'Majesty and love go ill together, nor can they long share one abode.'
>
> Ovid, *Metamorphoses*, II (page 72, Innes translation)

Much of the mythology concerning Zeus concentrates on his numerous love affairs. His first wife was Metis, goddess of Intelligence, mother of Athena, followed by Themis, who bore the Seasons and the Fates. With his sister Demeter Zeus fathered Persephone and with Memory, the Muses. Later Zeus married another sister, Hera, and their children were Ares, Ilithyia, Hephaestus and Hebe. Zeus was indeed majestic, but his failing was his predilection for nubile young females. His affairs so enraged Hera that he often transformed himself or his lovers to elude her. These were some of his lovers:

LEDA: The beautiful Queen of Sparta. Zeus desired her and persuaded Aphrodite to transform herself into an eagle and chase him, in the guise of a swan. The swan (Zeus) flew to Leda for protection and seduced her. She gave birth to two eggs, one containing Clytemnestra and Castor, the other containing Pollux and Helen.
DANAË: Princess of Argos. Zeus transformed himself into 'a shower of gold' to seduce her. Perseus, the famous hero, was the result of this union.
ALCMENE: Zeus transformed himself into an image of her husband to seduce her. Their son Heracles, the great hero, was named after Zeus's wife Hera in a vain attempt to appease her.
EUROPA: The Princess of Tyre was playing on a beach when Zeus, disguised as a bull, carried her off to Crete. There she bore him three sons, including King Minos (of minotaur fame).
IO: Princess of Argos. Zeus changed her into a white cow to conceal her from Hera.
ANTIOPE: Zeus disguised himself as a satyr to seduce this nymph.
SEMELE: Zeus accidentally killed her with a thunderbolt and their unborn child Dionysus, god of Wine, was sewn into Zeus's thigh until he was ready to be born.
GANYMEDE: A beautiful Trojan youth, abducted by Zeus (in the guise of an eagle). Ganymede became cupbearer to the gods.

Zeus as a Cameo Subject

Zeus, King of the gods. A regal, imposing, bearded male wearing an olive leaf wreath or a crown of oak leaves. Can hold a sceptre or a thunderbolt. An eagle, symbol of his strength and power, may be in the scene. See Plate 4.
Zeus with his daughter, Hebe, cupbearer to the gods. Zeus, in the form of an eagle, is offered nectar from a cup, pitcher or bowl by Hebe, a beautiful young girl. Nectar was the gods' elixir of eternal life. See Plate 9.
Zeus and Leda. The beautiful Queen of Sparta entwined with a swan (Zeus in disguise). See Plate 5.
Zeus and Europa. A woman riding a bull (Zeus) over the waves. See Plate 30.
Zeus and Antiope. A sleeping nymph is approached by a satyr (Zeus).
Zeus and Ganymede. A beautiful boy wearing a Phrygian cap (a folded, conical cap) is carried up into the sky towards Olympus by Hermes, or is entwined with an eagle. Or, a handsome youth gives an eagle (Zeus) nectar from a cup or bowl.
Zeus, in the guise of an eagle, with a Muse, maiden or nymph. See Plate 50.
Zeus and Danaë. A reclining female awaits a shower of gold from the sky.
Jupiter-Sarapis (Serapis). A god of Egyptian origin associated with both Zeus and Hades. Like Zeus, he was seen as a supreme ruler and his cult was popular at Alexandria. Distinguished from Zeus by the kalathos (basket or corn measure) on his head. See Plate 3.
See also: Athena, Dionysus, Hebe, Heracles.

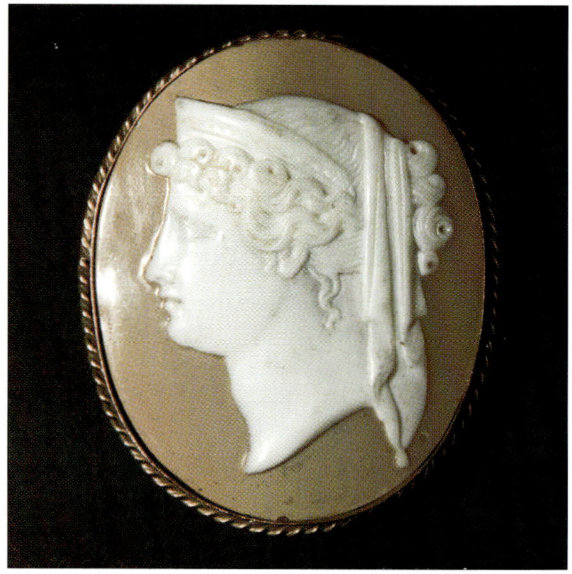

Plate 6. *Bull's Mouth shell, gold mount, mid-19th century. 2in. (5cm) x 1 3/16in. (3cm). Hera wears a diadem (Spartan crown) and a veil signifying her roles as Queen of Olympus and a marriage divinity. For similar, see Entry 889 in 'The Art of the Jeweller: A Catalogue Of The Hull Grundy Gift To The British Museum.' Editor, H. Tait.*

JILL BARNES, CENTRAL GALLERY, PORTOBELLO ROAD, LONDON £250

HERA (Greek), **Queen of Olympus**
JUNO (Roman)
Cameo Key: Regal female wearing a veil, or diadem

> 'I sing of golden-throned Hera whom Rhea bare Queen of the immortals is she, surpassing all in beauty.'
>
> Homeric Hymn XII *To Hera* (page 437, Evelyn-White translation)

HERA was Queen of Olympus and the sister and wife of Zeus. She was protector of marriage, children and families. A proud and regal goddess, Hera was often driven to despair by her husband's infidelities.

> 'She looked round to see where her husband was: for by now she knew well the deceptions practised by that husband, who had so often been caught behaving as he ought not. When she could not find him in the sky, "Unless I am mistaken", she said, "he is doing me some wrong".'
>
> Ovid, *Metamorphoses*, I (page 45, Innes translation)

When she discovered that Zeus had been unfaithful yet again, Hera became vengeful towards his lovers and their children. She especially despised Dionysus and Heracles, two of Zeus's offspring. Hera's own children were Ares, Hebe, Hephaestus and Ilithyia. The proud, regal peacock was her bird, reflecting her royal status. She put the eyes of her servant, Argus, into the peacock's one hundred-eyed tail so he could watch Zeus for her. The white lily, symbolising purity and majesty, was her sacred flower. Juno was Hera's Roman equivalent and her month, June, was most favoured for weddings.

Hera as a Cameo Subject

A regal, elegant female wearing a veil, symbolising her role as a marriage divinity, or a diadem, as she is Queen of Heaven. See Plate 6.

Hera portrayed with Zeus or an eagle, symbolising Zeus.

See also: Dionysus, Heracles, Zeus.

HERMES (Greek)**, Messenger of the gods**
MERCURY (Roman)
Cameo Key: Virile male, winged sandals, winged hat and caduceus

Hermes had many roles – chiefly he was god of Eloquence and Reason, Divine Messenger and Herald of the gods, god of Trade and Commerce. The son of Zeus, he had the gift of prophecy and was protector of mortal heroes. In his role as the gods' messenger, Hermes wore a petasus (brimmed, winged hat) and talaria (golden winged sandals). He carried a caduceus (a staff bearing entwined serpents), a magic rod, symbol of the messenger, of peace, prosperity and commerce. The caduceus also became the physician's symbol.

Hermes was a clever, inventive god:

> 'a robber, a cattle driver, a bringer of dreams, a watcher by night, a thief at the gates, one who was soon to show forth wonderful deeds among the deathless gods.'
>
> Homeric Hymn IV *To Hermes*
> (page 365, Evelyn-White translation)

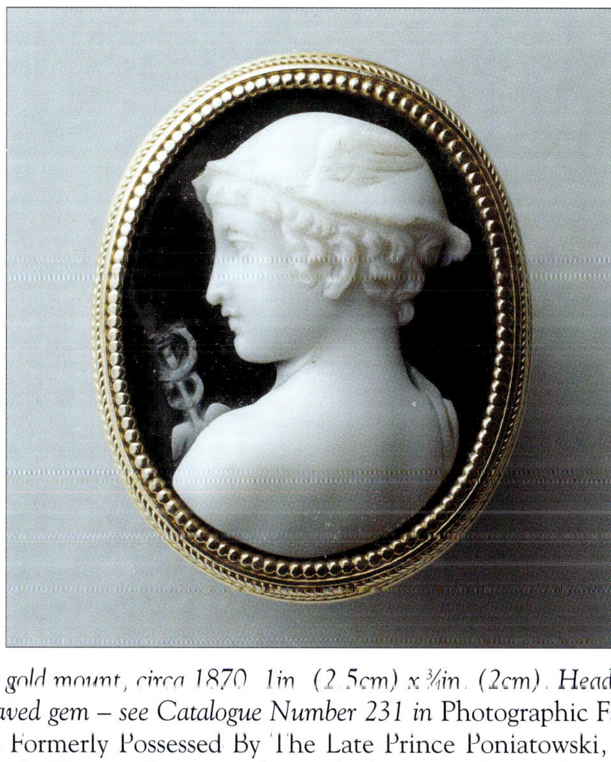

Plate 7 *Onyx, gold mount, circa 1870. 1in. (2.5cm) x ¾in. (2cm). Head of Hermes after an ancient engraved gem – see Catalogue Number 231 in* Photographic Facsimiles of the Antique Gems Formerly Possessed By The Late Prince Poniatowski, *Series I (1857) described as 'Head of Hermes by Pyrgoteles. Calcedony, partaking of the sapphire'.*

Private Collection

Within twenty-four hours of his birth, Hermes stole one hundred cattle from his brother Apollo and created a musical instrument, the lyre, from a tortoiseshell. He defended himself so eloquently against Apollo's charge of theft that Zeus made him his personal messenger. Apollo and Hermes reached an agreement – in return for the lyre, Apollo gave his brother his caduceus, a golden crook and the stolen cattle.

An amorous, young fertility god, Hermes had many lovers and children. His two best-known sons were Pan, a god of Nature and Hermaphrodite, who had the characteristics of both sexes. Statues called *Herms* – pillars with human torsos and male genitalia – stood at boundaries. In his role as 'Hermes Psychopompus', the god accompanied the souls of the dead to Hades (the Greek *psycho* meant 'soul').

Hermes as a Cameo Subject

As Divine Herald – A young, virile, naked god wearing his winged hat and winged sandals, holding a caduceus. See Plates 7 and 8.

Hermes Psychopompus – Hermes wears his winged hat and sandals and has a small figure or a butterfly on his arm, representing a soul.

The Judgement of Paris – Hermes is in the scene with Paris and the three goddesses, after delivering them to Paris to make his judgement. See Plate 29.

See also: Apollo, Pan.

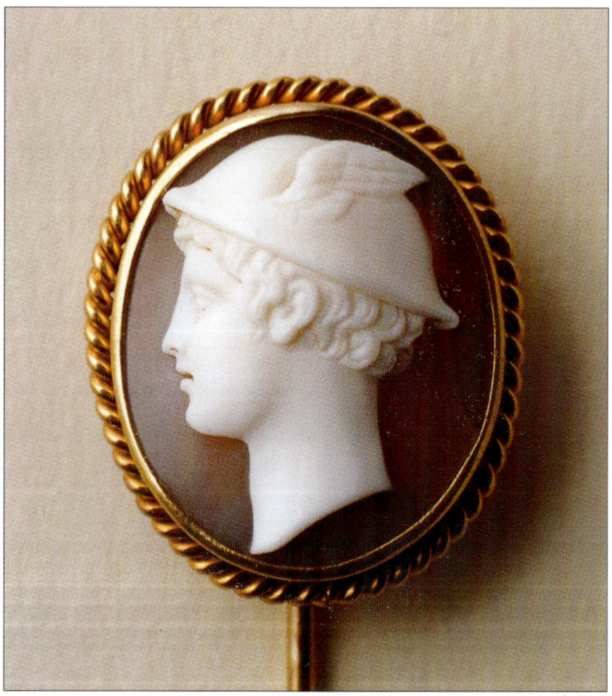

Plate 8. *Bull's Mouth shell, gold stickpin mount, late 19th century. 1in. (2.5cm) x ¾in. (2cm). Hermes, the gods' messenger portrayed wearing his winged hat. Representations of Hermes as a slender, beardless youth with short curly hair date from the 4th century BC.*

S. HARLOWE AT www.rowanandrowan.com £250

HEBE (Greek), **goddess of Youth**
Cameo Key: Young girl ministering nectar to an eagle

HEBE was goddess of Youth, the personification of eternal beauty. The daughter of Zeus and Hera, her role was cupbearer to the gods, serving them nectar as they feasted in Zeus's palace on Mount Olympus. Nectar was the gods' elixir of immortality. However, she lost this role after falling drunkenly at a feast and was replaced by Ganymede, a handsome youth whom Zeus desired. When the great hero Heracles died and ascended to Mount Olympus, Hebe became his wife.

Hebe as a Cameo Subject
Hebe is frequently portrayed on nineteenth century cameos, serving nectar to Zeus from a cup, bowl or ewer. Zeus is shown in the guise of an eagle. (Often mistaken for Leda and the swan.) See Plate 9.
A beautiful young goddess carrying a pitcher of nectar and a cup. See Plate 10.
Coronation of Hebe as cupbearer to the gods – Artemis and Hera present her with a cup.
Hebe dances with the Muses as Apollo plays his lyre.
See also: Zeus, Heracles.

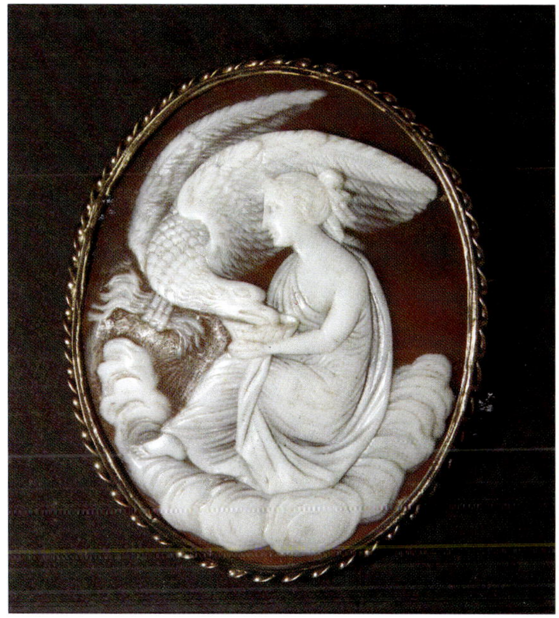

Plate 9 (above). *Black Helmet shell, gold mount, mid-19th century. 2½in. (6.5cm) x 2in. (5cm). Hebe, a young maiden, serves nectar to her father, Zeus (in the guise of an eagle).* M. ROWAN AT www.rowanandrowan.com £350

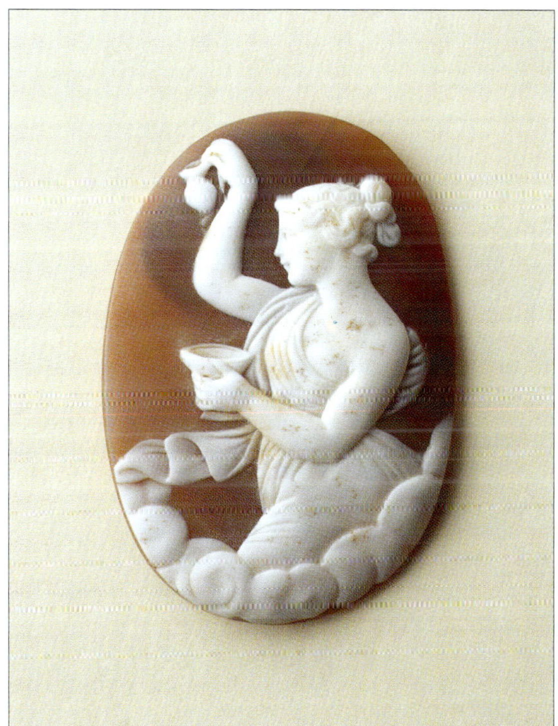

Plate 10 (right). *Bull's Mouth shell, mid-19th century. 1 3/16in. (3cm) x 1in. (2.5cm). Hebe, in her role as cupbearer to the gods, holding a ewer and goblet, after a statue by Antonio Canova, executed 1816-17.*
FOX COLLECTION

HEPHAESTUS (Greek), **Smith god**
VULCAN (Roman)
Cameo Key: A smith working at a forge

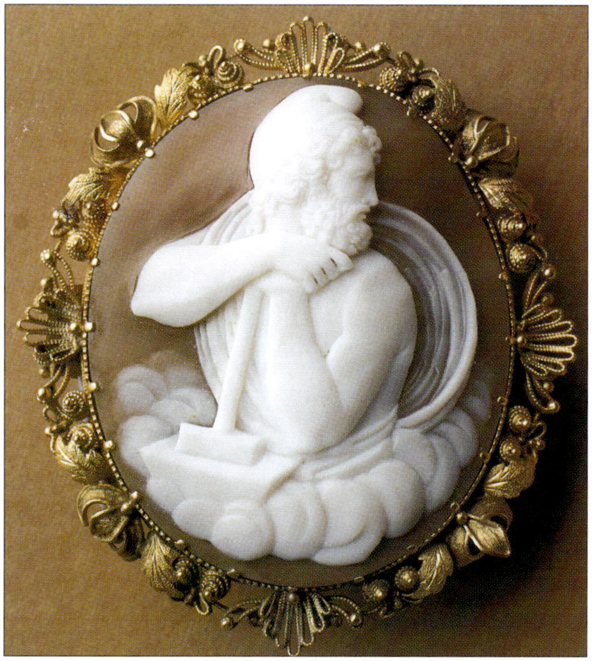

Plate 11. *Bull's Mouth shell, cannetille gold mount, circa 1830-40, the Smith god Hephaestus (Vulcan) wearing a conical cap, with his tools – a hammer and an anvil. 2⅜in. (6cm) x 2in. (5cm).*

RBR Group, Grays, London £675

Hephaestus was also god of Fire, son of Hera, Queen of Olympus:

> 'Hera, furying and quarrelling with her husband, gave birth to the renowned Hephaestus, who is endowed with skills beyond all the Celestials.'
>
> Hesiod, *Theogony* (page 30, West translation)

Hephaestus worked at his forge, making articles for the gods' use. He made Zeus's sceptre, arrows for Eros and chariots for the gods. After Aphrodite's rejection of Zeus, he punished her by forcing her to marry the lame and ugly Hephaestus, to whom she was unfaithful. Ovid describes Hephaestus's trap for Aphrodite after being informed of her infidelity with Ares:

> 'Vulcan's senses reeled, and the iron he was forging fell from his hand. At once, he began to fashion slender bronze chains, nets and snares which the eye could not see. The thinnest threads spun on the loom, or cobwebs hanging from the rafters are no finer than was that workmanship.
> When his wife and her lover lay down together upon that couch, they were caught by the chains, ingeniously fastened there by her husband's skill, and were held fast in the very act of embracing. Immediately, the Lemnian Vulcan flung open the ivory doors and admitted the gods. There lay Mars and Venus, bound together, a shameful sight.'
>
> Ovid, *Metamorphoses*, IV (pages 98-99, Innes translation)

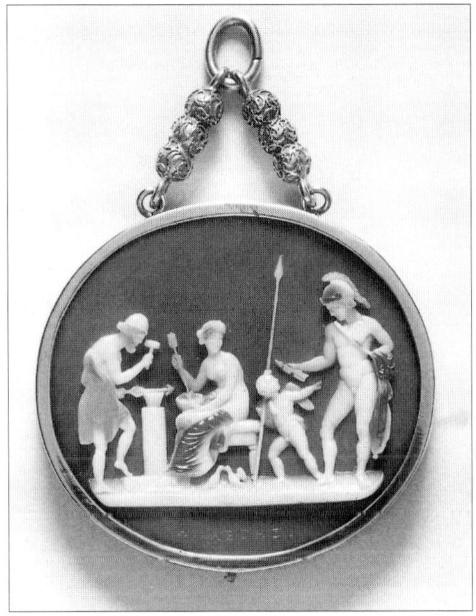

'Vulcan's Forge'

Plate 12. *Early 19th century sardonyx, later gold pendant setting. 1½in. (3.7cm) wide. Hephaestus (Vulcan) the Smith god in his forge with Aphrodite (Venus) his wife, her lover Mars, Cupid and two doves. Cameo by Domenico Calabresi, Roman gem-engraver. The source is a marble relief by Thorvaldsen completed in Rome in 1814.*

COURTESY OF THE BRITISH MUSEUM, HULL GRUNDY BEQUEST

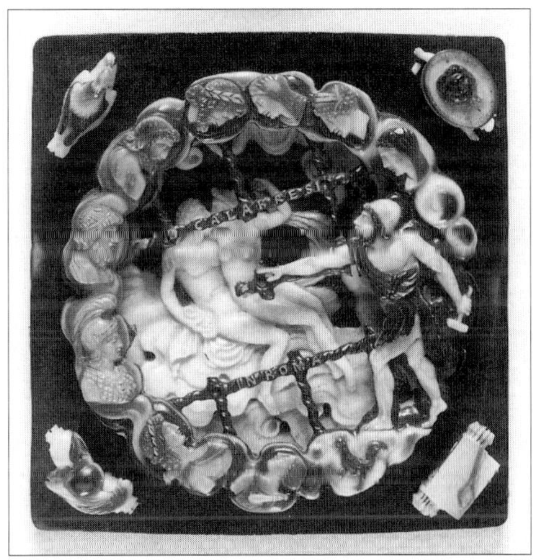

'Venus and Mars caught in Vulcan's Net'

Plate 13. *Agate, a remarkable carving in seven layers signed 'D. CALABRESI (FECE IN) ROMA'. 1⅝in. (4.1cm) wide. Portrays Venus and Mars caught in a net of chains devised by her husband, Vulcan. For further information see Entry 902 in* The Art of the Jeweller, *Ed. Hugh Tait. Around the edge of the carving the other Olympian gods look on:*

> 'The gods were highly amused; one of them prayed that he too might be so shamed.'
> Ovid, *Metamorphoses*, IV (page 99, Innes translation)

COURTESY OF THE BRITISH MUSEUM, HULL GRUNDY BEQUEST

The Romans called the god Vulcan and believed that he worked at his forge under volcanic Mount Etna.

Hephaestus as a Cameo Subject

Hephaestus, a bearded god in a workman's tunic and conical cap, shown working at his forge with blacksmith's tools. See Plate 11.

Hephaestus in his forge with Aphrodite, her lover Ares, and Eros. See Plate 12.

Hephaestus traps the lovers, Aphrodite and Ares, in a net of chains. See Plate 13.

See also: Aphrodite, Hera.

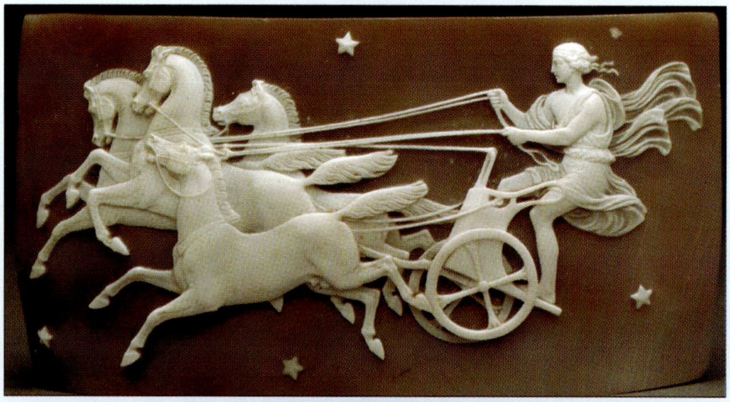

COSMOLOGICAL MYTHS

Helios and Phoebus Apollo, Sun gods

Eos, goddess of Dawn

Nyx, goddess of Night

Nyx's children: Hypnos (Sleep) Thanatos (Death)

Iris, the Rainbow goddess

Selene, Moon goddess (see Diana)

CHAPTER 2

COSMOLOGICAL MYTHS

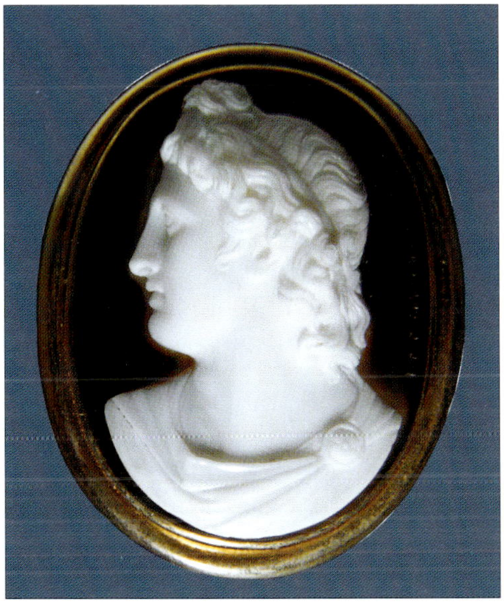

Plate 14. *Sardonyx, gold mount, early 19th century. 2⅜in. (6cm) x 2in. (5cm).Head of the 'Apollo Belvedere', signed 'Girometti' for Guiseppe Girometti (1779-1851), the celebrated Roman gem-engraver, sculptor and medallist who worked in Rome, or his son Pietro (1811-1859) who used the same signature.*
After the statue 'Apollo Belvedere', a Roman copy of a Greek 4th century BC bronze. Installed in the Vatican (Belvedere court) in 1509, ceded to Napoleon I, 1798, returned to Rome 1815.
S. J. PHILLIPS LTD., NEW BOND STREET, LONDON

These myths provided an explanation for the passage of day and night and the meaning of the cosmos. There were many nineteenth century cameos featuring this group of gods and goddesses, especially 'Day and Night' and extravagant scenes depicting chariots ascending the clouds, attended by nymphs and other figures.

HELIOS (Greek), **Sun god**
Cameo Key: Handsome male in chariot, light radiates around him

HELIOS, Titan god of the Sun, crossed the sky each morning in the splendid golden chariot of the sun as Homeric Hymn XXXI describes:

> 'As he rides in his chariot, he shines upon men and deathless gods, and piercingly he gazes with his eyes from his golden helmet. Bright rays beam dazzlingly from him, and his bright locks streaming from the temples of his head gracefully enclose his far-seen face: a rich, fine-spun garment glows upon his body and flutters in the wind: and stallions carry him. Then, when he has stayed his golden-yoked chariot and horses, he rests there upon the highest point of heaven, until he marvellously drives them down again through heaven to Ocean.'
>
> Homeric Hymn XXXI *To Helios*
> (page 459, Evelyn-White translation)

The Titan Helios later became identified with the Olympian god Apollo.

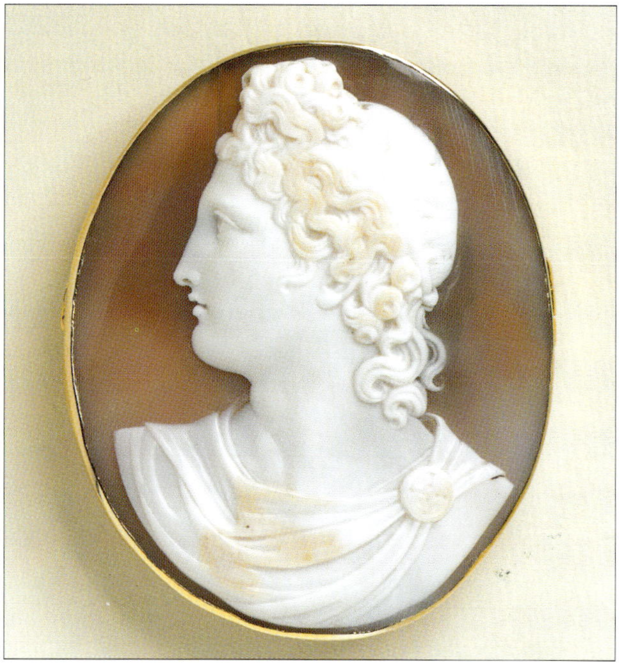

Plate 15. *Bull's Mouth shell, gold mount, 2⅜in. (6cm) x 2in. (5cm), circa 1860. After the statue 'Apollo Belvedere'. Cameos after this statue were extremely popular with visitors to Rome during the 19th century. A Scottish traveller to Rome in 1817-18 describes her first viewing of the celebrated statue:*

> *'Never, never was there revealed to the dreams of the gifted genius a vision of such celestial, such soul-beaming beauty!*
> *You will think me mad – but if I were, I am not the first person who has gone mad about Apollo*
> *But English maids don't die of love – neither for men nor statues – therefore I hope to live to admire the Apollo.'*
>
> Charlotte A. Eaton, *Rome in The Nineteenth Century* Vol. I, 5th Ed. 1860 (pages 104-6)

S. Harlowe at www.rowanandrowan.com £450

APOLLO (Greek and Roman)
Cameo Key: Handsome male, lyre, laurel wreath

'The god of light, and poesy, and imagination.'

Apollo, a handsome, virile, young god, personified culture, civilisation and ideal male beauty. He was a god of Light and became identified with Helios (the sun) as 'Phoebus Apollo' (bright, shining one).

Apollo was the son of Zeus and the Titaness Leto and the twin of Artemis, goddess of Hunting. After his birth, he went to Delphi, slew a dragon called 'Python' or 'Delphyne' and established sacred games called the

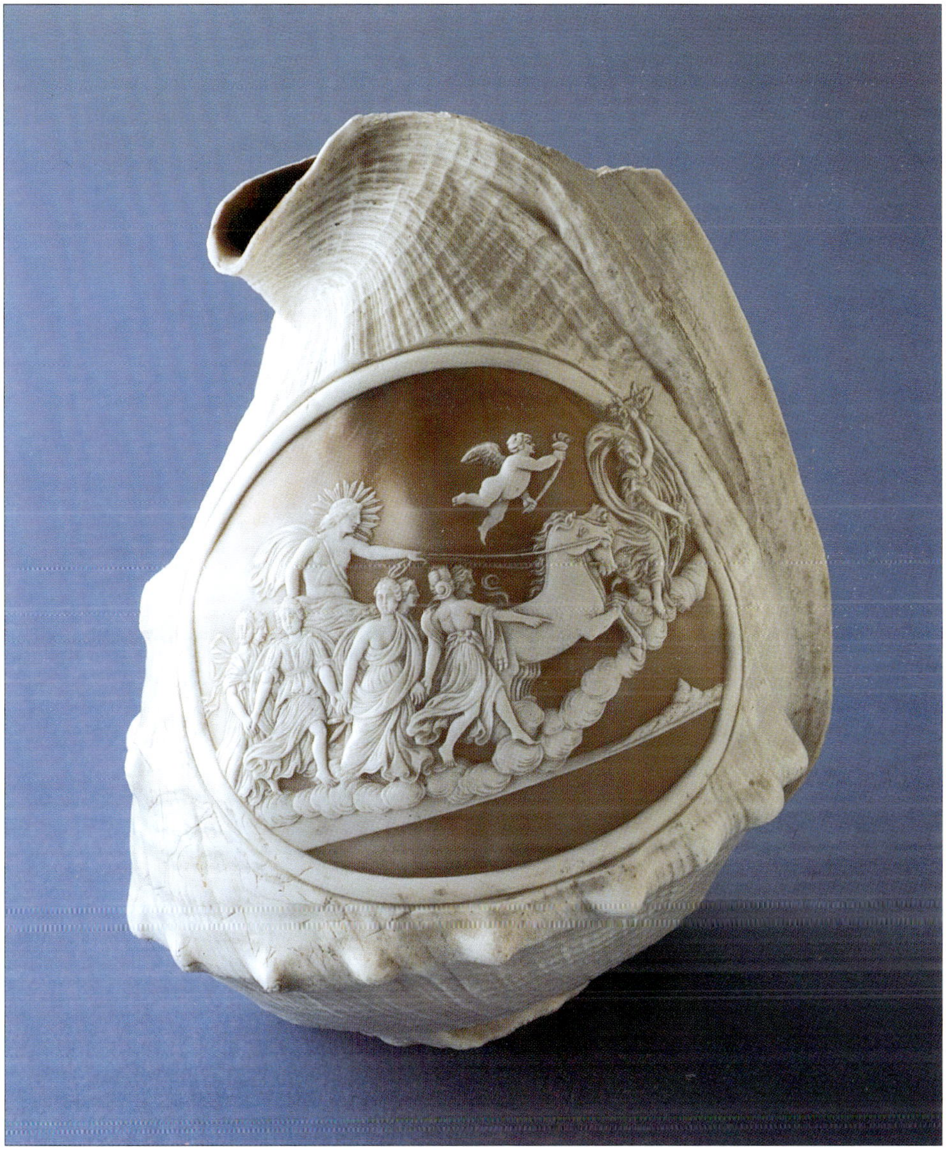

'Phoebus and the Hours preceded by Aurora'

Plate 16. *Carved Bull's Mouth shell, 7½in. (19cm) x 6in. (15cm), third quarter of 19th century, depicting 'Phoebus and the Hours Preceded by Aurora' based on a ceiling fresco by Guido Reni in 1613, in the Rospigliosi Palace, Rome. Phoebus ascends in his chariot, preceded by Eos (Aurora), goddess of Dawn, and the Genius of Light (a guardian spirit typically bearing a torch) described by Ovid as 'the daystar Lucifer.' The Horae (Seasons) and nymphs dance in attendance upon Apollo's chariot.* M. ROWAN AT www.rowanandrowan.com £1250

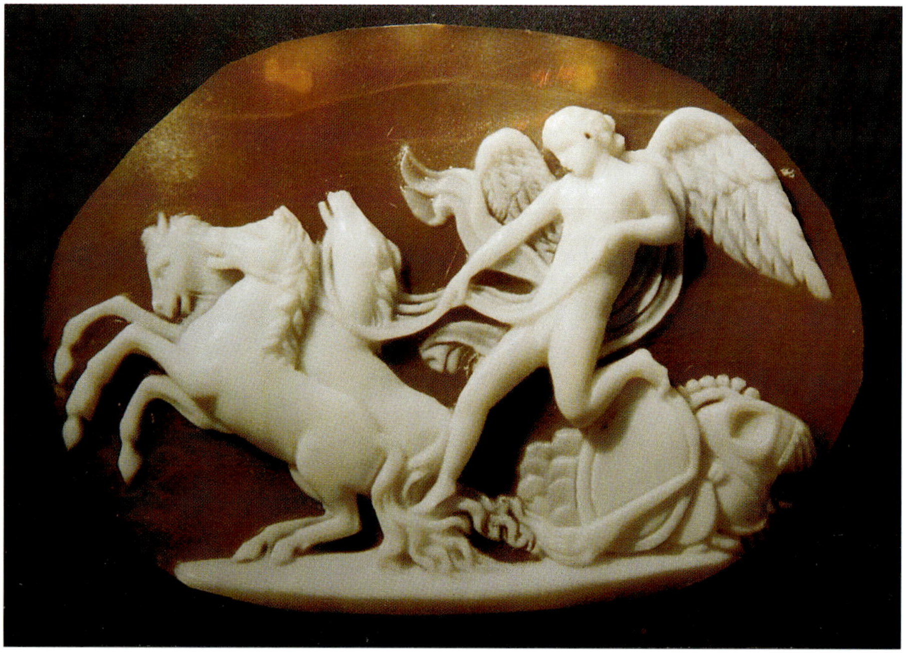

Plate 17. *Bull's Mouth shell, 2in. (5cm) x 2¾in. (7cm), after a cameo by Tommaso Saulini (1793-1864), 'Phoebus and His Horses', illustrated in Malcolm Stuart Carr's article 'Tommaso And Luigi Saulini' in The Connoisseur, November 1975. See also painting entitled* Peace Halting the Horses of Mars *by Benigne Gagneraux (1756-1795), Museum of Art and History, Geneva.* P.K. ANTIQUES, AVOCA BEACH, AUSTRALIA £850

Pythian Games, named after the monster he had killed. He was also god of Music and Poetry and Patron of the Arts. He tamed the Muses, nine wild goddesses who became his companions. In another role, he was god of Archery and protector of shepherds and their flocks. He was also god of Prophecy, with power over oracles, especially at Delphi, and was associated with medicine and healing as father of Asclepius, god of Healing.

Though Apollo was esteemed as a civilised god, he had a darker side and could be cruel and vindictive. When the satyr Marsyas boldly suggested they hold a musical contest, he defeated the satyr and then flayed him alive for challenging him. Despite his great beauty, Apollo's love affairs often ended tragically. The nymph Daphne spurned his love and her father turned her into a daphne (laurel) tree to escape Apollo's advances. As he possessed the gift of eternal youth, Apollo made the tree evergreen. It became an inspirational plant, communicating the spirit of prophecy and poetry, and a symbol of glory and victory.

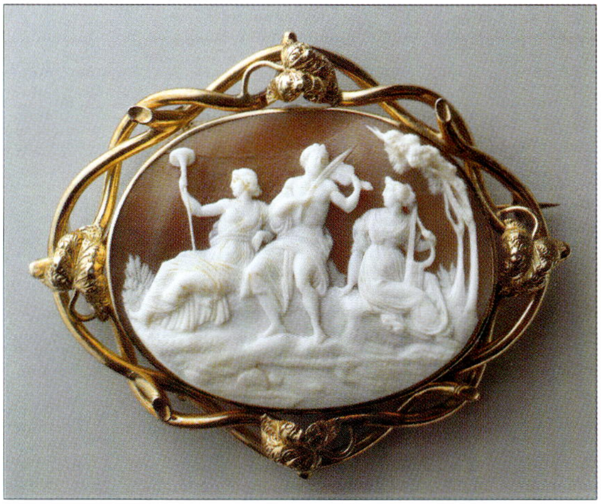

Plate 18. *Bull's Mouth shell, interlaced tubular gold frame with applied leaf decoration, circa 1860. 2in. (5cm) x 2⅜in. (6cm). After a work by Raphael,* Parnassus, *1510-11 (Stanza Della Segnatura, Vatican). Apollo, centre, playing a viol, flanked by two Muses, one holding a long horn, the other a lyre. Parnassus, a mountain north of Delphi, was the home of the Arts, frequented by Apollo and the Muses.*

PRIVATE COLLECTION

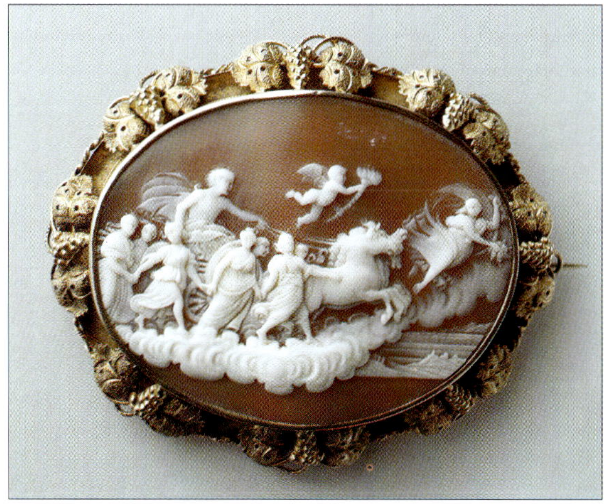

Plate 19. *Bull's Mouth shell, ornate gold mount, circa 1860. 2⅜in. (6cm) high x 2¾in. (7cm) wide. Based on a ceiling fresco by Guido Reni (1613) in the Rospigliosi Palace, Rome. Phoebus Apollo ascends in his chariot, preceded by Eos (Aurora), goddess of Dawn and the Genius of Light. The Horae (Seasons) and nymphs dance in attendance upon his chariot.*

PRIVATE COLLECTION

Helios/Apollo as Cameo Subjects

Helios – a beautiful, youthful male head in profile with flowing hair and light radiating around him.

Helios/Phoebus Apollo in the golden chariot of the sun. Sometimes the chariot is preceded by Eos, goddess of Dawn, and a torch-bearing cherubic figure (the Genius of Light/the daystar Lucifer). The Horae and nymphs accompany them. See Plates 16, 19, 61

Apollo Belvedere – after the celebrated statue of the god, depicted with one arm raised, in the Belvedere Gallery of the Vatican. See Plates 14 and 15.

Apollo wearing a laurel wreath, in his role as Inspiration of poetry and prophecy.

Apollo Musegete (conductor of the Muses) – Apollo playing the lyre in his role as god of Music. See Plate 98. Apollo accompanied by the Muses. See Plate 49.

Apollo, god of Archery – a handsome young male dressed in a chiton (short tunic), carrying a bow and arrows. Deer in scene. Sometimes with his twin Artemis, goddess of Hunting.

See also: Artemis, Asclepius, the Muses.

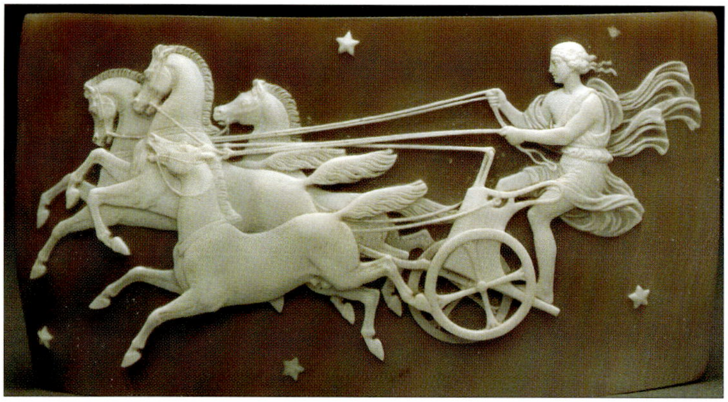

Plate 20. *Shell cameo panel, circa 1840, 3¾in. (9.4cm) wide, cut from an oblong designed to be set in an ornamental mount of a hair-comb, of a charioteer drawn by four horses, possibly a representation of Aurora, scratch-signed 'T. Saulini F.' for Tommaso Saulini (1793-1864), the prominent Roman gem-engraver. See Entry 912 in* The Art of the Jeweller, *Ed. Hugh Tait.*

COURTESY OF THE BRITISH MUSEUM, HULL GRUNDY BEQUEST

EOS (Greek), **goddess of Dawn**
AURORA (Roman)
Cameo Key: Female in chariot, or winged. Sun/moon/stars

Eos, the Titan goddess of Dawn, sister of Sun and Moon, supplied an explanation for the break of day. Her children were the winds and stars. This beautiful goddess, dressed in a saffron robe, preceded the chariot of the Sun god into the sky:

> '...from the summit of flower-decked Hymettus, saffron-robed Aurora, dispelling darkness with her morning light...She was fair to see, with her rosy lips, she was queen of the borderland of day and night, she was nurtured on draughts of nectar.'
>
> Ovid, *Metamorphoses*, VII (page 174, Innes translation)

Eos took many mortal lovers, among them the Trojan Prince, Tithonus. Their son, Memnon, was killed in the Trojan War. This caused the goddess such sorrow that her tears covered the world with dew. Often Eos carries or is preceded by a winged cherubic figure bearing a torch to light the day – 'the Genius of Light' (a guardian spirit, personifying the concept it was associated with), described by Homer as 'the daystar Lucifer'.

Eos as a Cameo Subject

Eos, sometimes in a horse-drawn chariot, flies across the clouds. Often she holds a torch, and flowers are scattered in her path. She can be accompanied by the Genius of Light, nymphs and the Horae (Seasons). See Plate 20.
Eos flies in front of the chariot of Phoebus Apollo. She holds a torch, or flowers. See Plates 16, 19, 61.
Eos in flight, accompanied by the Genius of Light. See Plates 21 and 22.
Eos flies through the sky carrying a hydria (water jug) as she covers the world with dew.
See also: Apollo, Cephalus and Procris, the Horae.

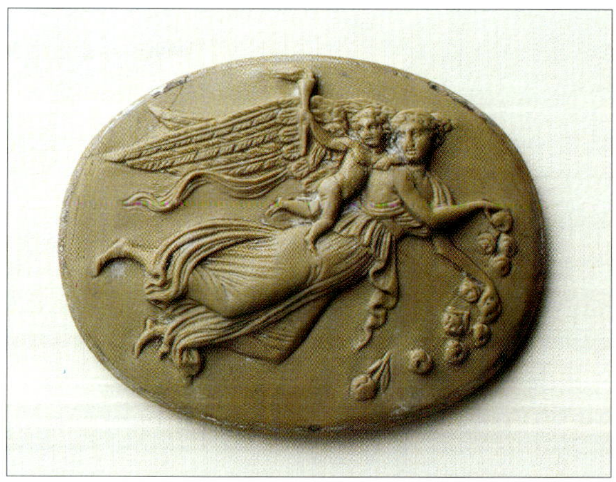

Plate 21. *Lava carving, circa 1870. 1³⁄₁₆in. (3cm) high x 1½in. (4cm) wide. Aurora, goddess of Dawn, accompanied by the Genius of Light, scatters flowers as she ushers in the day. Based on a relief by Thorvaldsen.*

PRIVATE COLLECTION

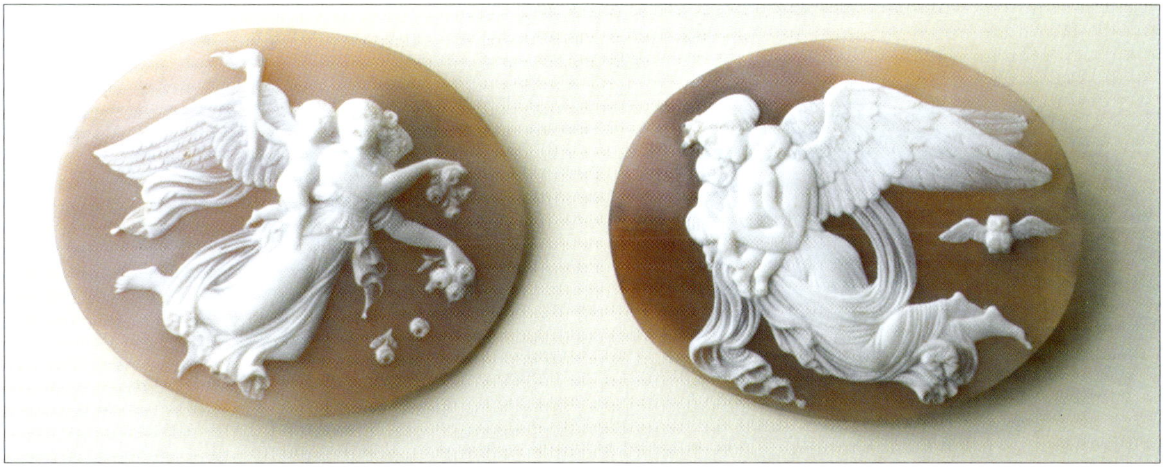

Plate 22. *Pair of Bull's Mouth shells depicting 'Day' and 'Night', 2in. (5cm) x 1½in. (4cm), based on a pair of bas-reliefs executed by Bertel Thorvaldsen in Rome, 1815. Thorvaldsen (1768-1844), a Danish sculptor, worked in Italy from 1797 to 1838, and was a leading figure of the Neo-classical movement. Hawks Le Grice describes 'Day and Night':*

> *'These two bas-reliefs are remarkable for delicacy of execution and poetic feeling. Aurora, with spreading wings, and drapery light as a summer breeze, seems to cleave the air in rapid flight, whilst with outstretched arm she scatters flowers on the earth; and Lucifer accompanies her in her aerial flight, ushering in the day. Night is represented under the form of a winged female; but the wings, to express repose, are collapsed, and the drapery hangs loosely, whilst the figure seems rather to float in the air than fly. Like Morpheus she wears around her head a wreath of poppies: the head droops; and the eyes are sealed in sleep. In her arms are infant twins hushed to dream in blissful innocence; whilst the night bird, making night hideous, screeches as he wings his way in regions of darkness.'*
>
> Count Hawks Le Grice, Walks Through The Studii Of The Sculptors At Rome, 1841 *(Vol. I, page 12)*

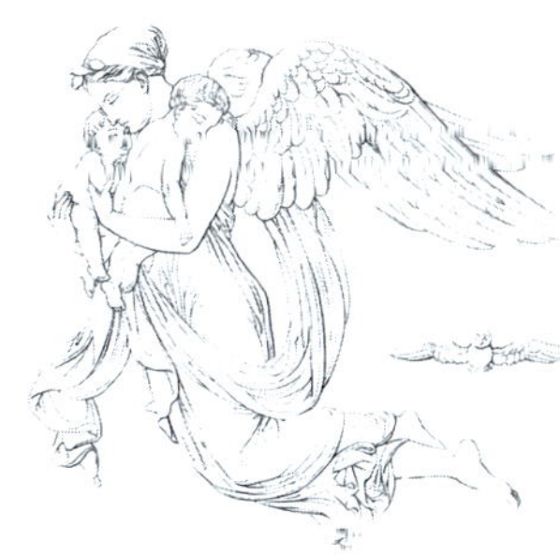

On the left shell, the goddess of Dawn, Eos (Aurora), accompanied by the Genius of Light, scatters roses as she ushers in the day. Homer described her as 'rosy-fingered'. The partner shell depicts Nyx, goddess of Night, carrying two sleeping children, whom Hesiod called 'Hypnos' (Sleep) and 'Thanatos' (Death). The chest of Cypselus (5th century BC) featured a carving of two infant figures, one black, one white, being carried in the arms of Night. PRIVATE COLLECTION

Thorvaldsen's bas-reliefs of 'Day' and 'Night' were extensively copied in cameo: 'Take only a stroll through the streets of Condotti, Babuina and Corso in Rome, and you will see them in every second window cut in stone or marine shells, or cut in plaster.'

J.M. Thiele, Thorwaldsen, 1869 *(Vol. II, page 7)*

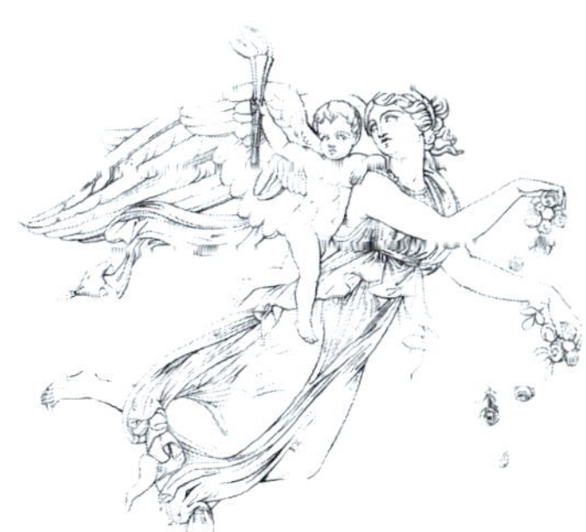

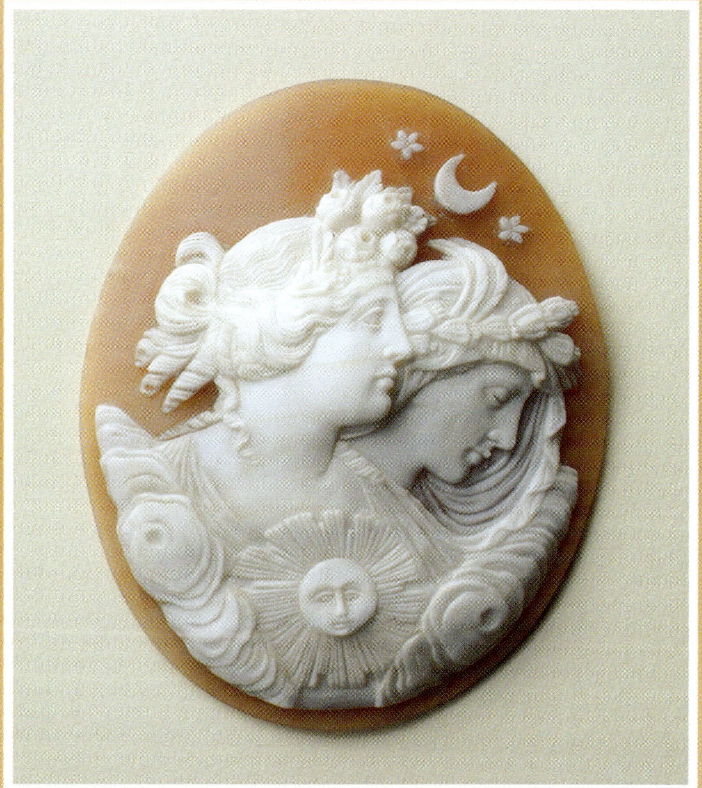

Plate 23. *Bull's Mouth shell, circa 1870, a personification of the goddesses 'Day and Night' with their respective attributes – the sun, a new moon and stars. 2⅜in. (6cm) x 2in. (5cm).* PRIVATE COLLECTION

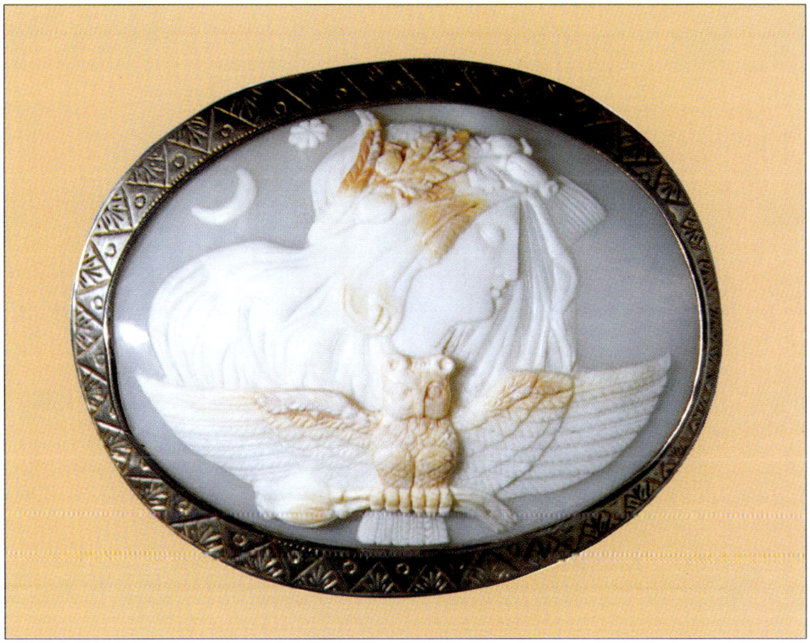

Plate 24. *Bull's Mouth shell, engraved silver mount, circa 1870. 2⅜in. (6cm) x 2in. (5cm). Veiled Nyx (Night) has her eyes closed in sleep, poppies in her hair and her attributes – an owl and moon – in the scene.*

BELLUM ANTIQUES, ANTIQUARIUS, LONDON £850

NYX (Greek)
'NIGHT'
Cameo Key: Female, hair dressed with flowers, or veiled

NYX, goddess of Night, was a feared goddess and mother of many powerful forces including Hypnos (Sleep), Thanatos (Death), Doom and the Tribe of Dreams. Hesiod describes her:

> 'One carries far-seeing light for those on earth, but the other, baleful Night, shrouded in clouds of mist, cradles Sleep, the brother of Death.'
>
> Hesiod, *Theogony* (page 25, West translation)

According to Homer, Nyx was feared and respected even by Zeus. Her attributes were the poppy – the narcotic, sleep-inducing plant – and nocturnal creatures such as the owl and bat.

Nyx as a Cameo Subject

Night is veiled or crowned with a wreath of poppies, her eyes are closed. Stars, sun, crescent moon, owl, flowers can be in the scene. See Plate 24.

'Day and Night' – the two goddesses, one veiled, the other with flowers in her hair, with their attributes in the scene. See Plates 23, 104.

Night in flight carrying two sleeping children in her arms – Sleep and Death. See Plates 21, 25.

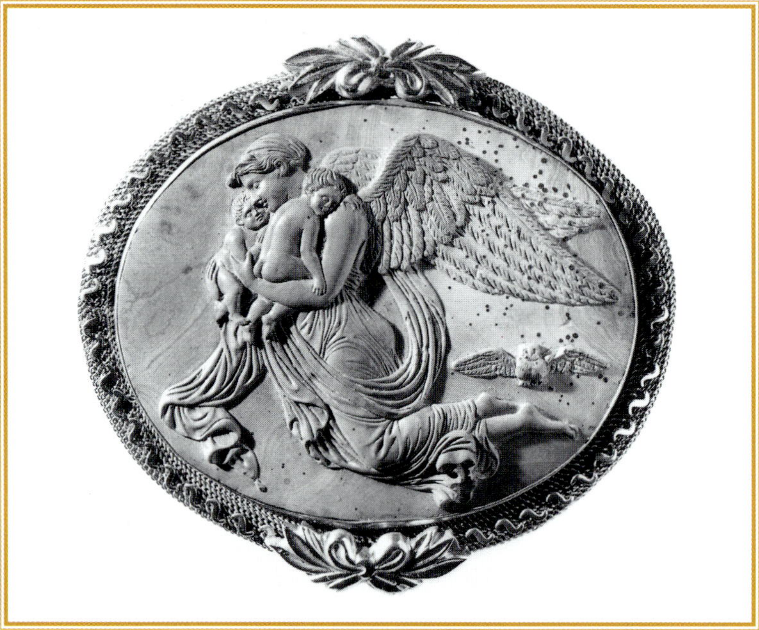

Plate 25. *Malachite, later set as a gold brooch. Italian cameo 1820-30, 2in. (5.1cm) high. A winged figure (Nyx) carrying her two sleeping children. Taken from a marble relief by Bertel Thorvaldsen executed in 1815, it remained a favourite subject for cameos throughout the 19th century. For further information, see Entry 901 in The Art of the Jeweller, Ed. Hugh Tait.* COURTESY OF THE BRITISH MUSEUM, HULL GRUNDY BEQUEST

Nyx's Children: Hypnos and Thanatos

Hypnos
God of Sleep, son of Night and brother of Death, who lived in Hades, the Underworld. He reputedly had one thousand children, including Morpheus (Dream) and Phoebotor (Nightmare). The Romans called this god 'Somnus'.

Thanatos
The personification of death. When the Moirae (Fates) decided that a person had completed his allotted time on earth, Thanatos cut off a lock of his hair and his soul was sent to Hades. Hesiod describes Thanatos:

> 'the other has a heart of iron and a pitiless spirit of bronze in his breast. That man is his whom he once catches, and he is hateful even to the immortal gods.'
>
> Hesiod, *Theogony* (page 25, West translation)

IRIS (Greek)
Cameo key: Winged female, caduceus, cornucopia

IRIS, goddess of the Rainbow, linked Olympus and the earth. She wore a multicoloured robe and was a messenger of the gods, especially Hera, Queen of Olympus.

Iris as a Cameo Subject
A winged goddess in a draped robe, sometimes carrying a caduceus to symbolise her role as the gods' messenger. See Plate 26.

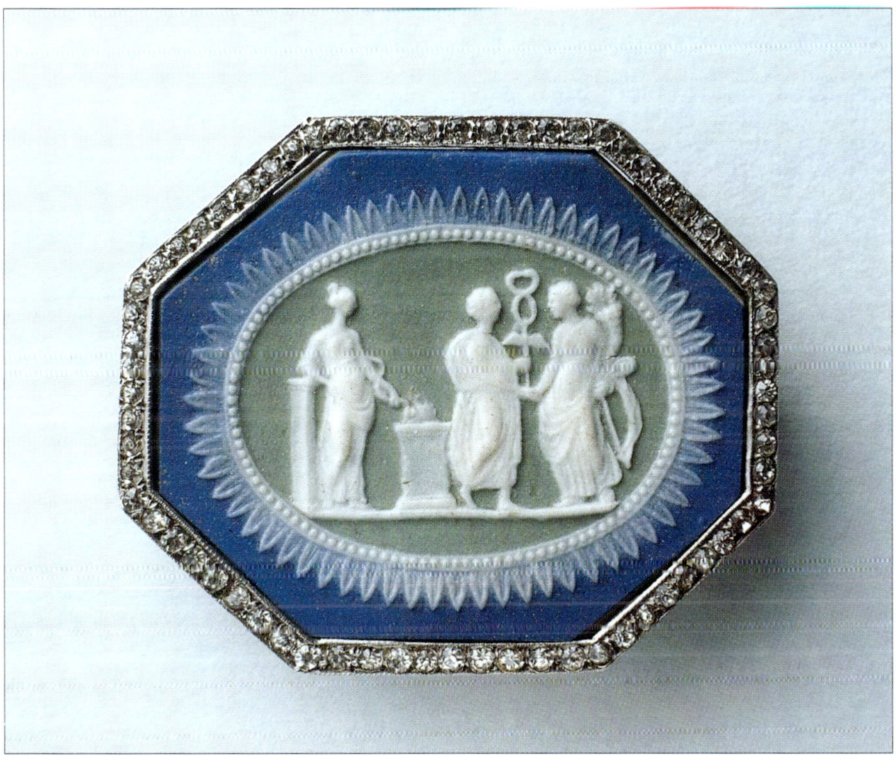

Plate 26. *Wedgwood cameo, circa 1790-1800, depicting Iris (with caduceus and cornucopia), Asclepius, god of Medicine, and his daughter Hygeia presenting a patera to a serpent, possibly an amalgamation of two separate subjects. 1³⁄₁₆in. (3cm) x 1½in. (4cm).* PRIVATE COLLECTION

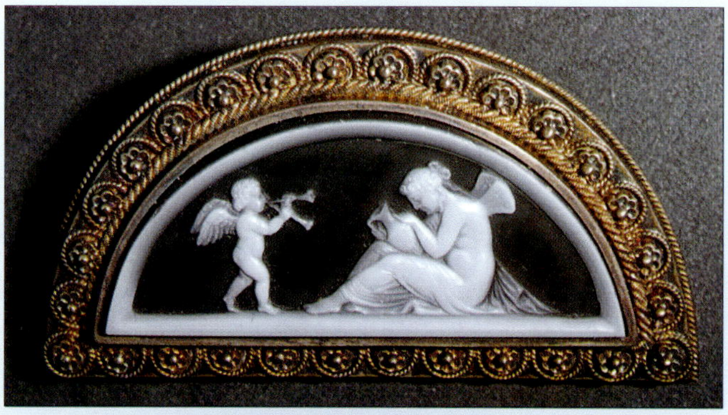

THE POWER OF LOVE

Aphrodite, goddess of Love

Eros, god of Love

Eros and Psyche, a tale about the soul

Clytia, a lovelorn nymph

Orpheus and Eurydice, a tale of love and loss

Flora, goddess of flowers

Cephalus and Procris, a tale of love and loss

– Chapter 3 –

THE POWER OF LOVE

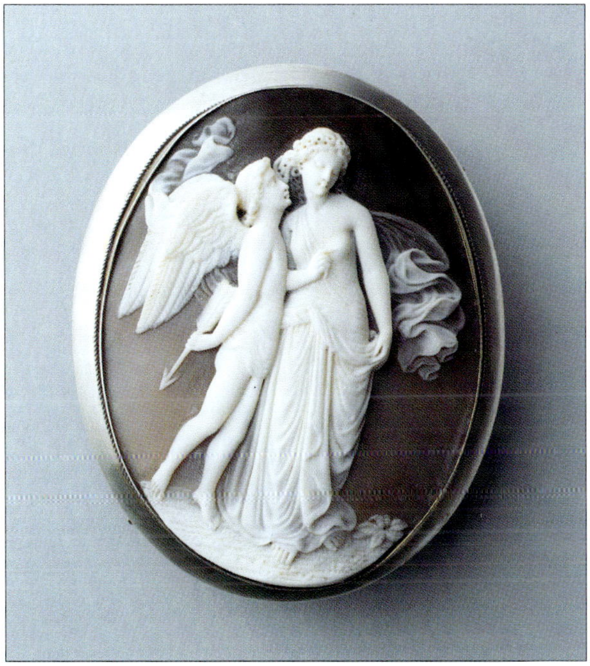

Myths demonstrating universal truths about love. Tales of romance, tenderness and passion, as well as stories of duplicity, jealousy, and loss. Nineteenth century cameos often portrayed Eros, and Eros with Psyche.

APHRODITE (Greek), **goddess of Love**
VENUS (Roman)
Cameo Key: A beautiful female, nude or wearing a diaphanous robe

'Goddess from Cyprus, cunning schemer, why did
Zeus honour you with this special privilege?
For you overpower men's reason; there is none
Clever or strong enough to get away.'

Anonymous, *Theognidea*, Greek, circa 6th century BC

APHRODITE, goddess of Love and Beauty, was the embodiment of ideal female beauty, her sole purpose to be adored by gods and men. She was sensual, vain, cruel and jealous; often encouraging her son, Eros, to play cruel tricks in love on gods and mortals. Her irresistible charm was the most formidable of her powers. Aphrodite was patron of fertility and marriage and of courtesans and prostitutes. According to Homer, she was the daughter of Zeus and the nymph Dione. Hesiod's version of her birth saw her arise naked and fully formed from the foam

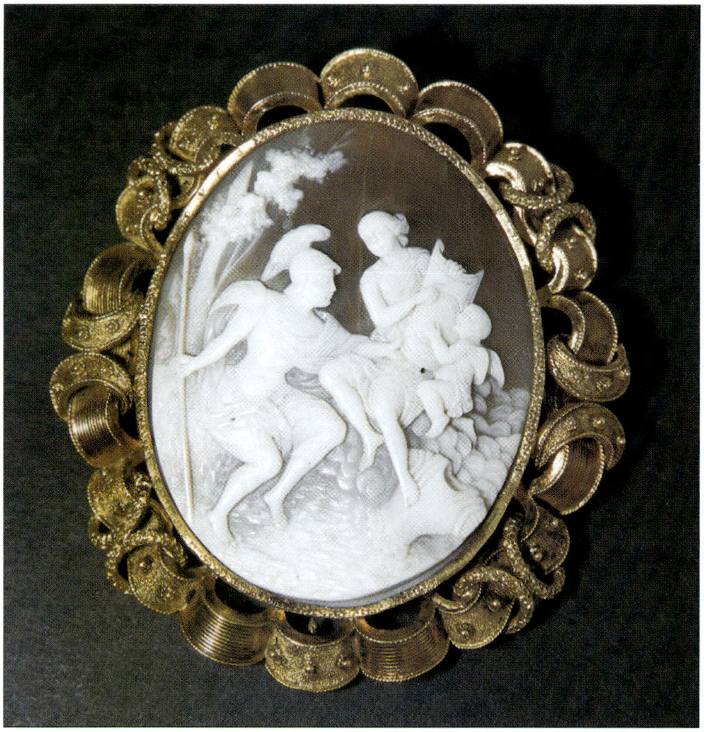

Plate 28. *Black Helmet shell, ornate High-Victorian gold mount, circa 1860. 3⅛in. (8cm) x 2⅜in. (6cm). Aphrodite with her lover Ares, god of War and her son Eros, god of Love. Aphrodite and Eros tease Ares and withhold his shield.*
SPICER WARIN ANTIQUES, SILVER FOX GALLERY, PORTOBELLO ROAD, LONDON £950

produced when the castrated phallus of the Titan Uranus was thrown into the sea. (Greek *aphros*, foam.) Gentle breezes carried her to the island of Cyprus where the Horae (Seasons) clothed and bejewelled her before presenting her to the gods on Mount Olympus.

Aphrodite wore a magic breastband, a *cestus* that made everyone fall in love with her:

'she loosed from her breasts the breastband, pierced and alluring, with every kind of enchantment woven through it...There is the heat of Love, the pulsing rush of Longing, the lover's whisper irresistible – magic to make the sanest man go mad.'

Homer, the *Iliad*, XIV (page 376, Fagles translation)

Previous page:
Plate 27. *Black Helmet shell, silver mount, 2¾in. (7cm) x 2in. (5cm), circa 1880. Aphrodite and Eros, after the statue 'The First Whisper of Love' (1846) by William Calder Marshall (Royal Dublin Society, Dublin). Possibly inspired by a literary source. The words of Ovid may be applicable here:*

> *'For, while her son Cupid was kissing Venus ... he unwittingly grazed her breast with an arrow...the wound was deeper than it seemed...[she was] captivated by the beauty of a mortal [Adonis].'*
>
> *Ovid,* Metamorphoses, *X (page 239, Innes translation)*

PRIVATE COLLECTION

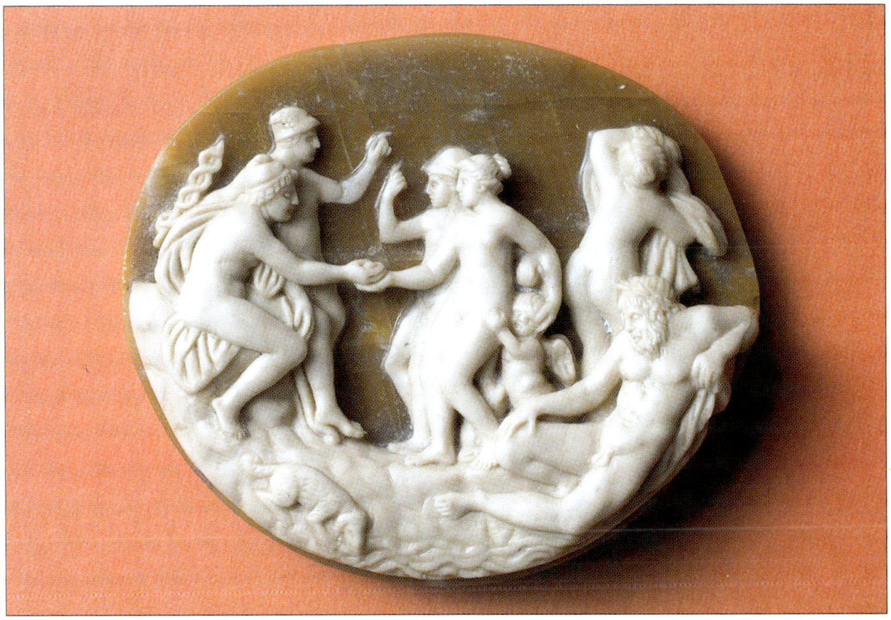

'The Judgement of Paris'

Plate 29. *Unmounted jasper ground with figures carved in calcite. Italian, circa 1710. 2¾in. (7cm) x 2⅜in. (6cm). Paris, wearing the Phrygian cap of a Persian soldier, is seated, awarding the prize of beauty to Aphrodite. Paris had asked the goddesses to undress so he could judge them fairly. The gods' messenger, Hermes, who brought the goddesses to Paris, looks on. Zeus reclines to the right of the scene, having commanded Paris to make the judgement. Aphrodite is accompanied by her son Eros and Hera composes herself behind Zeus.*
See the 'Early' London Judgement of Paris, *1602-03 by Peter Paul Rubens.*

PETER SZUHAY GRAYS LONDON £4500

Aphrodite rejected Zeus's advances so he gave her in marriage to the Smith god, Hephaestus. She took many lovers, including Ares, Dionysus, Hermes and Adonis. Aphrodite and Ares were caught together 'in flagrante' in a net of chains devised by her husband and were ridiculed by the other gods (see Plate 13):

> 'The gods were highly amused; one of them prayed that he too might be so shamed.'
> Ovid, *Metamorphoses*, IV (page 99, Innes translation)

The bird sacred to Aphrodite in antiquity was the dove (love and constancy). The Romans knew the goddess as Venus. Her son, Aeneas, a Trojan War hero, was the founder of Lavinium, capital of Latium.

The Judgement of Paris

Eris, the goddess of Strife, slighted by not being invited to the wedding of Thetis and Peleus, threw a golden apple amongst the guests. The apple was inscribed 'Let it be given to the fairest'. Aphrodite, Hera and Athena all claimed it as theirs so Zeus, not foolish enough to choose one over the others, instructed a handsome youth, Paris, Prince of Troy, to decide which goddess was the fairest. All three tried to bribe Paris – Hera promised him wealth and power, Athena wisdom and victory. Aphrodite offered him the love of the most beautiful woman on earth. Paris chose Aphrodite, who awarded him the love of the beautiful Helen, Queen of Sparta. Paris's seduction and abduction of Helen led to the Trojan War. See Plate 29.

Aphrodite and Adonis

Grazed by Eros's arrow, Aphrodite fell in love with Adonis, a youth as beautiful as an immortal. Adonis was the son of the Cypriot King, Cinyras and his daughter Myrrah, a union contrived by Aphrodite after Myrrah offended her. To save her from death when the incestuous act was discovered, Myrrah was transformed into a myrrh tree. The tree burst open and Adonis was born. Aphrodite, besotted with Adonis, accompanied him everywhere, preferring his company to that of the other gods. Ares, god of War and Aphrodite's lover, became jealous and while the youth was out hunting, Ares transformed himself into a boar and gored Adonis. Aphrodite, in her swan-drawn chariot, heard his cries and flew down to find him dying. She sprinkled Adonis's blood with sweet nectar and anemone flowers appeared, symbolic of abandonment and despair. Bereft, Aphrodite begged Zeus to restore Adonis to life. Zeus agreed, but only on condition that he spent part of the year on earth and part in the underworld, with Persephone, Queen of Hades, who had also loved him.

Aphrodite as a Cameo Subject

Aphrodite and Eros: A beautiful female, nude or in a diaphanous robe, often portrayed with her son Eros, god of Love, a cherubic figure. See Plate 27.

The Triumph of Aphrodite: A beautiful female in a swan-drawn chariot, or accompanied by Eros and other 'erotes' such as Himeros (carnal desire), Pothos (love and desire) and various muses and nymphs, or the Charites.

Aphrodite and Adonis as lovers: Adonis in a *chiton* (short tunic) with bow and arrow/dogs. Eros is in the scene.

Aphrodite at toilet: The goddess bathing/attended by nymphs pouring water from a *hydria* (jug), or dressing her hair, presenting her with articles such as a mirror. Eros is in the scene.

Aphrodite and Ares: The lovers, Ares (in armour) and Aphrodite, representing beauty and valour with Eros in the scene. See Plate 28.

Reclining Aphrodite: The nude goddess, representing ideal female beauty.

The Judgement of Paris: Paris, a youth in a *chiton*, to one side of the scene. The three goddesses, Athena, Aphrodite and Hera, stand before him. Hermes, Divine Messenger, is also present. Sometimes Zeus is in the scene as well. See Plate 29.

At the forge of Hephaestus, Aphrodite, Eros and Ares are in the scene. See Plate 12.

Birth of Aphrodite: The goddess rises from the waves on a shell.

See also: Ares, Charites, Eros, Hephaestus, Paris, The Trojan War.

Plate 30. *Bull's Mouth shell cameo suite, circa 1820. A festooned gold necklace, bracelet and earrings depicting various mythological scenes:*

Necklace, from clasp, clockwise: maenad, Eros and butterfly (Psyche); Eros in swan-drawn chariot; triton and Genius of Light precede Aphrodite; Aphrodite and Eros in the forge of Hephaestus; Poseidon in seahorse-drawn chariot; Eros in swan-drawn chariot; Aphrodite and Eros.

Bracelet: Eros and Psyche before an altar of love; Europa on a bull (Zeus in disguise); a libation to love; centaur and nymph; Eros with a dog at play.

Earrings: Apollo playing a double-pipe and a Muse. The earring tops depict theatre masks.

LANDSBERG AND SON (ANTIQUES LTD.), HATTON GARDEN, LONDON

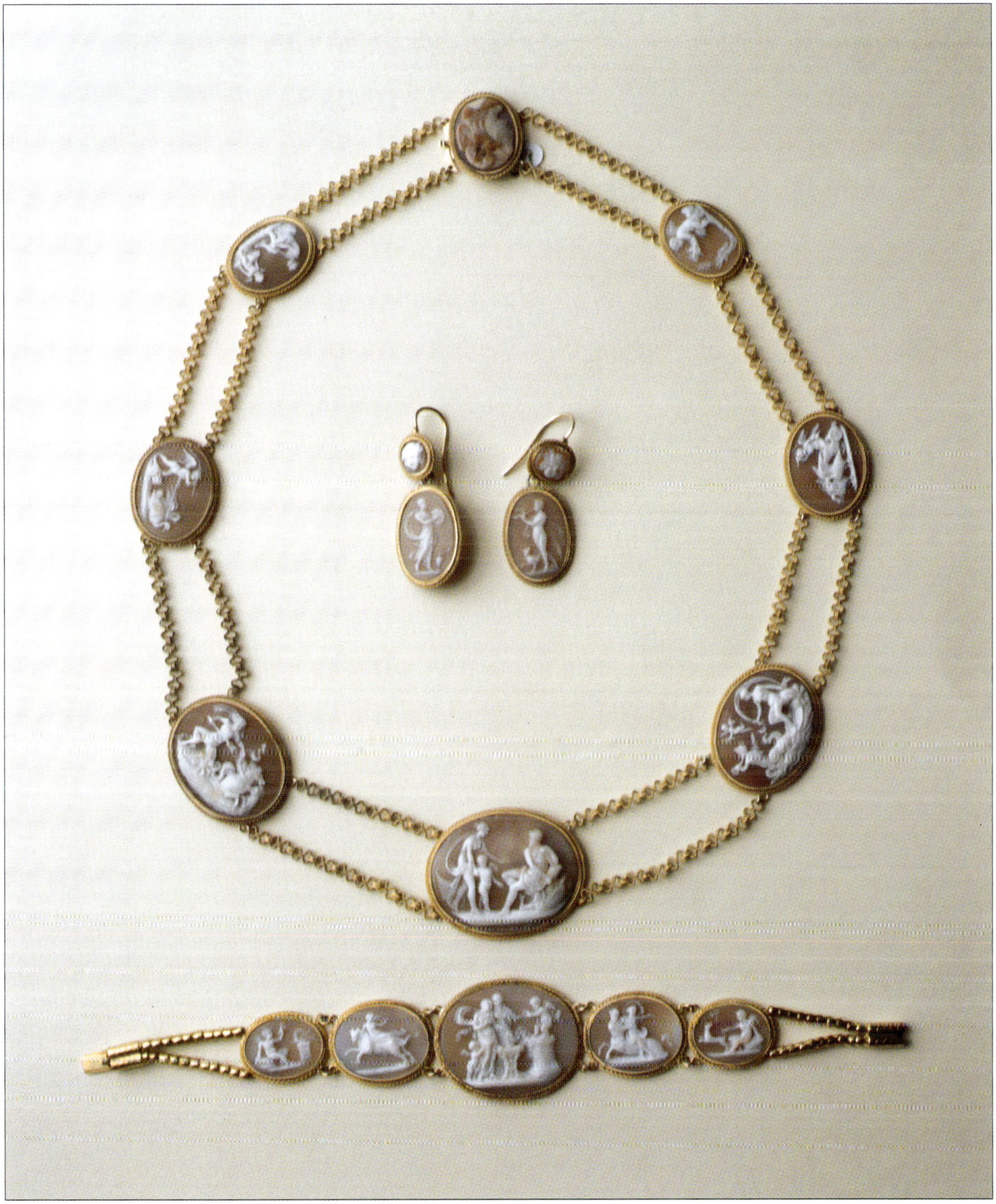

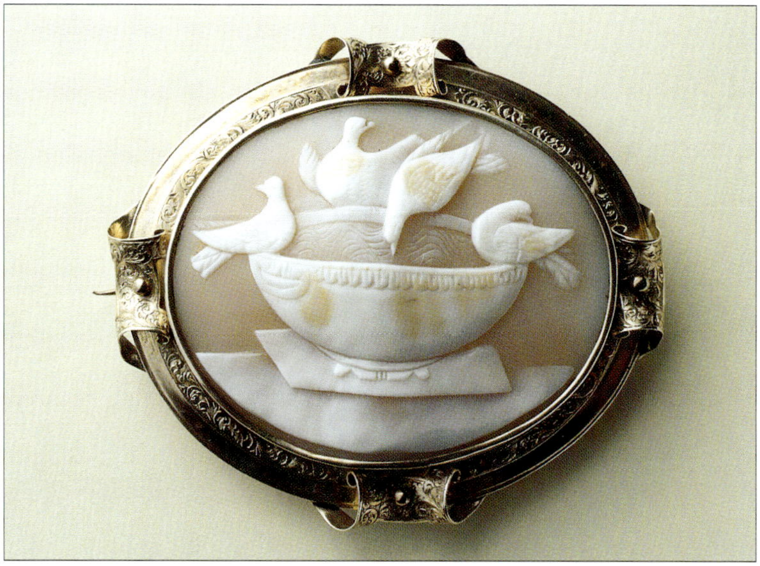

Plate 31. *Bull's Mouth shell, engraved gold mount, circa 1870, 2in. (5cm) x 2¾in. (7cm). 'The Doves Of Pliny'. This popular cameo subject was also widely depicted on mosaics, pietra dura and ivory carvings during the 19th century.* M. ROWAN AT www.rowanandrowan.com £550

THE DOVES OF PLINY
THE DOVES OF APHRODITE (Venus)

Aphrodite, originally an Eastern deity, came to the island of Cyprus, the main point of contact for the Greeks with the East. Doves were her sacred birds and flocks of white doves were kept in her temple at Paphos. In *The Golden Ass*, a Roman tale (circa A.D. 158), Apuleius describes Aphrodite (Venus) preparing to mount her chariot:

> 'Four white doves from the flock in constant attendance on her flew happily forward and offered their rainbow-coloured necks to the jewelled harness, and when Venus mounted, drew the chariot along with enthusiasm.'
>
> Lucius Apuleius, *The Golden Ass* (Cupid and Psyche 111) (page 90, Graves translation)

The subject of doves drinking from a bowl became fashionable after the discovery in 1737 at Hadrian's Villa near Rome of a Roman copy of a Greek mosaic, 'the finest ever found', mentioned by Pliny the Elder as the work of Sosus at Pergamus (2nd century BC). Pliny wrote:

> 'There is a dove also, greatly admired, in the act of drinking, and throwing the shadow of its head upon the water: while other birds are to be seen sunning and pluming themselves, on the margin of a drinking bowl.'
>
> Pliny, *Natural History* (XXXVI.184)

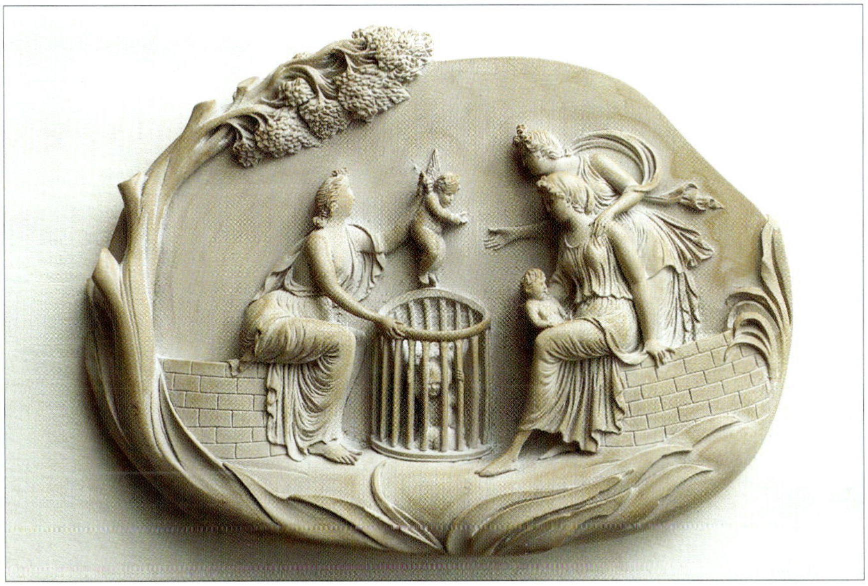

Plate 32. *Lava cameo plaque, circa 1870, 3⅛in. (8cm) x 4in. (10cm), based on a Pompeian wall painting from Stabiae discovered in 1759, depicting a woman selling cupids as love tokens, now in the Naples Museum. The subject held an added significance for Pompeii, whose patron was Venus. C. Nolli's etching from the album* Pitture antiche d'Ercolano *(1762) popularised the subject. The design is presented in 18th century French paintings, for example* La Marchande D'Amours *by Joseph-Marie Vien (1763), now in the Chateau de Fontainebleau. In the 19th century the subject decorated not only jewellery but also textiles, porcelain and objects of virtue.*

PRIVATE COLLECTION

EROS (Greek), **god of Love**
CUPID (Roman)
Cameo Key: Winged cherub or beautiful youth, with bow and arrow or torch

Hesiod described **EROS** as a cosmogonic force, 'the most handsome among the immortal gods'. Often in art and myth, the god of Love was portrayed as the son of Hermes and Aphrodite, goddess of Love, in the form of either an exquisitely beautiful youth or a winged cherub. Beneath his cherubic exterior, Eros

A bas-relief by Bertel Thorvaldsen, 1824, interpreting this popular Herculaneum subject as the different ages of love. He presents the vendor as Psyche, taking a little Cupid from the cage by his wings to offer him for sale. The tableau depicts all ages as being subject to the power of the god of Love.

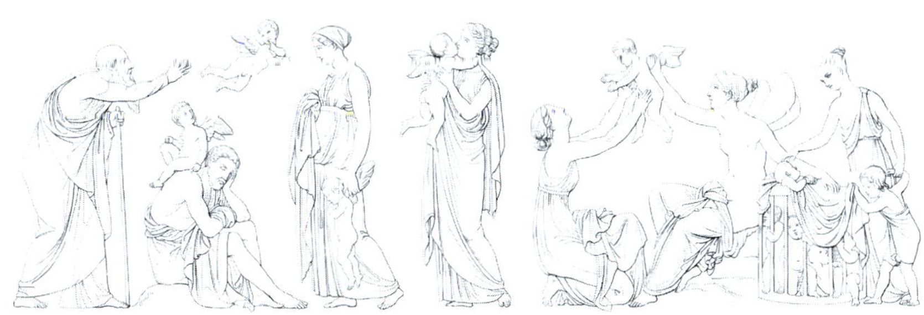

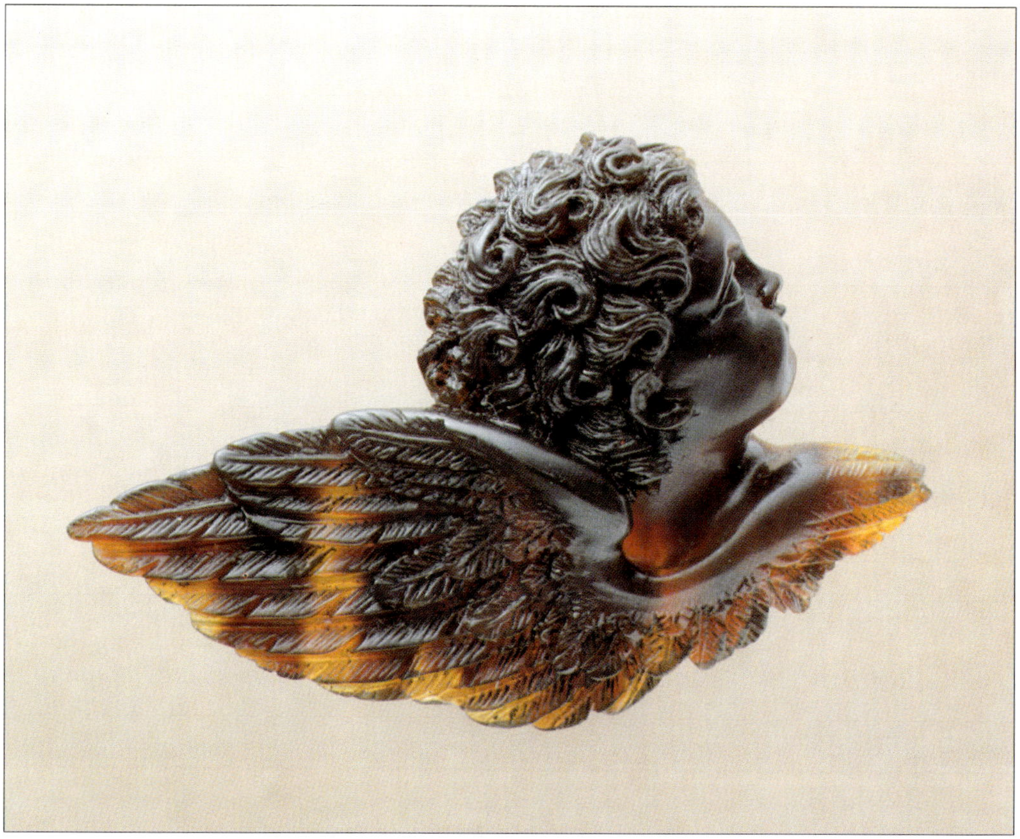

was the author of mischief, a devious god who took malicious pleasure in causing heartache and turmoil, and often a tool for his mother, Aphrodite:

> 'My son, you who are arms and hands to me, and all my power, take those all-conquering darts, my Cupid, and shoot your swift arrows into the heart...'
>
> Ovid, *Metamorphoses*, V (page 126, Innes translation)

Eros wounded gods and mortals with his arrows or used his flaming torches to arouse passion. He used golden arrows to encourage virtuous love, lead-tipped ones to encourage passion, and he sharpened his arrows on a whetstone stained with the blood of hearts. 'Erotes', a number of Eros figures in a scene, personify the many aspects of love. Cupid, the Roman version of Eros, was chiefly a god of passionate and carnal love. The term 'cupid' or 'putti' is also used to describe purely decorative motifs in art.

Eros as a Cameo Subject

A winged cherub or handsome youth with a bow and arrows, or a flaming torch, arouses love and passion. See Plates 98, 124.

Eros is often portrayed in the company of his mother, Aphrodite. See Plate 27.

Triumph of Eros: He is in a chariot, shooting arrows. See Plate 30.

Eros with a blindfold on, or with his hands tied behind his back, to show that love chooses randomly.

Education of Eros: With Hermes, Aphrodite or a nymph and a book or tablet.

Plate 33 (left). *Tortoiseshell carving of Eros, circa 1860-70. 1½in. (4cm) x 2⅜in. (6cm).*
CHARLOTTE SAYERS, GRAYS, LONDON £1950

Plate 34. *Bull's Mouth shell, silver mount, circa 1870. Eros, after Raphael. 2⅜in. (6cm) x 2in. (5cm).*
MARIAD, ANTIQUARIUS, LONDON £300

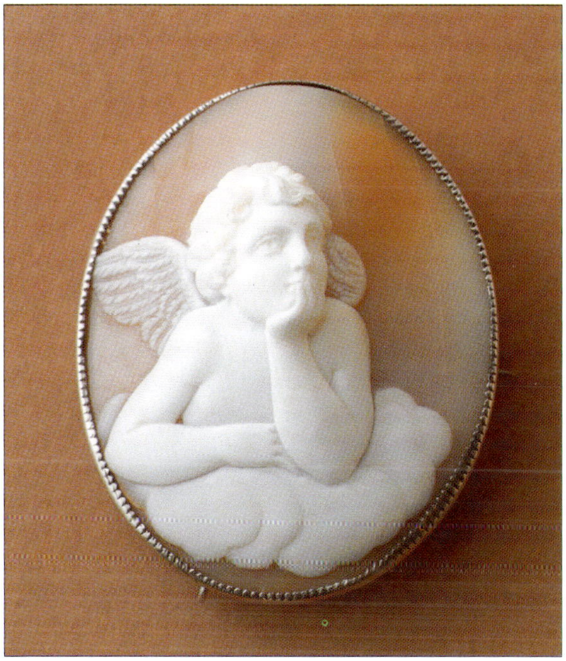

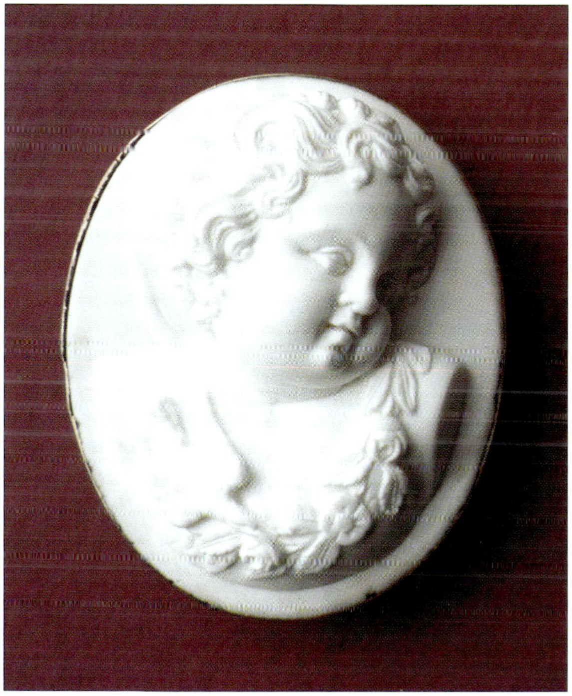

Plate 35. *White lava, gold mount, circa 1860. A flower-bedecked cherub with dove and quiver. 2in. (5cm) x 1½in. (4cm).*
S. HARLOWE AT www.rowanandrowan.com £375

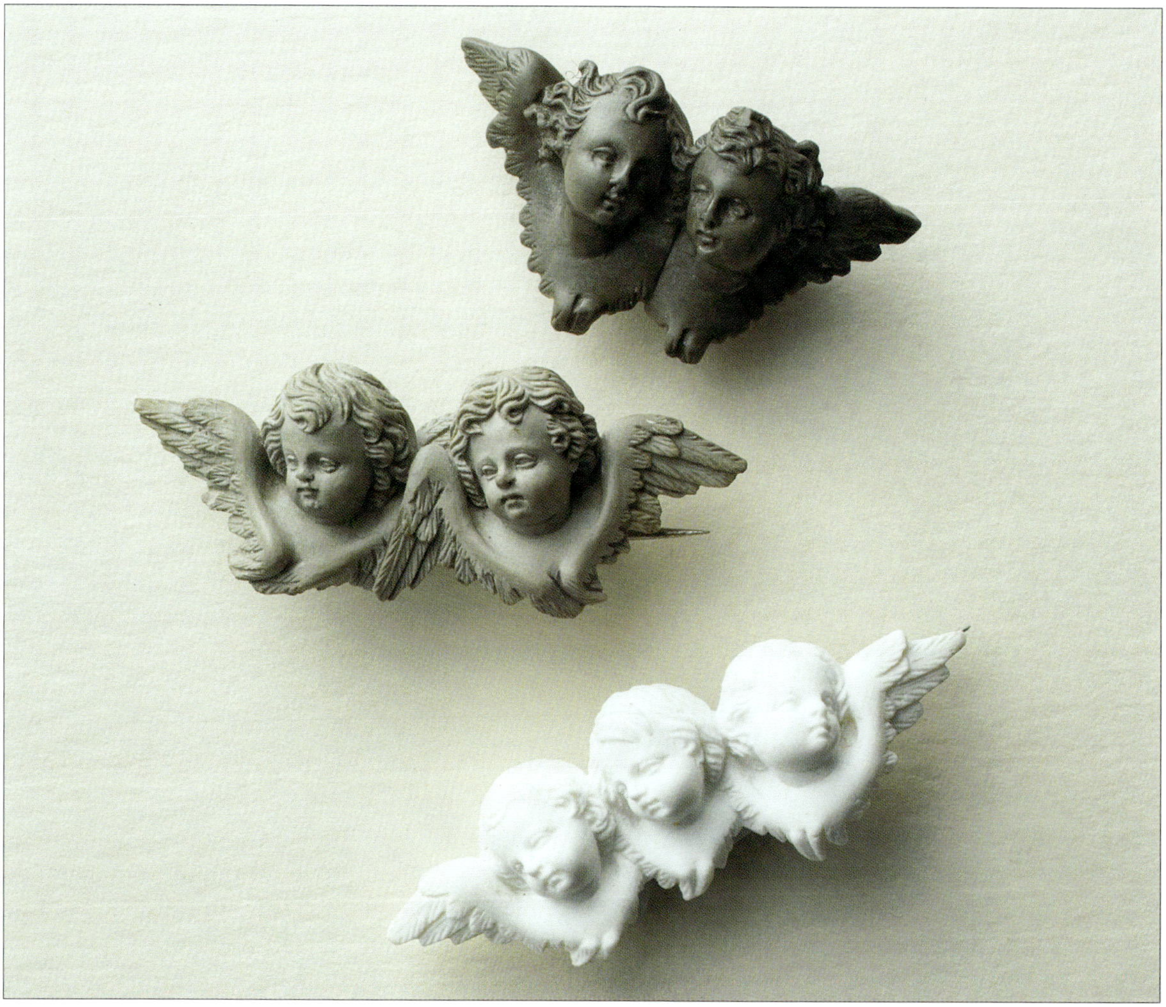

Erotes

Plate 36. *Lava carvings, circa 1860, cherubic heads in flight. 1in. (2.5cm) x 1½in. (4cm).* PRIVATE COLLECTION

Punishment of Eros: His mother, or a nymph, takes away his arrows/chastises him.
Eros and Anteros. With his identical brother.
Love vanquished – Eros chained to a wall, weeping.
Eros at play: Variously with nymphs/a swan/a goat/a panther. See Plate 30.
Cupids being released from a cage by the vendor of love. See Plate 32.
Eros with a lion/on a dolphin/with Cerberus/an eagle: Allegories of the power of love over the four elements – earth, ocean, fire and air. See Frontispiece and Plate 91.
If Eros appears in a scene with others, it indicates that love is present.
See also: Aphrodite, Dionysus, Hades, Psyche.

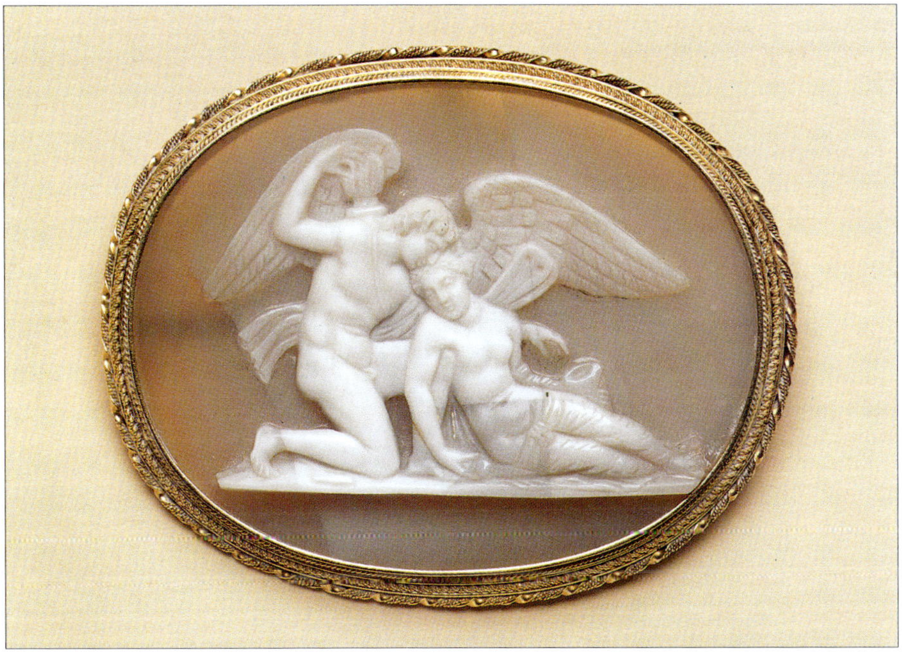

Plate 37. *Chalcedony, gold ropework frame, circa 1810. Eros and Psyche in Hades. Eros cradles his unconscious lover and withdraws an arrow from his quiver with which to revive her. 3in. (7.5cm) x 2in. (5cm).* PETER SZUHAY, GRAYS, LONDON £1600

EROS AND PSYCHE

Cameo Key: Female with butterfly wings

A story often portrayed on nineteenth century cameos, an allegorical tale of love conquering the soul. It is from a Roman fable, *The Golden Ass* by Lucius Apuleius, circa AD 158. *Psyche* in Greek means both 'soul' and 'butterfly' – the soul was seen as a butterfly which left the body after death. Here, after a lifetime of trials and tribulations, the soul ultimately found true happiness.

Aphrodite, jealous of the mortal Psyche's beauty, ordered Eros to punish her, but he pricked himself with his own arrow and fell in love with her. Every night the invisible god visited Psyche. One night, unable to resist any longer, she lit an oil lamp to see what her lover looked like, but a drop of hot oil fell on the sleeping Eros who angrily abandoned her. Love deserted the soul.

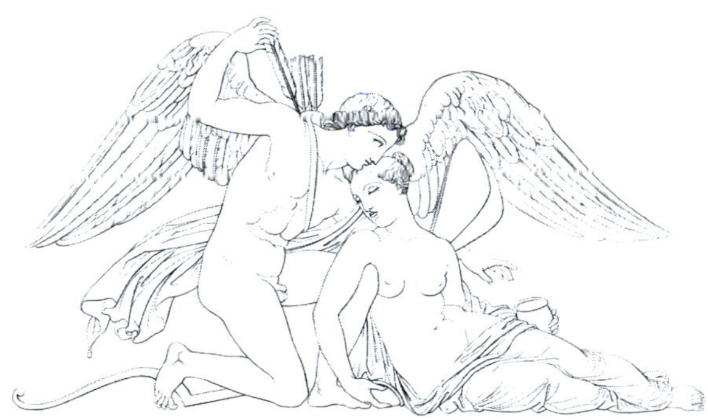

A bas-relief by Bertel Thorvaldsen, executed in 1810.

Plate 38. *Onyx, archaeological revival gold mount, circa 1870, 1⅛in. (3cm) x 1½in. (4cm). depicting Eros and Psyche, based on an 18th century intaglio of* Amor and Psyche *by Giovanni Pichler, after a composition by Angelika Kauffmann, late 18th century interior designer and painter.*

S. J. PHILLIPS LTD., NEW BOND STREET, LONDON

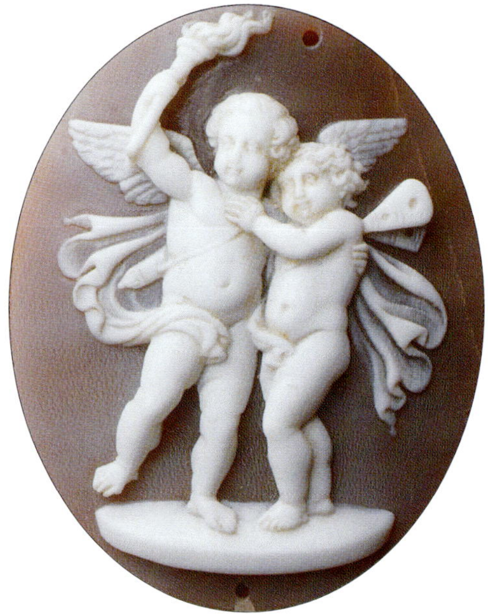

Plate 39 (below). *Black Helmet shell, late 19th century, 1½in. (4cm) x 1⅛in. (3cm), depicting the infant Eros and Psyche. Their pouting lips and dimpled cheeks impart a warning – do not be seduced by the dangerous sweetness of this budding flower.*

ANTIQUARIUS, LONDON £150

Psyche, distraught, wandered the world searching for her lost lover. Aphrodite caught and tormented her, forcing her to perform many difficult tasks. Eventually, in Hades, Psyche fell into a comatose sleep. Eros revived her with his golden arrow. Zeus gave him permission to marry Psyche and she became an immortal. The soul found eternal love.

Eros and Psyche as Cameo Subjects

Psyche as a young maiden with butterfly wings, or symbolised as a butterfly. See Plates 30, 38, 40.

Eros and Psyche: A young girl with butterfly wings and a handsome young god embrace and kiss/hold a bow and arrow/ascend towards Olympus. See Plates 39, 45.

Eros arouses the unconscious Psyche. See Plate 37.

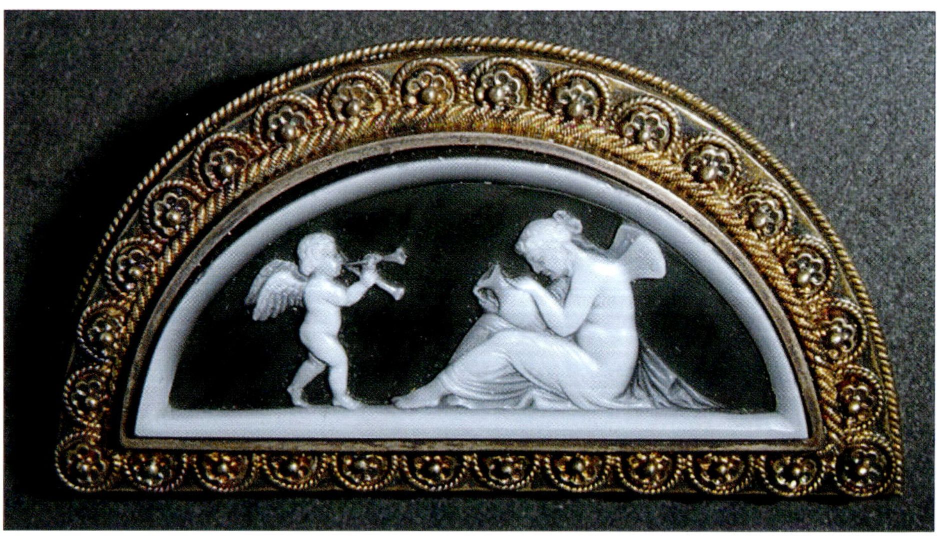

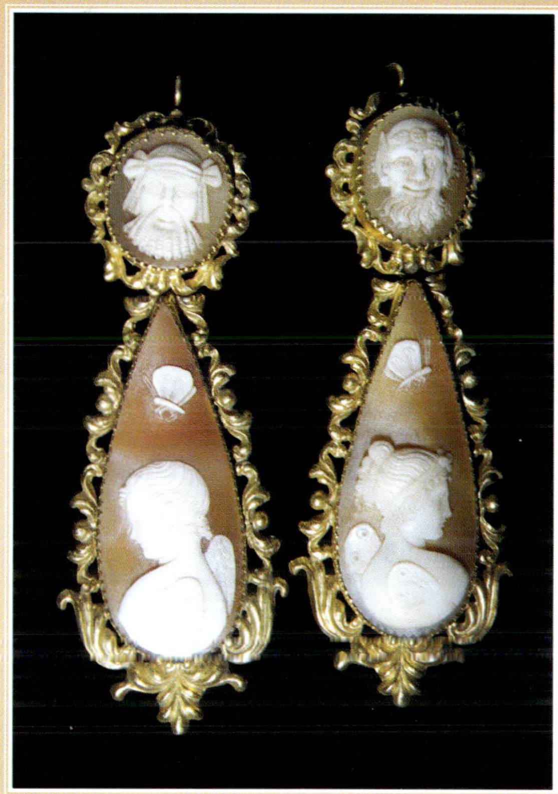

Plate 40. *Bull's Mouth shell, gold repoussé earring mounts, circa 1850, portraying the winged god Eros and Psyche (with butterfly wings) beneath butterflies (love conquers the soul). The tops depict theatre masks.*

CHARLOTTE SAYERS, GRAYS, LONDON £1250

CLYTIA (Greek)
CLYTIE (Roman)

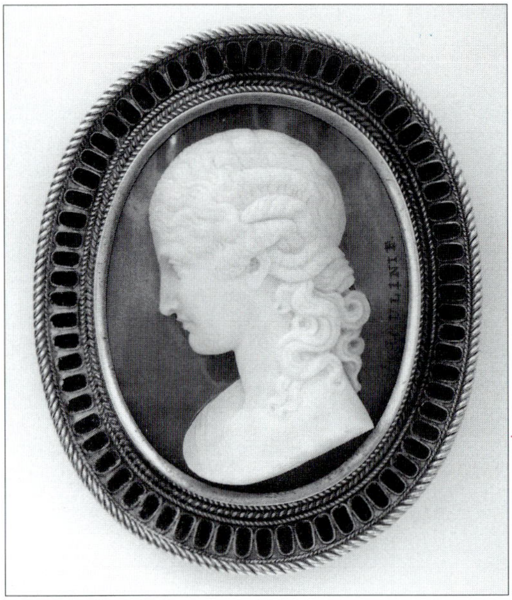

Plate 41. *Bust of a young girl known as 'Clytie', sardonyx in a silver-gilt setting, ornamented with corded wire and ovals of wirework containing deep blue enamel. Engraved signature 'L.SAULINI F.' for Luigi Saulini (1819-1883), the prominent Roman gem-engraver. Cameo circa 1855, the setting probably English, mid-19th century. 1½in. (3.7cm) high. Based on a Roman marble sculpture, wrongly identified in the 18th century as Clytie. The bust in now thought to represent Antonia (36BC-AD38), daughter of Mark Antony and Octavia, and mother of the Emperor Claudius. For further information, see Entry 919 in* The Art of the Jeweller, *Ed. Hugh Tait.*

COURTESY OF THE BRITISH MUSEUM, HULL GRUNDY BEQUEST

CLYTIA, a water nymph, fell in love with the handsome Sun god, who spurned her. She sat pining for him, as Ovid describes:

> 'She had no use for the company of the nymphs, but sat upon the bare ground, night and day, under the open sky, her head uncovered, and her hair all disarrayed. For nine days she tasted neither food nor drink, but fed her hunger only on dew and tears. She never stirred from the ground: all she did was to gaze on the face of the sun god, as he journeyed on, and turn her own face to follow him. Her limbs, they say, became rooted to the earth, and a wan pallor spread over part of her complexion, as she changed into a bloodless plant: but in part her rosy flush remained, and a flower like a violet grew over her face. Though held fast by its roots, this flower still turns to the sun, and although Clytie's form is altered, her love remains.'
>
> Ovid, *Metamorphoses*, IV (page 101, Innes translation)

Clytia became, according to different versions, a sunflower or heliotrope. She symbolises love and devotion.

Clytia as a Cameo Subject

A fair young nymph, with Eros. A sunflower may be in the scene.

The profile of a beautiful, young woman with curled hair frequently described as 'Clytie' is thought to be Antonia, daughter of Mark Antony and Octavia. (*The Art of The Jeweller*, Ed. H. Tait, Vol. 1, p.138.) See Plate 41.

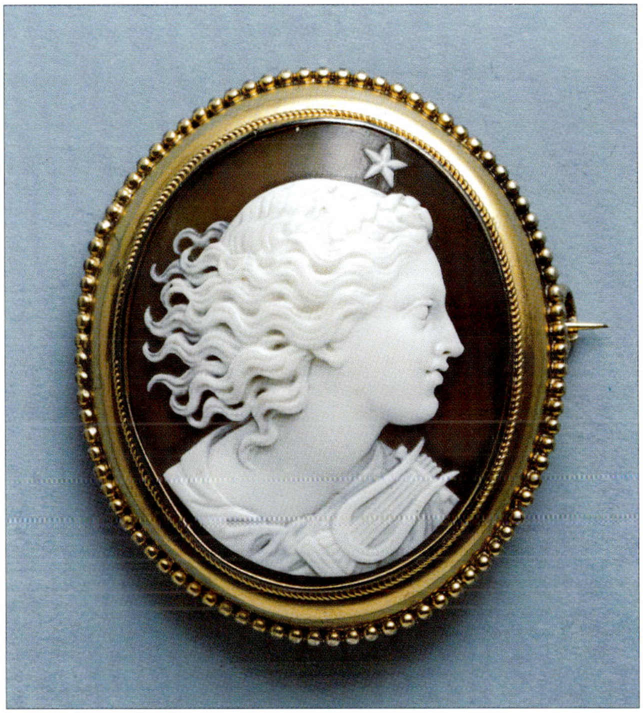

Plate 42. *Bull's Mouth shell, gold beaded mount, circa 1870. Orpheus with lyre and star, wearing a laurel wreath symbolic of poetic inspiration.* M. ROWAN AT www.rowanandrowan.com £550

ORPHEUS AND EURYDICE

Cameo Key: Male with a lyre

ORPHEUS, son of the Muse Calliope, played the lyre and sang so sweetly that all were enchanted by his song. It was said that his music had the power to soothe savage beasts. When his wife, the nymph Eurydice, was bitten by a snake and died, Orpheus travelled to Hades and begged the god of the Dead to let his wife live again. Hades and Persephone were so moved by his music that Hades agreed, providing that Orpheus did not turn and look at Eurydice until they had left the realm of the dead. Unfortunately his concern for his wife overcame him, he disobeyed the command and she was lost to him forever.

> 'Eurydice, dying now a second time, uttered no complaint against her husband. What was there to complain of, but that she had been loved?'
>
> Ovid, *Metamorphoses*, X (page 226, Innes translation)

Orpheus returned to earth, inconsolable. Thracian women, jealous of the power of his music and his

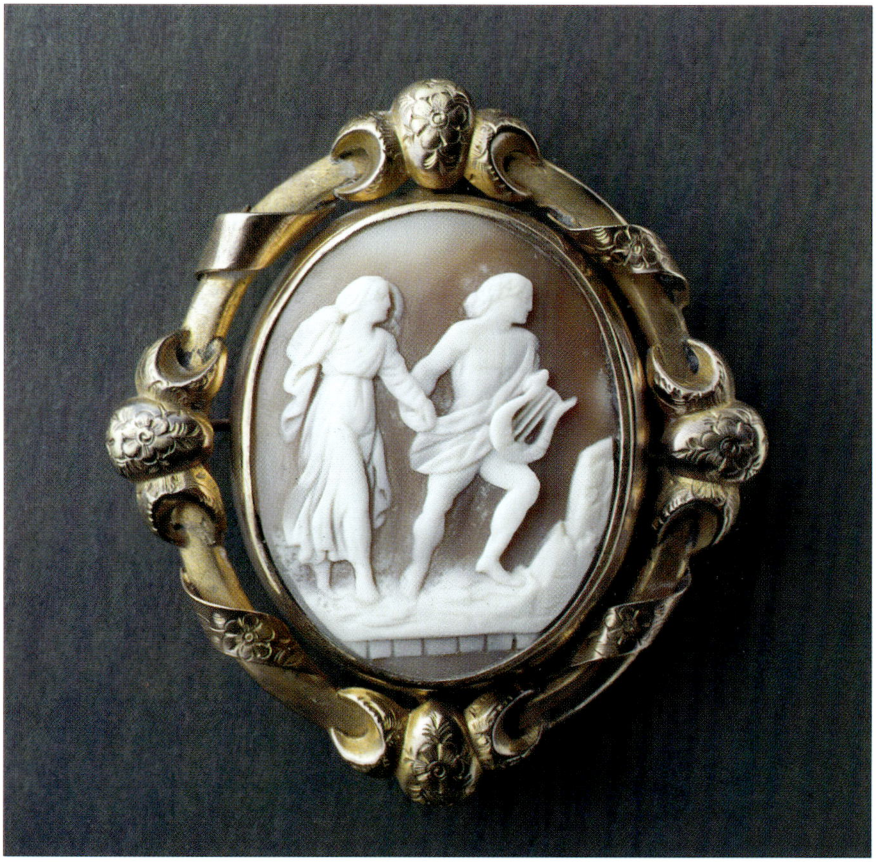

Plate 43. *Bull's Mouth shell, ornate gilt metal mount, circa 1880. 2⅜in. (6cm) x 2in. (5cm). Orpheus with lyre leads his wife, the nymph Eurydice, out of Hades (the Underworld).* M. ROWAN AT www.rowanandrowan.com £250

love for his wife, tore him limb from limb. The Muses placed his body and his lyre in the sky and his soul returned to Hades, where he was reunited with his beloved Eurydice.

> 'There they stroll together, side by side: or sometimes Orpheus follows, while his wife goes before, sometimes he leads the way and looks back, as he can do safely now, at his Eurydice.'
>
> Ovid, *Metamorphoses*, XI (page 247, ibid.)

Orpheus and Eurydice as Cameo Subjects

Orpheus with his lyre, wearing a laurel wreath to symbolise poetic inspiration. See Plate 42.

Death of Eurydice: She lies on the ground while Orpheus weeps over her.

Orpheus holding his lyre, with Eurydice. See Plate 43.

FLORA (Roman)
Cameo Key: Nymph with flowers

The Roman goddess of Flowers, associated with the Greek Chloris, made flowers blossom and grow. Zephyr, the wind, fell in love with this nymph and made her 'mistress of the flowers', symbolising new life, spring, regeneration and hope. Her festival, the Floralia, was celebrated from 28 April to 3 May each year.

Flora as a Cameo Subject

A lovely young nymph adorned with garlands of flowers, or with flowers entwined in her hair. Sometimes she holds a crown of blossoms or a cornucopia filled with flowers. See Plates 44, 101.

Triumph of Flora: In a procession of nymphs, sometimes led by Aphrodite. She holds a crown of flowers or wears them in her hair.

Flora and Zephyr: Two embracing figures intertwined, Zephyr has wings and holds a crown of flowers above her head.

Flora also personified 'Spring' on cameos.

See also: Zephyr.

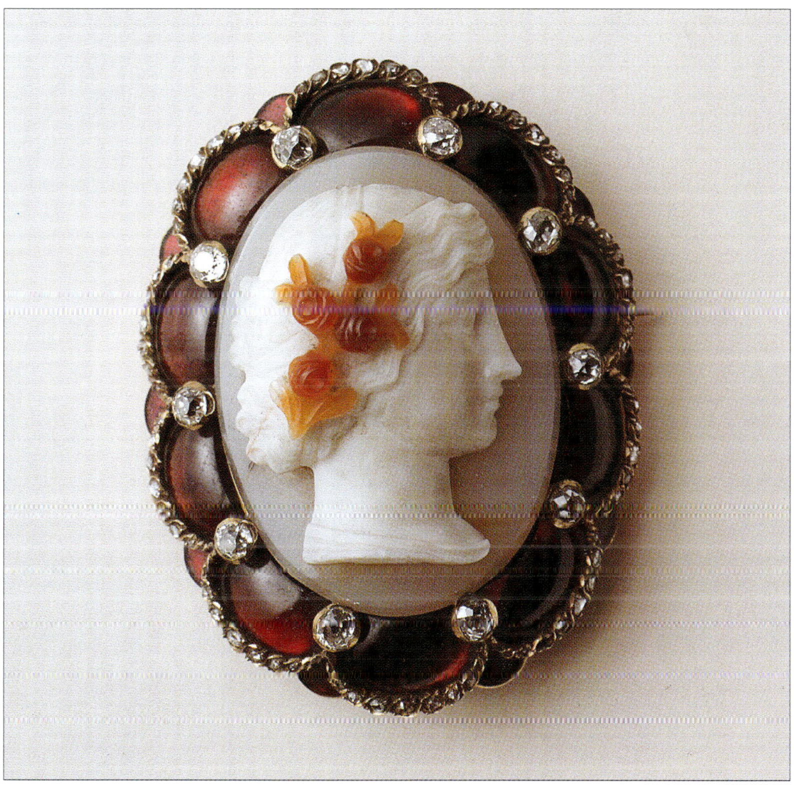

Plate 44. *Hardstone cameo, circa 1870, in a high-Victorian cabochon garnet and diamond mount. 3in. (7.5cm) x 2⅜in. (6cm). A young lady depicted as Flora.* S. J. PHILLIPS LTD., NEW BOND STREET, LONDON

CEPHALUS AND PROCRIS

Cameo Key: A pair of lovers

CEPHALUS, son of Hermes, deeply loved his wife Procris, Princess of Athens. However Eos, goddess of Dawn, abducted Cephalus to be her lover. He spurned her, swearing undying love for his wife; so the disgruntled goddess transformed him into a handsome youth called Pteleon and sent him back to Procris. Grieving for her lost husband, she rejected his advances, but eventually surrendered. Cephalus revealed his true identity, reviled her for her unfaithfulness and deserted her. Procris forswore the company of men and went to live with Artemis, virgin goddess of Hunting.

Cephalus later met a handsome youth called Pterelas, who owned a marvellous hound. He tried to buy the beast, but was told it could only be bought for love. Cephalus offered his love, the youth threw off his disguise and Procris stood before him. They were reunited and lived happily for some time. However, Procris could not forget the episode with the Dawn goddess and followed her husband when he went hunting. She hid in a bush and when he called for a breeze to cool him she assumed he was calling a lover. Cephalus saw a movement in the bush and hurled his spear, killing his wife. Inconsolable, Cephalus threw himself into the sea.

Cephalus and Procris as a Cameo Subject

A warrior holds a dying maiden, pulling a spear shaft from her breast. A herm may be in the scene to show that Cephalus is Hermes' son.

Cephalus, a youth, with the goddess of Dawn, Eos (Aurora). See Plate 45, 46.

See also: Eos.

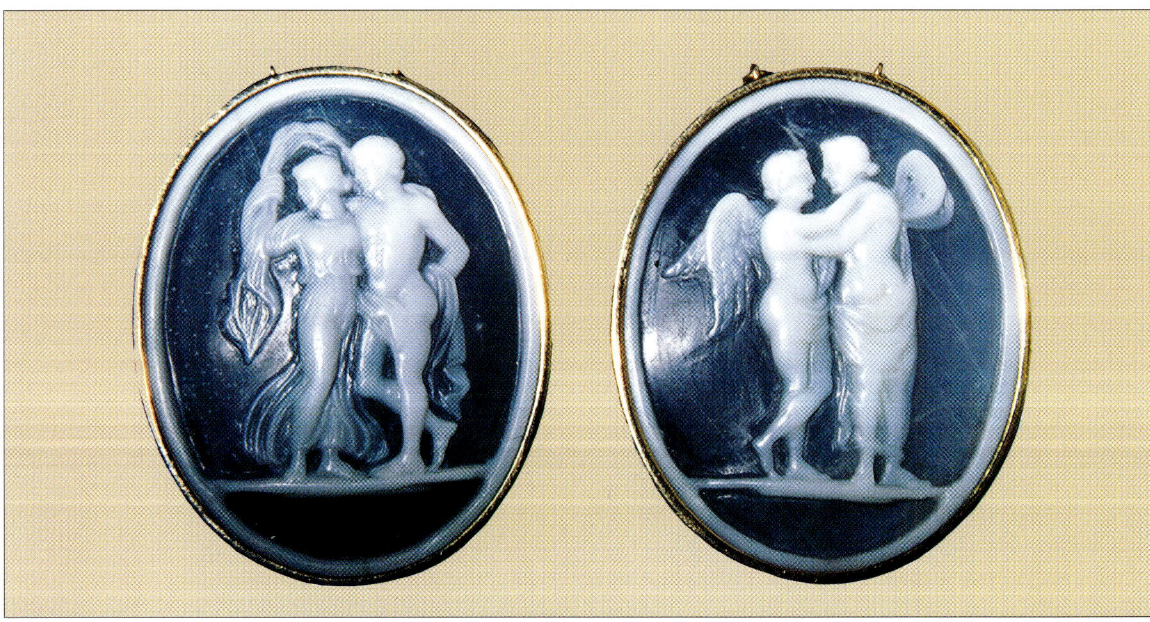

Plate 45. *Two 18th century French tinted shell cameos in gold channel-set mounts, 2in. (5cm) x 1½in. (4cm), depicting, on the left, Eos (Aurora) embracing Cephalus; and on the right Cupid and Psyche, 'The Kiss'. Based on antique Roman pastes.* S. J. PHILLIPS LTD., NEW BOND STREET, LONDON

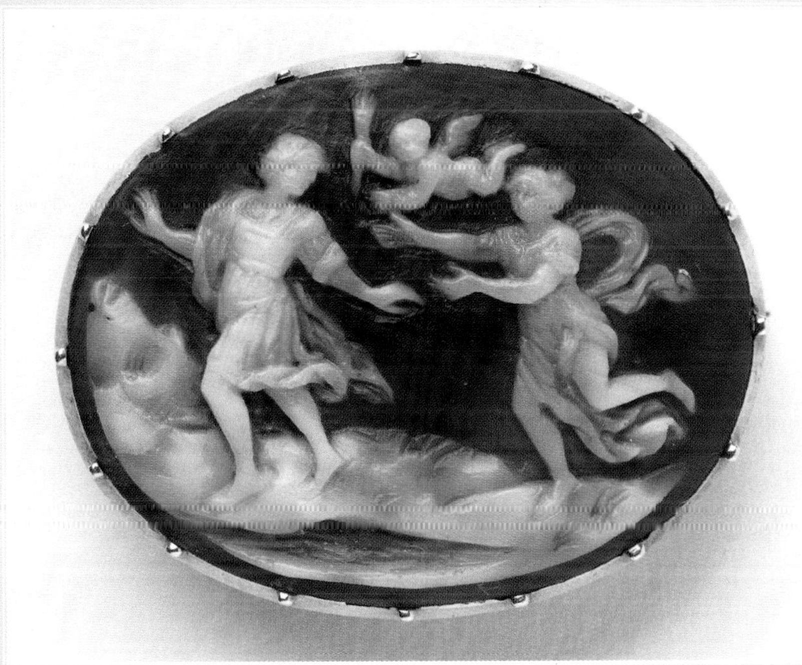

Plate 46. *Cowrie shell, closed-back gold mount, cut-down setting, circa 1820. 1½in. (4cm) x 1⅛in. (3cm). The goddess of Dawn, Eos (Aurora) pursues the youth Cephalus. She is accompanied by the Genius of Light.*

S. HARLOWE AT www.rowanandrowan.com £475

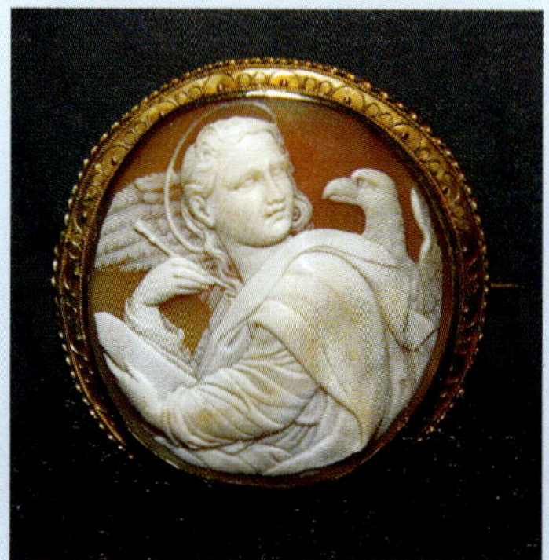

THE ARTS

Apollo: god of the Arts (see Cosmological Myths)

Charites: 'The Three Graces'

Muses: Inspirers of Creativity

Asclepius: god of Medicine

CHAPTER 4

THE ARTS

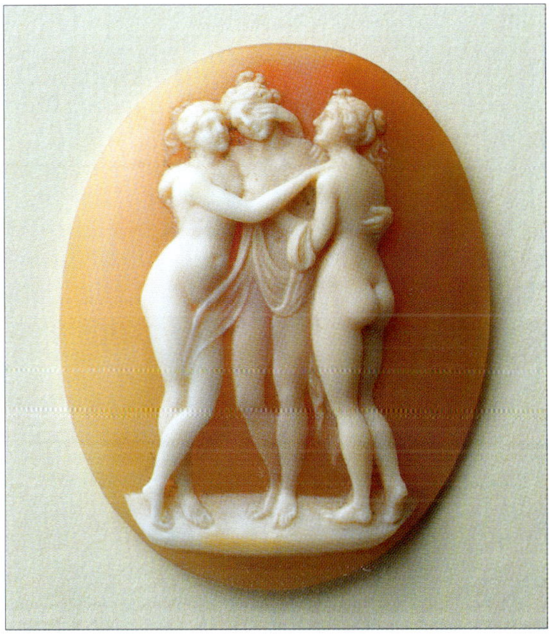

Plate 47. *Horned Helmet shell, mid-19th century. The Three Graces after a statue by Antonio Canova (1813). Based on a 1st century BC Pompeian fresco from the House of Titus Dentatus Panthera (Museo Nazionale, Naples). 1½in. (4cm) x 1⅛in. (3cm).*
CHARLOTTE SAYERS COLLECTION

Poetry and music played a vital role in worship of the gods and formed part of religious rituals. Poetry contests were considered to be of parallel importance to athletic contests. Apollo and the Charites ('The Three Graces') were popular nineteenth century cameo subjects.

CHARITES (Greek)
THE THREE GRACES
Cameo Key: Three beautiful females

These three elegant goddesses lived on Mount Olympus and presided over all the arts and social activities. They symbolised the beauty and grace of young women. Hesiod called them Euphrosyne (serenity), Aglaia (splendour) and Thalia (prosperity) and described their influence:

> 'From their eyes love that dissolves the flesh seeped down down as they looked; beautiful is their glance from their brows.'
> Hesiod, *Theogony* (page 30, West translation)

The Charites as Cameo Subjects
Three beautiful women, either nude or clothed in diaphanous robes, stand with their arms on each other's shoulders, facing each other. This shows that their gifts were given, shared and returned. See Plate 47.
They can appear as attendants of Aphrodite, or with Apollo or the Muses.
See also: Aphrodite, Apollo, Muses.

MUSES (Greek)
MUSAE (Roman)
Cameo Key: Beautiful maidens with various instruments, books, etc.

> 'every man is fortunate whom the Muses love;
> the voice flows sweet from his lips.'
> Hesiod, *Theogony* (page 6, West translation)

These nine beautiful daughters of Zeus and Mnemosyne (Memory) were goddesses who patronised art, music and literature and inspired creativity. They lived wild on Mount Parnassus until Apollo tamed them and made them his companions. The Muses were very wise, imparting their gifts to chosen men. Accounts of their roles and attributes vary, but generally they were believed to be fulfill the following roles, with the following attributes:

Calliope: The most important Muse, of Epic Poetry. Portrayed holding a trumpet, or tablet, books and a

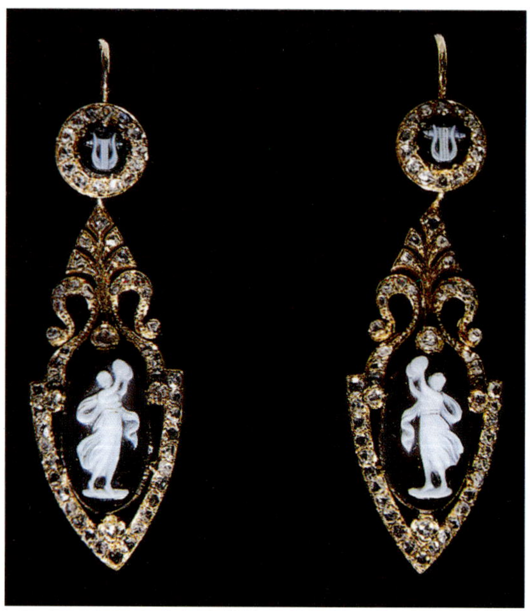

Plate 48. *Onyx earrings, French gold and diamond mounts, late 19th century. The Muse Terpsichore holds a tambourine aloft. The earring tops depict a lyre, symbolising the Muses' connection with Apollo and music. ⅜in. (1cm) x 2in. (5cm) long.* KIKUCHI TRADING CO. LTD., GRAYS, LONDON £2500

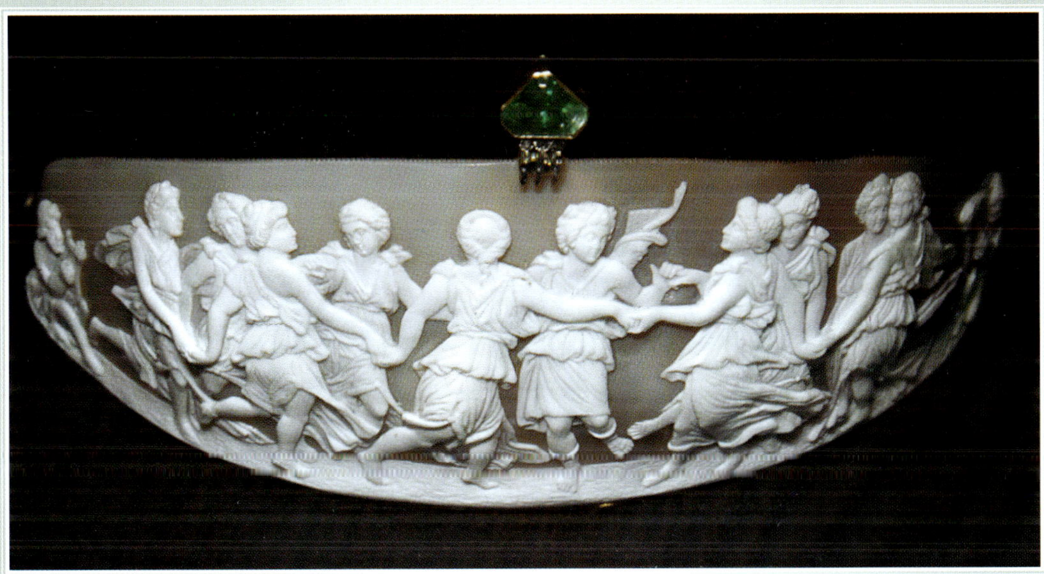

Plate 49. *Bull's Mouth shell, designed as a hair ornament, circa 1840, depicting Apollo and the Muses. From left to right: Calliope, Cleio, Erato, Melpomene, Terpsichore, Apollo, Polymnia, Euterpe, Thalia and Urania. The hairpiece later set with an emerald centrepiece. See painting* Apollo and The Muses *by Baldassare Peruzzi (1481- 536). 2in. (5cm) x 6¼in. (16cm).*

DIEM FINE JEWELLERY, GRAYS, LONDON

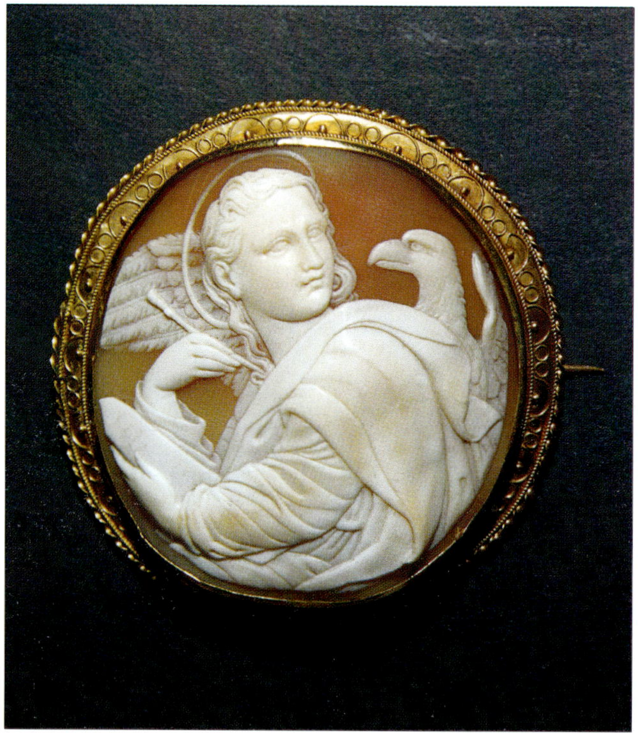

Plate 50. *Bull's Mouth shell, archaeological revival gold mount, circa 1870. A Muse (Calliope?) holding a stylus and tablet with Zeus in the guise of an eagle. 2⅜in. (6cm) x 2in. (5cm).* M. ROWAN AT www.rowanandrowan.com £450

stylus; she has a crown of laurel leaves on her head. The trumpet symbolises fame, the books poetry and the laurel, poetic inspiration.

Cleio: Muse of History. She holds a pen and book, scroll or tablet to record heroic deeds.

Polymnia: Muse of Sacred Poetry, Hymns and Pantomime. Veiled, she holds a book (of sacred poetry) or a sceptre. She is often found posing in meditative mode.

Euterpe: Muse of Music. She wears a crown of laurel leaves and holds a flute.

Melpomene: Muse of Tragedy. Often veiled, she holds a tragic mask or a lyre and plectrum.

Terpsichore: Muse of Lyric Poetry and Dancing. She wears a crown of flowers and holds a musical instrument.

Erato: Muse of Lyric Poetry and Love Poetry. Crowned with roses, she appears with Eros or a swan (symbol of love and the poet) and holds a lyre.

Urania: Muse of Astronomy. She wears a crown of stars and holds a globe or a compass.

Thalia: Muse of Comedy. She holds a scroll, a comic mask, or musical instruments.

Muses as Cameo Subjects

The Muses with Apollo. See Plate 49.

The Muses with their attributes. See Plate 49, 50.

See also: Apollo.

GENIUS (sing.) Genii (plural): Roman

Genii were guardian spirits, either of a concept or an individual. They were personifications rather than mythological characters. The Romans believed that two genii accompanied every man from birth to death, one of them good and one of them evil. Genii were usually portrayed as cherubic winged figures or winged youths, carrying the attributes of that which they protected – the Genius of Light carried a torch, the Genius of Music carried a musical instrument, etc.

Genii as Cameo Subjects

Usually depicted as winged cherubic figures, carrying the attributes of that which they protect. See Plates 16, 19, 21, 22, 46.

ASCLEPIUS (Greek)
AESCULAPIUS (Roman)

Cameo Key: Male with a serpent-entwined staff

Asclepius was the son of Apollo and god of Medicine and Healing. Chiron the centaur taught him how to make potions to cure ills. He carried a staff entwined with a serpent. This symbolised medicine and healing, as the Greeks regarded snakes as regenerative creatures, who gained new strength and vigour by the casting-off of their skins. It was said he could even restore the dead to life by using the blood of the Gorgon Medusa, given to him by Athena. This upset Hades, god of the Dead, who complained that the Underworld was being robbed of its inhabitants, so Zeus killed Asclepius with a thunderbolt and he became a constellation. Hygeia, goddess of Health, was his daughter.

Asclepius as a Cameo Subject

A bearded man wearing a long draped robe and carrying a snake-entwined staff. His daughter is usually portrayed holding a snake. See Plate 26.

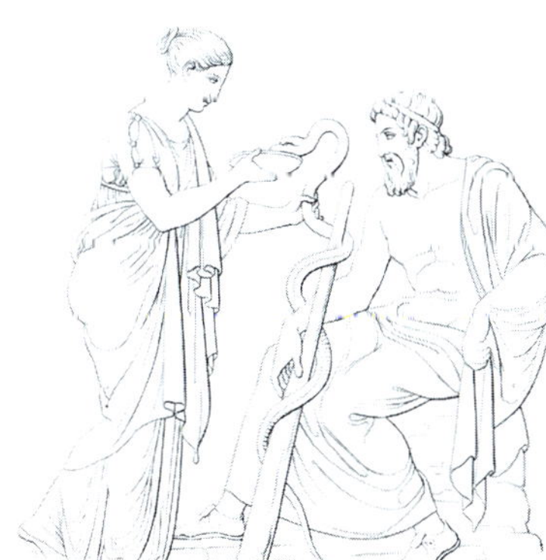

Bas-relief by Bertel Thorvaldsen, completed in 1810.

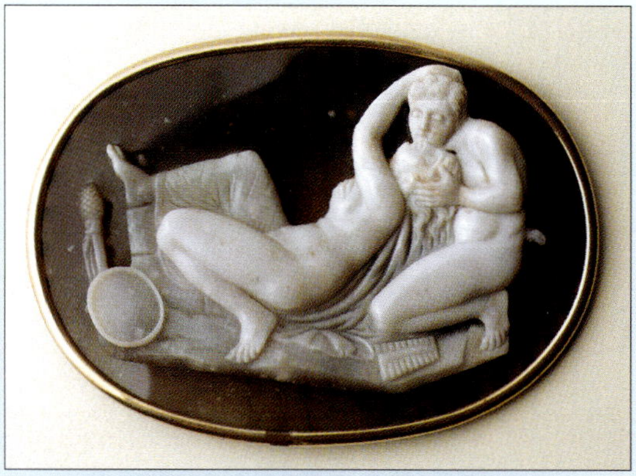

TALES FROM THE LAND

Demeter and Persephone: goddesses of Agriculture

Dionysus: god of Wine

Maenads, satyrs: followers of Dionysus

Horae: the Seasons

Pan: a god of Nature

Nymphs: spirits of Nature

Centaurs: fierce creatures

Grylli: grotesque figures

CHAPTER 5

TALES FROM THE LAND

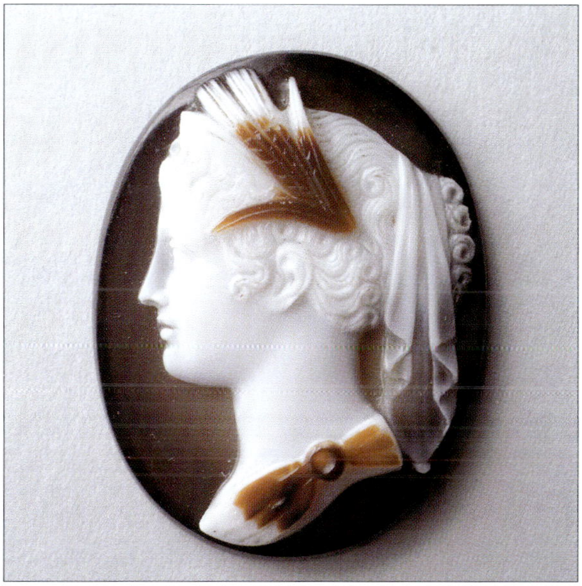

Plate 51. *Onyx, circa 1800, classical head of Demeter wearing a crown of wheat-sheaves. 1½in. (4cm) x 1⅛in. (3cm).* PETER SZUHAY, GRAYS, LONDON

Many Greek myths described deities associated with fertility, plentiful harvests and the cycle of the seasons. Strange, mythical creatures were also thought to inhabit the land. Dionysus and his followers were popular nineteenth century cameo subjects. The nymphs and Horae appear on cameos as attendants to other deities.

DEMETER AND PERSEPHONE (Greek)
CERES AND PROSPERINE (Roman)

Cameo Key: Female figures, with wheat-sheaves or ears of corn in their hair

This myth concerned life and death, rebirth and the passage of the seasons. Demeter was goddess of Agriculture and Vegetation, a beneficent earth goddess who made everything grow and ripen and brought corn, symbol of civilisation, to the world. She was the daughter of the Titan rulers and the sister of Zeus, Hades, Hera and Poseidon. A kind, gentle goddess, with the help of her beloved daughter Persephone, she ensured that mortals always had plentiful harvests.

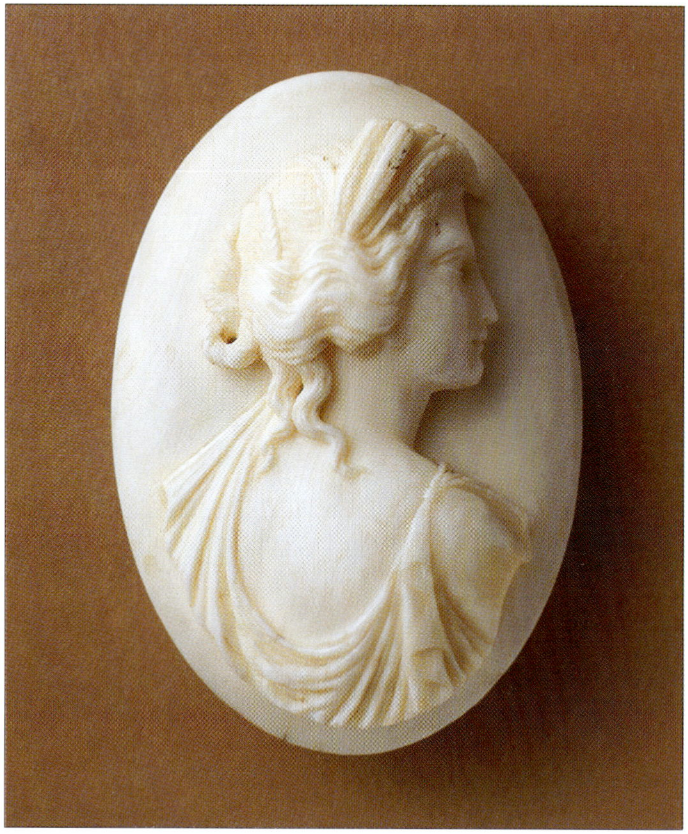

Plate 52. *Ivory carving, circa 1860-70 of the goddess Demeter in Greek dress. She wears a polos (crown) and ears of corn in her hair. 2⅜in. (6cm) x 1¾in. (4.5cm).* RBR GROUP, GRAYS, LONDON £375

However, Hades, god of the Dead, wanted Persephone for his wife, so he abducted her and took her to the Underworld. Demeter abandoned her work and wandered the world with a torch, searching for her lost daughter, with grave consequences for mankind:

'But golden-haired Demeter...caused a most dreadful and cruel year for
mankind over the all-nourishing earth: the ground
would not make the seed sprout, for rich-crowned
Demeter kept it hid.... So she
would have destroyed the whole race of man with
cruel famine and have robbed them who dwell on
Olympus of their glorious right of gifts and sacrifices.'

Homeric Hymn II, *To Demeter* (page 311, Evelyn-White translation)

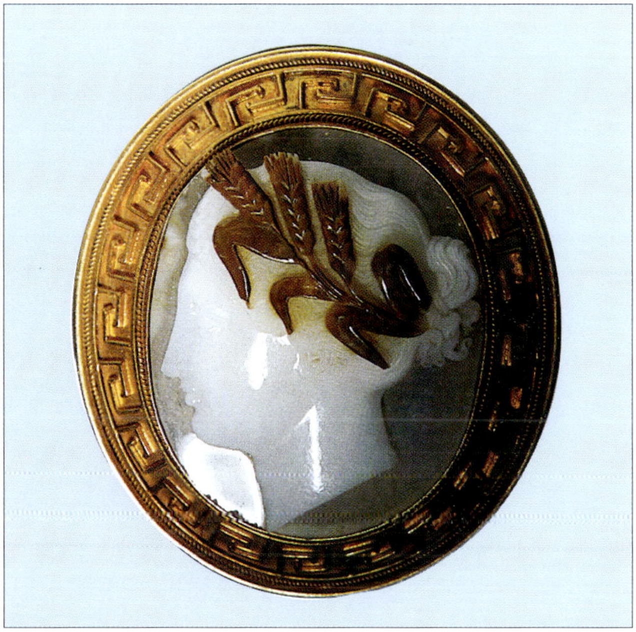

Plate 53. *Agate, gold mount with Greek key design. Demeter (Ceres) in profile with a crown of wheat-sheaves. 2⅜in. (6cm) x 2in. (5cm). Signed 'E. Pistrucci' – Elena Pistrucci (1822-1886), a gem-engraver who worked in Rome, daughter of the famous carver Benedetto Pistrucci.* A Handbook Of Rome And Its Environs *by J. Murray (1881) includes an entry for 'The Misses Pistrucci, 16 Via delle Quatro Fontane, the daughters of the late engraver to the Mint in London, for engraving of gems and cameos'.*

S. J. PHILLIPS LTD., NEW BOND STREET, LONDON

Zeus realised he needed to act, as the gods were going to suffer too. Not wishing to offend his brother Hades whilst appeasing his sister Demeter, he agreed to allow Persephone to return to earth provided she had not tasted the food of the dead. She had however eaten a pomegranate or pomegranate seeds, symbolic of marriage and fertility, so was forced to remain in Hades for three months of the year, when winter came. On her return to earth, spring arrived. Ceres and Prosperine were the Roman names for the two goddesses.

Demeter and Persephone as Cameo Subjects

Demeter: a regal goddess wearing a polos (a cylindrical headdress), or a crown of wheat-sheaves. Sometimes with a torch. See Plates 51, 52, 53, 122, 126.

Triptolemus: Prince of Eleusis sent by Demeter in a dragon-drawn chariot to spread the secret of growing corn across the world. A male figure accompanied by Demeter and Persephone.

Persephone – a beautiful young girl wearing a wreath of wheat-sheaves, sometimes mixed with poppies (the flower of sleep).

See also: Hades.

DIONYSUS (Greek), **god of Wine**
BACCHUS (Roman)
Cameo Key: Sensual male with grapes or vine leaves

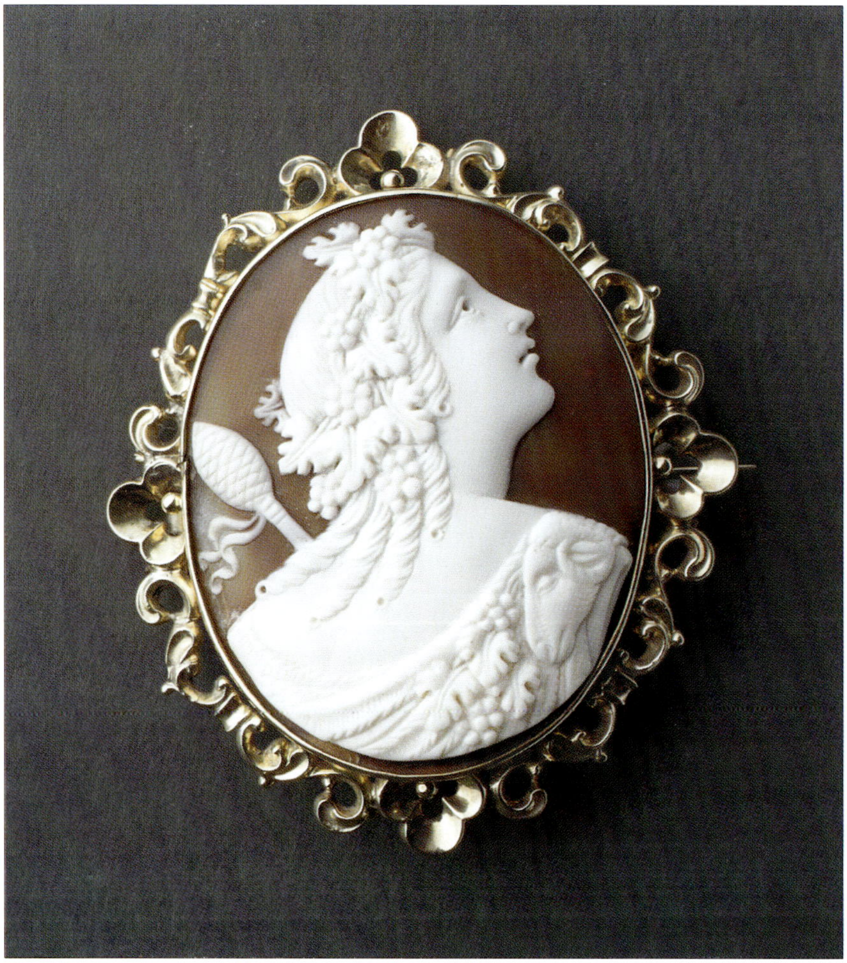

Plate 54. *Black Helmet shell, gold repoussé mount, circa 1850. The god of Wine is softly modelled as a beautiful youth with long, flowing hair crowned with a vine wreath and wearing a pelt. He holds a thyrsus. 2¾in. (7cm) x 2⅛in. (5.5cm).*

TOM SADDINGTON LTD., SILVER FOX GALLERY, PORTOBELLO ROAD, LONDON £950

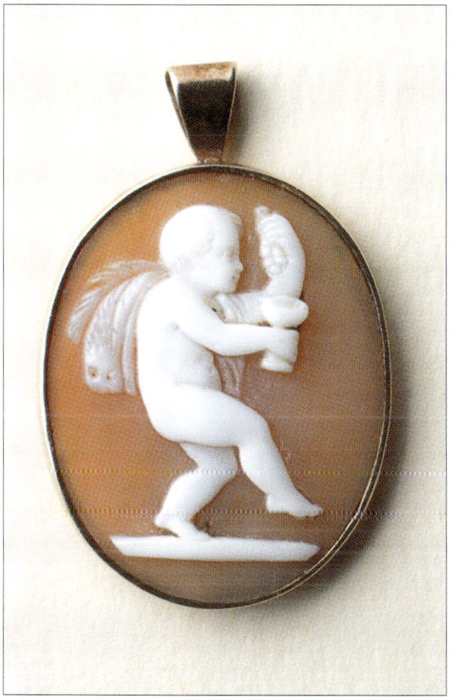

Plate 55. *Bull's Mouth shell, late 19th century, later gold pendant setting. The infant Dionysus holds a bunch of grapes and a cup, an animal pelt over his shoulder. 1½in. (4cm) x 1⅛in. (3cm).* FOX COLLECTION

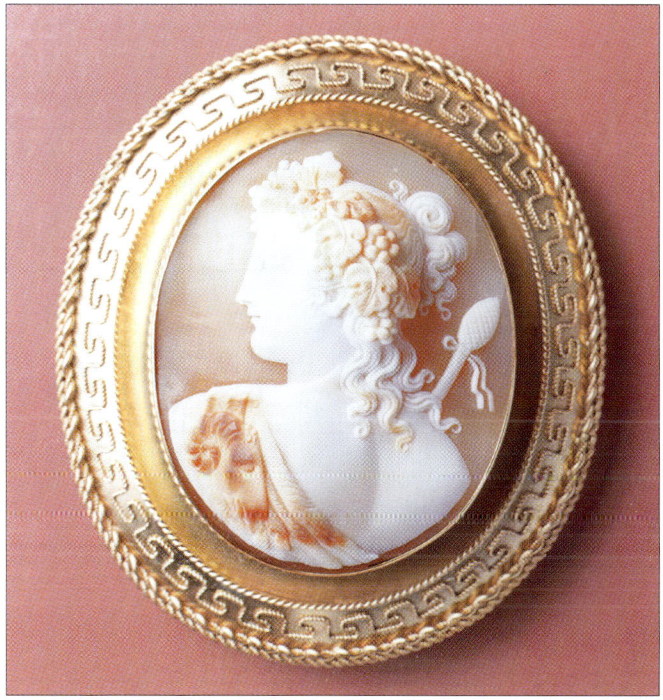

Plate 56. *Bull's Mouth shell, gold mount with stylised Greek key applied decoration, circa 1870. Dionysus (Bacchus), holding a thyrsus, wears an animal pelt and has a crown of vine leaves on his head. 3½in. (9cm) x 2¾in. (7cm).*

'The god himself wreathed his head with bunches of grapes, while in his hand he flourished a wand draped with vine leaves.'
Ovid, Metamorphoses, *III (page 91, Innes translation)*

LYNN LINDSAY, WIMPOLE ANTIQUES, GRAYS, LONDON £2450

'Wine puts cares out of mind, gift of a god to men.'
Alcaeus, Greek poet, circa 625-620 BC

DIONYSUS was the hedonistic god of the Vine, Wine and Fertility, the son of Zeus and the mortal Semele. The power of Zeus's thunderbolt accidentally killed the pregnant Semele, so Dionysus was sewn into his father's thigh until he was ready to be born. Zeus's wife Hera was so enraged by her husband's affair with Semele that she pursued Dionysus relentlessly, at one point driving him to insanity. Accounts of his life vary, but generally he travelled the world, his journeys rich in adventure. The satyr Silenus taught him how to make wine and in Asia he learned the art of mysticism. On his return to Greece the god travelled

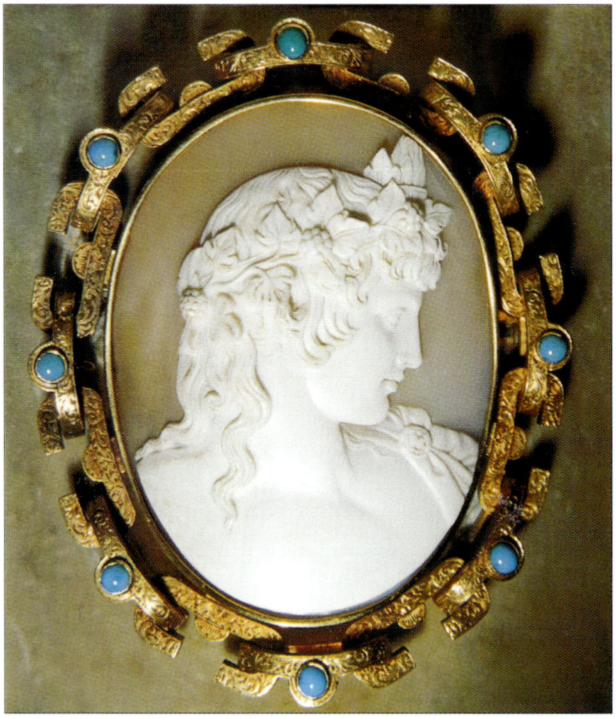

Antinous Vertumnus

Plate 57. *Bull's Mouth shell, elaborate gold and turquoise mount, circa 1850-60. 4in. (10cm) x 2¾in. (7cm). The subject is a Bacchic youth known as 'Antinous', wearing a wreath and a cloak. Signed 'JHW' (possibly as an item of the stock of Watherston of the firm Watherson and Brogden) in original fitted case. The carving is based on a marble bas-relief found in Hadrian's Villa near Rome in 1735, subsequently published in the collection of Cardinal Albani in Venuti's Collectanea Antiquitarum Romanorum. Antinous, a young slave, was a favourite of the Emperor Hadrian and idealised as an example of perfect male beauty. After his mysterious death in AD 130, Antinous was deified by Hadrian.*

ANTHEA A.G. ANTIQUES, GRAYS, LONDON £5500

across the land in triumphant procession, in a panther-drawn chariot bedecked with ivy. His cult of mysticism with its elements of revelry and drunkenness was extremely popular, attracting a wild band of attendant revellers – maenads and satyrs, playing music and dancing with abandonment. Dionysus established his cult at Thebes. Often his followers wore masks and from choragic literary contests known as 'Dionysia', tragedy and comedy evolved. Once his cult was secure, he went to live on Mount Olympus. A kind god, he married Ariadne when Theseus abandoned her. Dionysus's attribute was the vine (the ambrosial plant) and the animals associated with him were the panther, bull and goat. Bacchus, his Roman equivalent, was chiefly god of Wine. His followers indulged in debauched and drunken orgies known as 'Bacchanalia'.

Dionysus as a Cameo Subject

The Triumph of Dionysus: The god, wearing a vine-wreath crown, rides on a panther, or is accompanied by maenads and satyrs dancing and playing musical instruments. Silenus and/or Ariadne may be in the scene. Dionysus or his followers hold a thyrsus (ivy-entwined staff topped with a pinecone, a fertility symbol). Grapes, ewers, cornucopia can be in the scene.

The head of Dionysus: A sensual young god with long, flowing hair, wearing a vine-wreath crown. Usually holding a thyrsus. See Plates 54, 56.

Dionysus as an infant: A chubby child stretches out to reach a bunch of grapes/holds a bunch of grapes/rides on a goat/with a nymph. See Plate 55.

Dionysus/Demeter/Aphrodite: Representing wine, food and love.

Dionysus holding a theatre mask, or a theatre mask: Symbolising the link between Dionysia and the development of Greek theatre. See Plate 97.

A goat or bull standing on a thyrsus: Representing Dionysus.

Dionysus can also personify 'Autumn' on cameos.

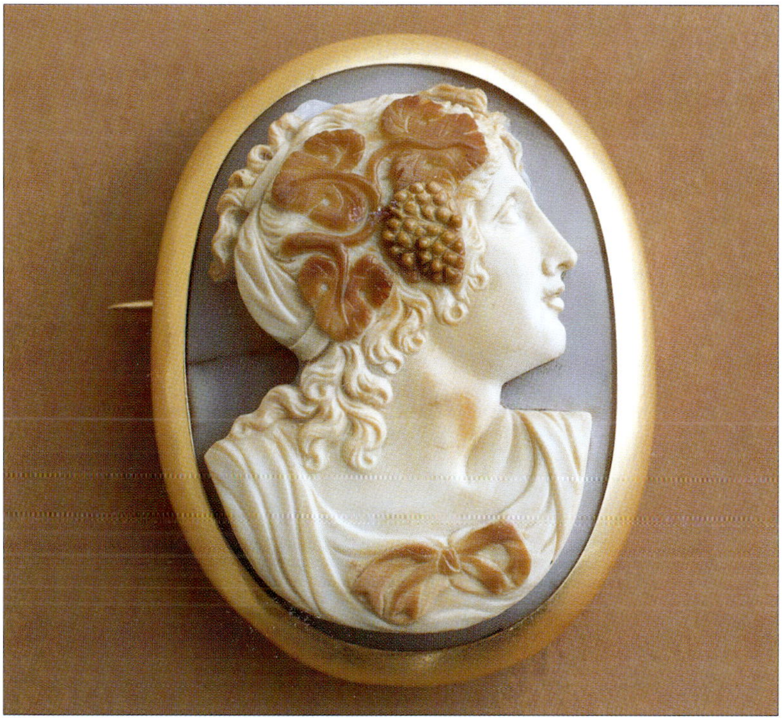

Plate 58. *Agate, gold mount, circa 1790-1800, depicting a bacchante. 2⅜in. (6cm) x 2in. (5cm). Fine carving similar in style to the work of Nicolo Morelli* JILL GAINE COLLECTION

The Train of Dionysus:
MAENADS (Greek)
BACCHANTE (Roman)
Cameo Key: Females with vine leaves or grapes

These female followers of Dionysus were frequently depicted on Victorian cameos as pretty, decorative maidens with vine leaves trailing through their hair. In mythology they were somewhat different – wild women who danced frenziedly, cavorted with satyrs and beasts and devoured raw flesh. They carried a thyrsus – a staff bedecked with ivy and topped with a pine-cone, a fertility symbol. The thyrsus could be used as a weapon against anyone who angered them.

Maenads as Cameo Subjects

A beautiful, young female head with vine leaves or grapes entwined in her hair. See Plates 58, 59, 103, 108, 114, 115, 116, 117, 118.

Young female, naked or dressed in diaphanous robe, with a satyr, or panther, or goat. See Plate 60.

Young female wearing the pelt of an animal, holding a thyrsus. See Plate 113.

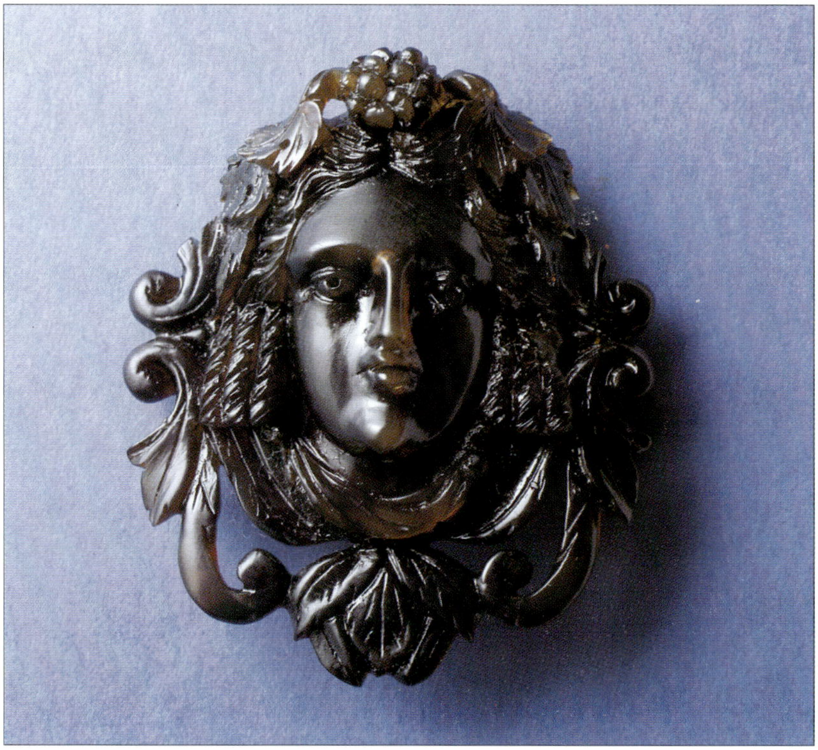

Plate 59. *Tortoiseshell carving, circa 1850-70, of a female follower of Dionysus with fruit and vine leaves in her hair. 3⅛in. (8cm) x 2¾in. (7cm).*

PUSHKIN ANTIQUES, GRAYS, LONDON £950

Train of Dionysus:
SATYRS (Greek)
BACCHAE (Roman)
Cameo Key: Half man, half goat

SATYRS, the male attendants of Dionysus, were characterised by their lasciviousness. They had the horns, tails and hooves of goats and the upper bodies of men. Satyrs hunted wild animals and chased mænads and nymphs after drinking wine. Silenus, an elderly satyr, raised Dionysus and taught him how to make wine.

Satyrs as Cameo Subjects

Half man/half goat figures leaping, dancing with maenads, playing musical instruments.

A satyr approaches a nymph with the intention of ravishing her. See Plate 60.

Silenus: An aged satyr with a snub nose, pot-belly, sometimes riding on a donkey, falling drunkenly to one side. See Plate 97.

Triumph of Silenus: He wears a crown of vine leaves on his head and is surrounded by maenads and satyrs.

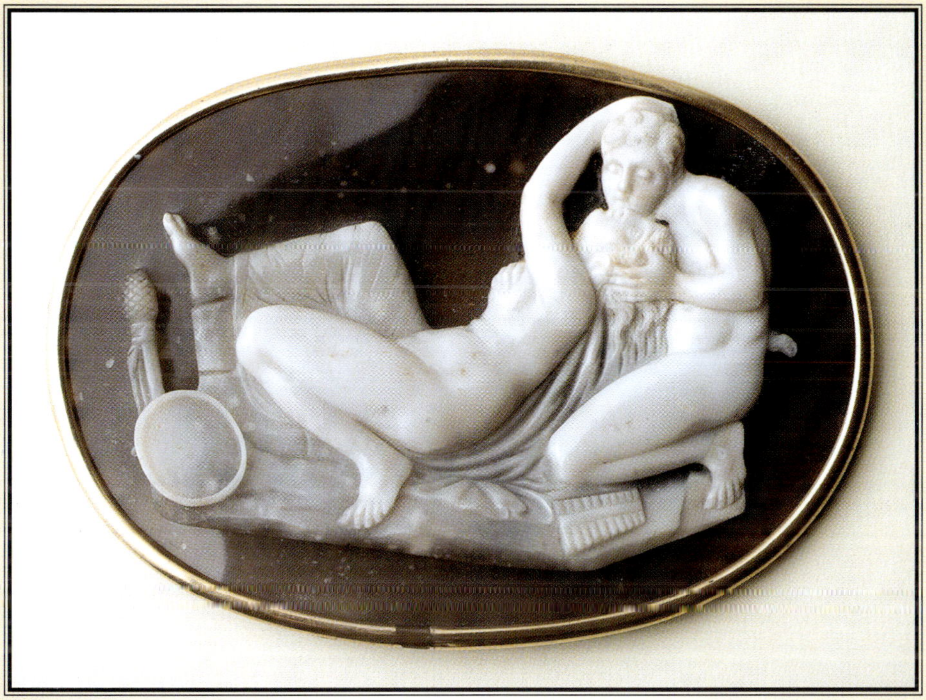

Plate 60. *Agate, gold mount, circa 1800. 2½in. (6.25cm) x 3½in. (8.75cm). From the 4th century BC satyrs were depicted as almost human, with only minor bestial features, perhaps sprouting horns, a small tail, or animal ears. Depicted here, a lascivious satyr and willing bacchante – their pan-pipe, thyrsus and tambourine abandoned in pursuit of erotic pleasure. Based on a Pompeian fresco illustrated in the 1762* Pitture Antiche d'Ercolano.
PETER SZUHAY, GRAYS, LONDON £4500

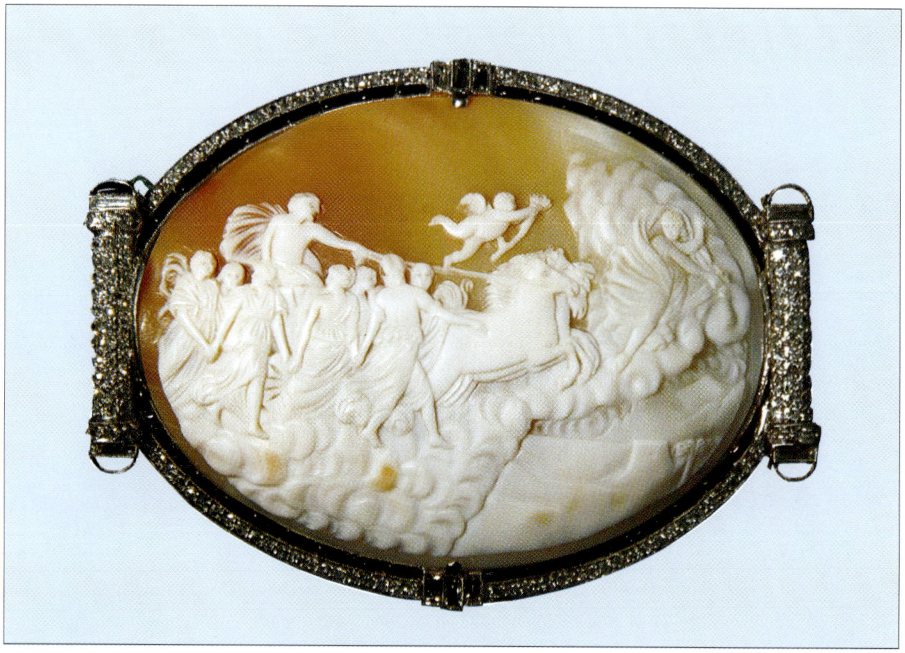

Plate 61. *Late 19th century Horned Helmet shell, early 20th century black enamel and diamond mount, depicting 'Phoebus and The Hours, Preceded by Aurora' after a ceiling fresco by Guido Reni, 1613, in the Rospigliosi Palace, Rome. The Dawn goddess, harbinger of light, leads the chariot of Phoebus into the sky. The Genius of Light (also known as the daystar Lucifer) bears his torch. The Horae (Seasons) and nymphs dance in chorus around Apollo's chariot. 2¾in. (7cm) x 2⅜in. (6cm).* S. J. Phillips Ltd., New Bond Street, London

HORAE (Greek)
'THE SEASONS' (Roman)
Cameo Key: Three young maidens

These three deities were goddesses of Nature and guardians of order and stability. They ruled over the seasons and the natural course of birth, growth and decay. Their name means 'hours' in Greek and Hesiod called them:

Thallo (bloom); Auxo (grow); Karpo (fruit)

They guarded the cloud gates of Mount Olympus, rolling them aside for the chariots of the gods, and guided the chariots of Hera and Athena. The Horae clothed and bejewelled Aphrodite after her birth and took her to Olympus. From the Hellenistic period onwards, there were four seasons.

Horae as a Cameo Subject

Three beautiful young goddesses in draped robes, sometimes holding flowers. Can appear in scenes with Aphrodite, Apollo, Flora. The Horae are often indistinguishable from nymphs in cameo scenes. See Plates 16, 19, 61.

The following deities were also representative of the seasons: Flora – Spring (flowers); Demeter – Summer (the harvest); Dionysus – Autumn (wine); Hephaestus – Winter (fire).

See also : Aphrodite, Apollo, Demeter, Dionysus, Flora.

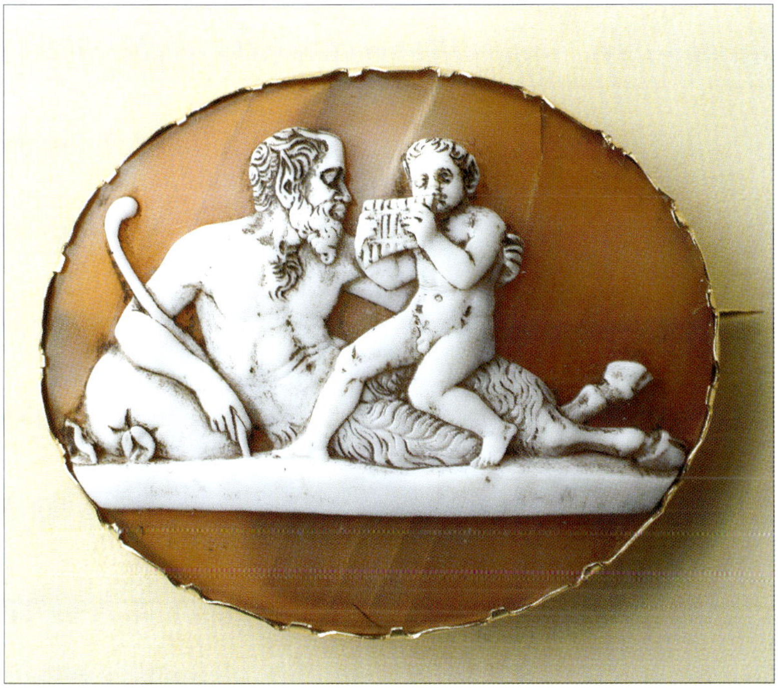

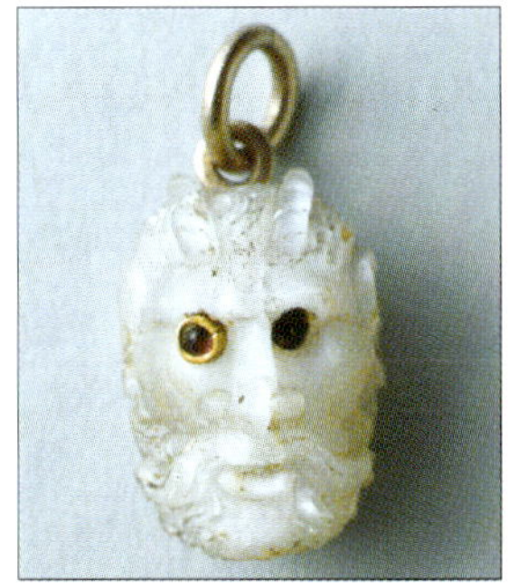

Plate 62. *Moonstone carving of the god Pan, with cabochon garnet eyes, second half of 19th century, ¾in. (2cm) high.* PRIVATE COLLECTION

Plate 63. *Bull's Mouth shell, gold mount, late 19th century. The sage instructor Pan instructs a dutiful faun to play the pan-pipe. 2in. (5cm) x 2¾in. (7cm).*
ANGELA MEECH, SILVER FOX GALLERY, PORTOBELLO ROAD, LONDON £275

PAN (Greek)
FAUNUS/SILVANUS (Roman)
Cameo Key: Goat-like male

PAN was a god of Nature, of the fields and woods, of shepherds and flocks. Pan means 'all' and a Homeric Hymn offers an explanation for his name:

> 'Then all the immortals were glad in heart and Bacchic Dionysos in especial and they called the boy Pan because he delighted all their hearts.'
>
> Homeric Hymn XIX, *To Pan* (pages 445-447, Evelyn-White translation)

Pan was half-human, half-beast, with a human face and the horns, ears and hooves of a goat. He lived in a pastoral paradise called Arcadia where he hunted and frolicked with nymphs, centaurs and satyrs. He represented male sexuality, always pursuing nymphs and mortal maidens. The nymph Syrinx only escaped his unwanted advances by turning into a bed of reeds. The reeds plaintively made a sweet, sad sound as the wind blew through them, so Pan fashioned them into a musical instrument, the syrinx or pan-pipe. His attributes were the goat (lust) and the pine (fertility). Pan's Roman counterparts were Silvanus and Faunus.

Pan as a Cameo Subject

Pan, half-human, half-goat, plays pan-pipe/plays with a goat/stealthily approaches a nymph.

Triumph of Pan: Satyrs and maenads dance and play musical instruments with Pan, or before a statue of Pan, worshipping him as a representative of nature, fertility, sexuality.

Pan often accompanies Dionysus, where he symbolises nature.

Pan giving instructions on the pan-pipe to a faun. See Plate 63.

See also: Dionysus, Hermes.

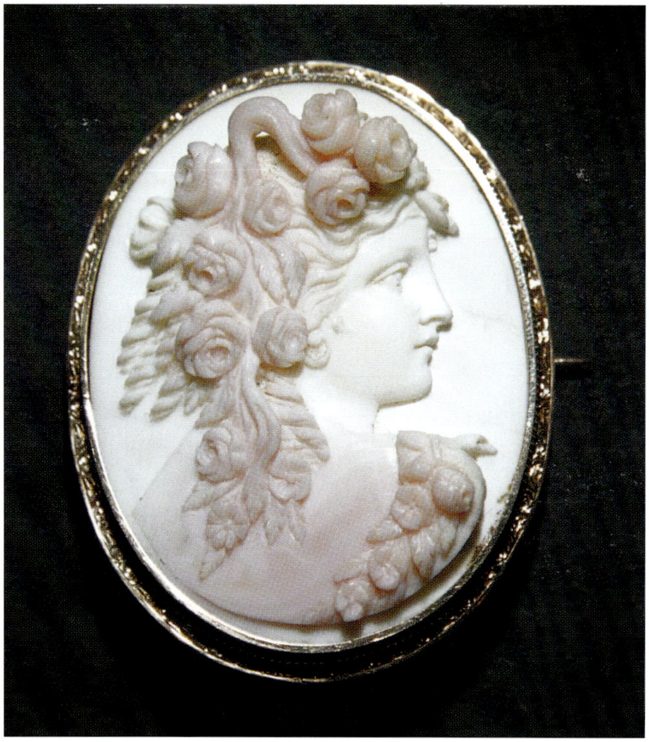

Plate 64. *Queen Conch shell, engraved gold mount, circa 1860. A nymph bedecked with garlands of flowers. 2½in. (6.5cm) x 2⅛in. (5.5cm).* M. ROWAN AT www.rowanandrowan.com £550

NYMPHS (Greek)
Cameo Key: Female figures, diaphanous robes

These female deities, daughters of Zeus, were spirits of nature. Hesiod called them 'shining goddess children'. They were depicted as beautiful, eternally youthful maidens. There were four different categories of nymphs:

Naiads were water nymphs of rivers, fountains, streams and springs, controlling the life-giving properties of water.

Nereids were sea nymphs who lived at the bottom of seas and oceans.

Oreads were mountain nymphs and companions of the god Pan.

Dryads were tree nymphs, who died when the tree they lived in died.

Nymphs as Cameo Subjects

Young females in diaphanous robes, representing nature when they appear with Aphrodite, Dionysus, Artemis, Eos. It is difficult to distinguish nymphs on cameos as they are often attendants to a scene. See Plates 16, 19, 64, 66, 108, 109, 123.

Nereids frolicking in the sea with tritons and dolphins in the realm of Poseidon.

Naiads portrayed as young maidens holding urns, or pouring water from an urn.

See also: Aphrodite, Apollo, Dionysus, Eos, Pan, Poseidon.

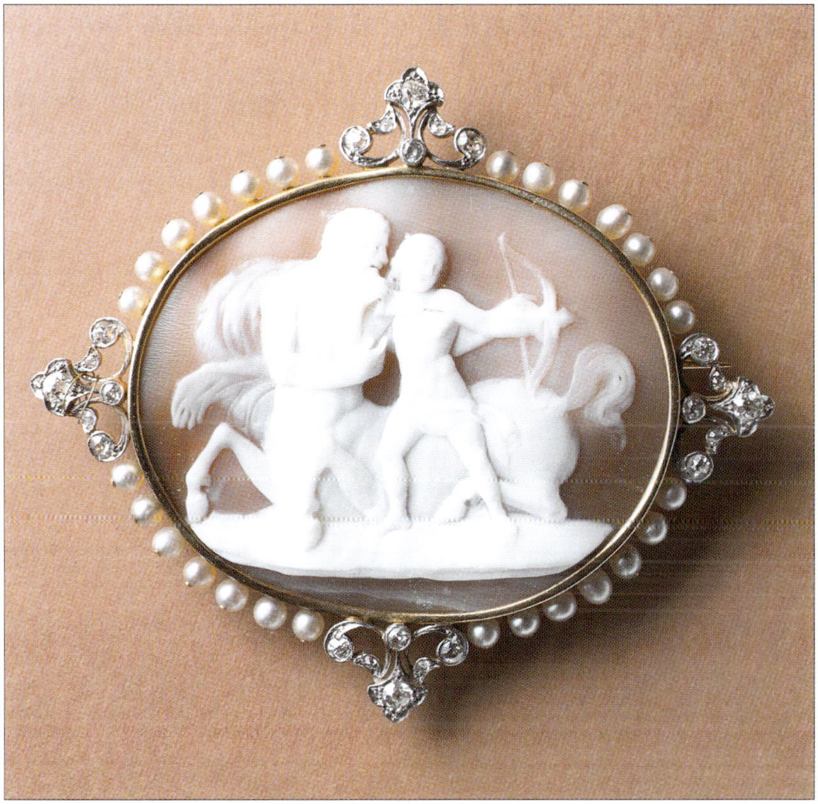

Plate 65 *Bull's Mouth shell, late 19th century gold pearl and diamond mount. The centaur Chiron instructs Achilles in the use of the bow. See painting* The Centaur Chiron Instructing Achilles *by Jean-Baptiste Regnault, circa 1783, The Hermitage. 2in. (5cm) x 2¾in. (7cm).* RBR Group, Grays, London £2325

CENTAURS (Greek)
Cameo Key: Half-man, half-horse

These wild and savage creatures represented the most primitive and basic human instincts. They had the torsos of men and the legs of horses and inhabited the mountain regions of Thessaly where they were fierce hunters, living on raw flesh. They were thought to be the offspring of the Lapith King and Hera, Queen of the gods. Chiron, a civilised centaur, had been instructed by Apollo and Artemis and was wise in the arts of medicine, music and prophecy. He raised Asclepius and Jason (of the Argonauts). When he died he became the constellation Sagittarius.

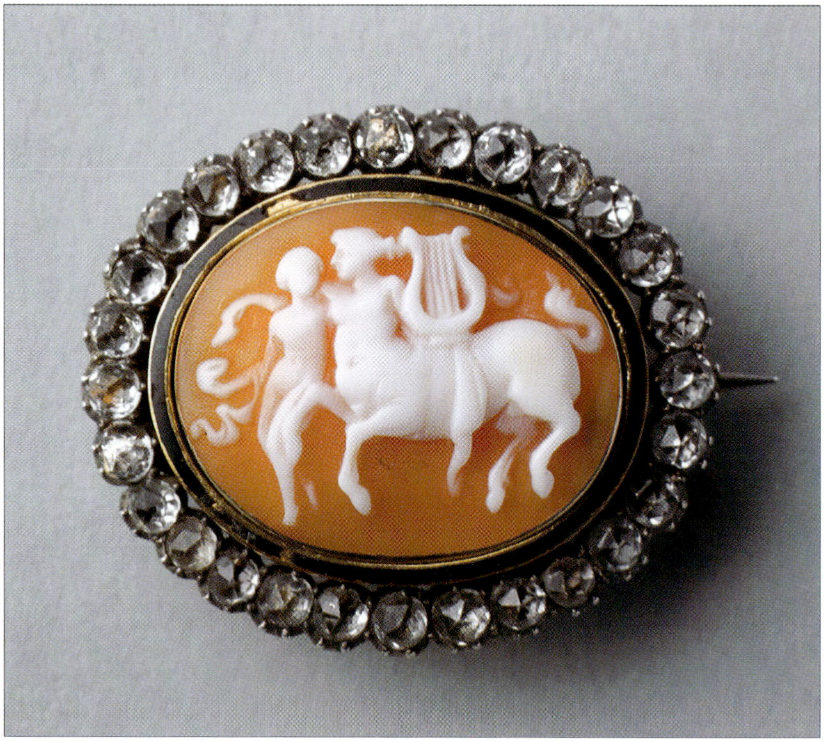

Plate 66. *Horned Helmet shell, enamel and paste mount, early 19th century. A centauress with the lyre of Apollo (centaurs being descended from Centaurus, a son of Apollo) cavorts with a nymph. 1⅛in. (3cm) x 1½in. (4cm).*

LOWTHER ANTIQUES, CENTRAL GALLERY, PORTOBELLO ROAD, LONDON £350

The other centaurs were characteristically violent. At the wedding feast of the Lapith King Pirithous and Hippodamia they drunkenly tried to rape and carry off the Lapith women. A fierce battle ensued and finally the centaurs were driven out of Thessaly. They appear in other myths, usually involved in rape, abduction or murder.

Centaurs as Cameo Subjects
Half-man, half-horse.
Half-female, half-horse. See Plate 66.
Chiron instructs Achilles. See Plate 65.
A centaur and a warrior holding a club – the warrior Theseus defeating the centaurs in the battle of Lapiths and centaurs.
See also: Apollo.

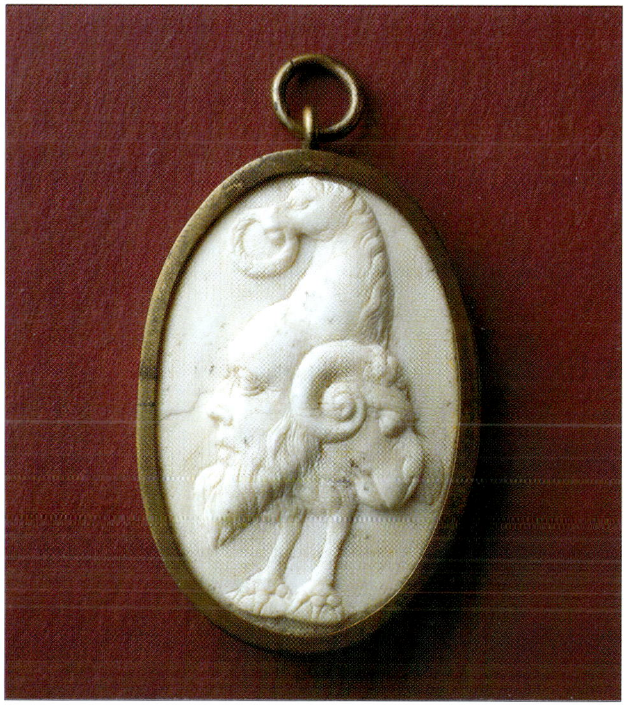

Plate 67. *Marble, metal mount, 2in. (5cm) x 1½in. (4cm), circa 1800, similar to an unusual sardonyx model of a gryllus, illustrated and described in C. W. King's* Antique Gems, *1860 (page 329): 'the head and neck of a horse, a complete animal* sui generis *which was next supplied with legs… an old man's head is backed by that of a ram.'* PRIVATE COLLECTION

GRYLLUS (sing.) GRYLLI (plural) (Roman)

From the Latin *gryllus* meaning caricature. C.W. King refers to *gryllus* as meaning 'both a cricket and a caprice'. They derived from ancient paintings called 'capricci' – conjoined grotesque figures with both human and bestial features. Various models exist, features often include the head of an elderly man, a ram's head, a horse's head, animal legs. In *Antique Gems*, King cites Pliny as using the expression *pinxit et Gryllum ridiculi habitus*, translated as 'he painted a gryllus (a cricket, grasshopper or type of comic figure in art) of ridiculous appearance.' King illustrates a number of these models. They were believed to protect the wearer from harm.

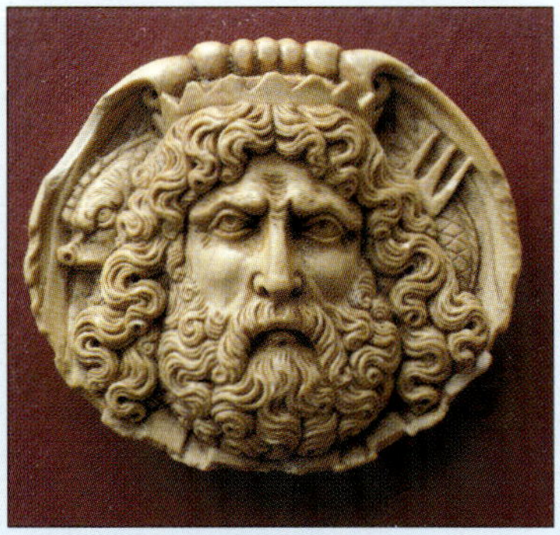

TALES FROM THE SEA

Poseidon, god of Seas and Oceans

The Winds

Chapter 6

TALES FROM THE SEA

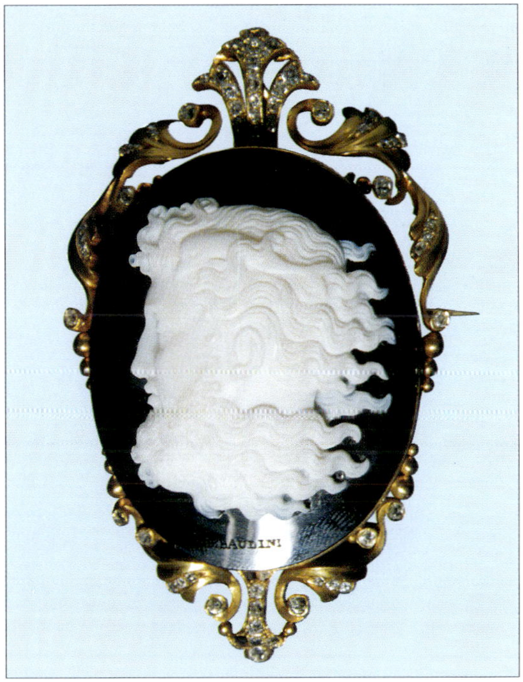

Plate 68. *Onyx, French gold and diamond* fin de siècle *mount, signed 'L. Saulini' for Luigi Saulini (1819-1883), the prominent Roman gem-engraver, renowned for his portrait cameos. The wind-swept god Poseidon is vividly portrayed with a dolphin leaping through his hair. 2¾in. (7cm) x 2⅛in. (5.5cm).*
S. J. Phillips Ltd., New Bond Street, London

The sea played an elemental role in ancient Greek life, largely due to the island geography of the country and its seafaring traditions. The Greeks were a sailor people, in ceaseless relations with the seas. Gods and other fabulous creatures were thought to inhabit the seas and oceans.

POSEIDON (Greek)
NEPTUNE (Roman)
Cameo Key: Regal male with trident

Poseidon reigned over seas and oceans. He was assigned ruler of these realms when the Olympian gods defeated the Titans. He was an ill-tempered, volatile god who sent calm seas if feeling beneficent, but caused storms and earthquakes when enraged. Poseidon lived in an underwater palace with his wife Amphitrite and his son Triton, his trumpeter. Clad in a robe of gold, he traversed his kingdom in a golden chariot drawn by white horses. Poseidon took many lovers who bore him numerous children. His attributes were the trident and the horse, representing warfare and royalty. The Romans knew him as

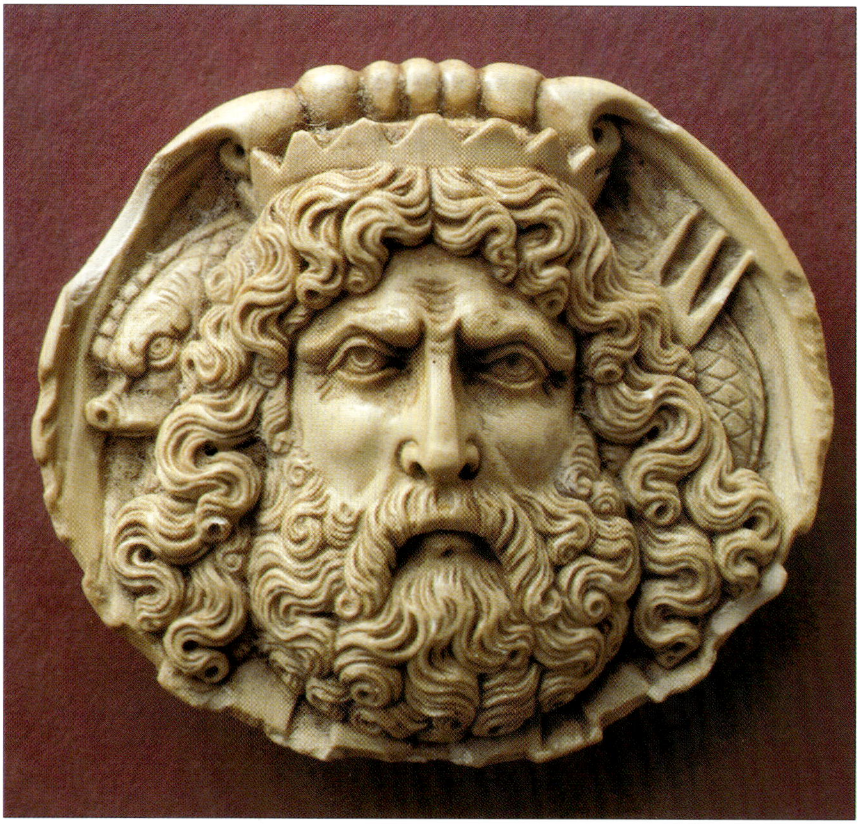

Plate 69. *Lava carving, circa 1840, a crowned Poseidon facing, with full beard and ringlets. His attributes, a dolphin and trident, are behind him. The whole carving in the shape of a clam. 1½in. (4cm) x 2⅛in. (5.5cm).* PRIVATE COLLECTION

Neptune. Homer describes the god in all his glory:

> 'Going there he harnessed under his chariot his bronze-shod horses,
> flying-footed, with long manes streaming of gold; and he put on
> clothing of gold about his own body, and took up the golden
> lash, carefully compacted, and climbed up into his chariot
> and drove it across the waves. And about him the sea beasts came up
> from their deep places and played in his path,
> and acknowledged their master,
> and the sea stood apart, before him, rejoicing.'
>
> Homer, the *Iliad*, XIII (lines 23-29, Lattimore translation)

Poseidon as a Cameo Subject

A regal male with long hair and a flowing beard holding a trident. See Plates 68, 69.

Triumph of Poseidon: In a chariot with Amphitrite being drawn over the waves by horses or seahorses. Tritons (mermen) and nereids (sea nymphs) are in attendance. Dolphins/fish in scene. See Plate 30.

Poseidon rescues Amymone: He rides on a dolphin carrying a maiden away from a satyr.

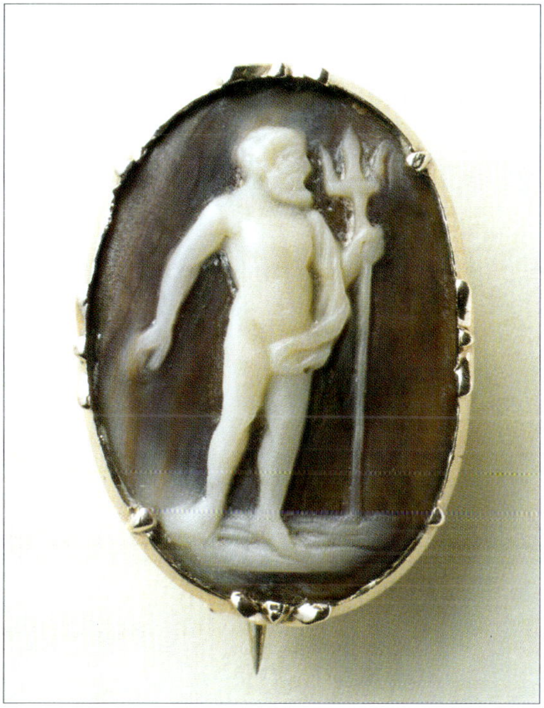

Plate 70. *Cowrie shell, closed-back gold mount, cut-down setting, lace pin, circa 1820. A triton depicted with trident.*
PRIVATE COLLECTION

THE WINDS

Cameo Key: Puff cheeked heads

The Greeks were sailors and regarded the winds as divinities who aided navigation. They were seen as four quarrelsome brothers who were under the care of Æolus, a son of Poseidon. He had great difficulty keeping them under control. They were named:

Boreas – the cold North wind
Notus – the warm South wind
Eurus – the blustery East wind
Zephyr – the mild, warm West wind

Ovid describes their violent nature:

> 'they can scarcely be prevented from tearing the world apart, even as it is, although each blows in a different direction so violent is the strife between the brothers. The East wind withdrew to the lands of the dawn, to the kingdoms of Arabia and Persia... the West, and the shores which are warmed by the setting sun, are subject to Zephyr. Boreas, who makes men shudder with his chill breath, invaded Scythia and the North, while the lands opposite to those are continually drenched with rain and clouds, brought by the South wind.'
>
> Ovid, *Metamorphoses*, I (pages 30-31, Innes translation)

The Winds as Cameo Subjects
The winds can appear on cameos as puff-cheeked heads blowing breezes.
See also: Aphrodite, Flora.

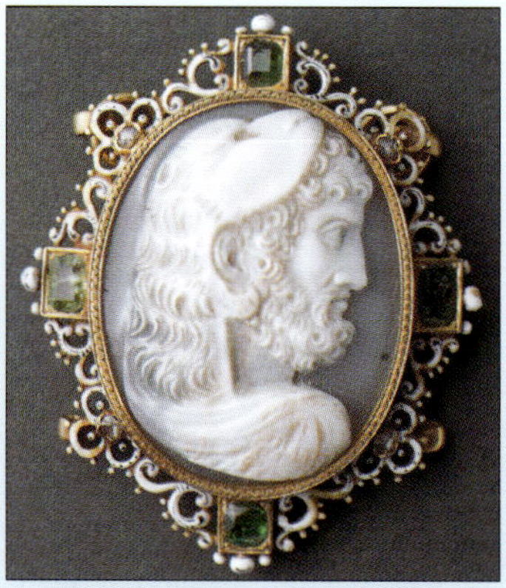

HUNTERS, WARRIORS AND HEROES

Apollo, god of Archery (see Cosmological Myths)

Ares, god of War

Artemis, goddess of Hunting

Athena, goddess of War and Wisdom

Nike, goddess of Victory

Heracles, a Hero

The Trojan War

CHAPTER 7

HUNTERS, WARRIORS AND HEROES

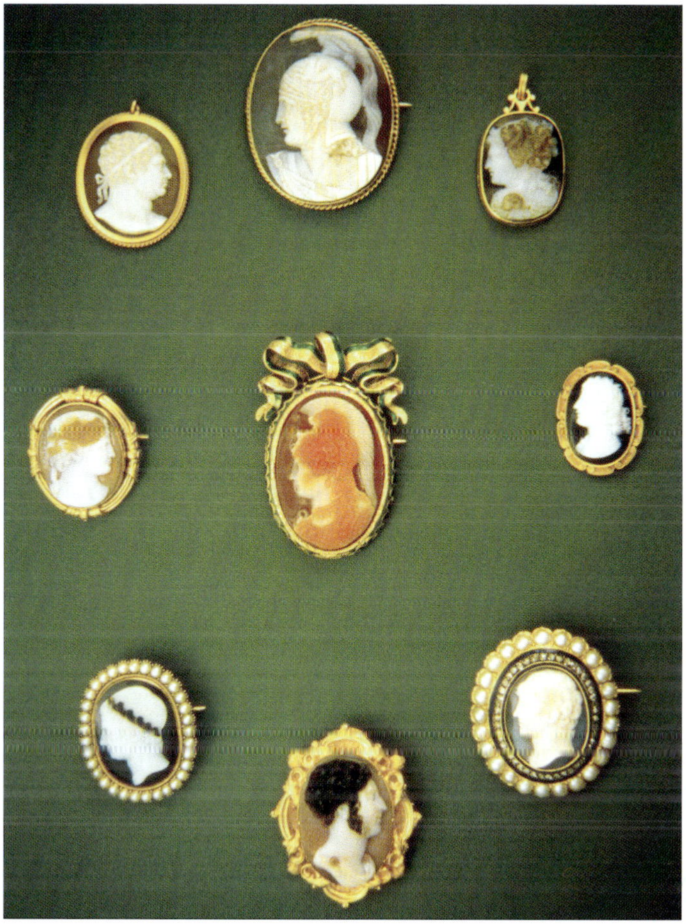

Plate 71. *Cameo group: The centre top cameo, a warrior in a helmet, is possibly Mars. The cameo subjects are from left to right, top to bottom, George III, Mars?, Bacchus, Bacchus, Minerva, classical head, said to be Lord Nelson, portrait head and Alexander The Great(?).* COURTESY OF THE BRITISH MUSEUM, HULL, GRUNDY COLLECTION

Hunting gods were brave heroes armed with bows and arrows who protected mortals from fierce and dangerous beasts. Heroes, the sons of gods who distinguished themselves by their deeds, were cult figures, revered for displaying exemplary courage. Myths about war gods described examples of bravery and cowardice and the influence of the gods on mortal warriors. An ambivalent attitude towards war is apparent in these myths, as the ancient Greeks were so often at war. Athena and Heracles in particular were popular nineteenth century cameo subjects.

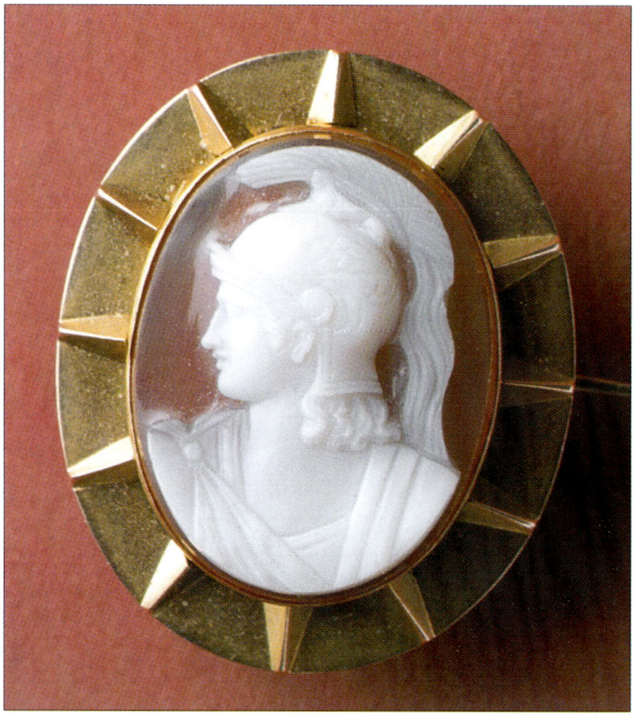

Plate 72. *Agate, gold archaeological revival mount, dated 1894 on the reverse. A warrior, possibly Ares, or Achilles. For similar see Catalogue Entry 126 in* Geschnittene Steine des 18. bis 20. Jahrhunderts *by Ingrid S. Weber. 2⅜in. (6cm) x 2in. (5cm).*

JEAN A. BATEMAN, GRAYS, LONDON £550

ARES (Greek), **god of War**
MARS (Roman)
Cameo Key: Rugged warrior

ARES, the predatory god of War, was ruggedly handsome, unscrupulous and violent. He epitomised brute strength. The son of Zeus and Hera, Ares was portrayed in armour or with armour in the scene. He killed Adonis, a rival for his lover Aphrodite's affection. The Romans called the god 'Mars' and believed he was the father of Romulus and Remus. Homer describes him as the least favoured Olympian god:

> 'But Zeus who marshals storm clouds lowered a dark glance
> at Ares : 'No more, you lying two-faced...
> no more sidling up to me, whining here before me.
> You – I hate you most of all the Olympian gods.
> Always dear to your heart,
> strife, yes, and battles, the bloody grind of war.'
>
> Homer, the *Iliad*, V (page 193, Fagles translation)

Ares as a Cameo Subject
Handsome, rugged male head in profile, wearing a helmet. See Plates 71, 72.
Handsome, virile male figure, nude or in a chiton (short tunic), wearing a cuirass (tightly fitted body armour) and a helmet, with a sword/spear/shield.
Ares and Aphrodite – the lovers together, Ares often in a helmet, his armour nearby. Eros in the scene. See Plate 28.
Ares, Aphrodite and Eros at the forge of Hephaestus. See Plate 12.
See also: Aphrodite, Hephaestus, The Trojan War.

ARTEMIS (Greek), **goddess of Hunting**
DIANA (Roman)
Cameo Key: Young female with crescent moon/ hunting symbols

Goddess of the Hunt who became identified with the Titan moon goddess, Selene, hence the crescent moon as her attribute. Artemis was a beautiful wild maiden, a virgin huntress bearing a silver bow and a quiver of golden arrows, living in the forest with an attendant band of nymphs and hunting dogs.

> 'In Zeus' presence then Artemis swore with the gods' great oath:
> "By thy head, I will keep myself virgin evermore,
> roaming free in the heights of the mountains, the lonely peaks.
> Nod now, grant me this favour!" she said, and the blessed gods'
> father nods, confirming it. Therefore do gods and men
> call her virgin and deershooter, goddess of all the wild;
> noble titles; and Eros can never go near her...'
> Sappho (44A), Greek poet, 7th century BC

Artemis was the daughter of Zeus and Leto, and the twin sister of Apollo, the Sun god. Contrary and wilful, she could cure mortals, or kill them. She was also protector of children and young animals and patron goddess of the Amazons, a race of warrior women. Men were not allowed to approach her, so when the hunter Actæon spied her bathing, the enraged goddess transformed him into a stag and set his own pack of hounds upon him. Artemis was called Diana by the Romans.

In another myth, Selene (the Moon) fell in love with Endymion, a handsome young shepherd. She asked Zeus to grant him the gift of eternal sleep so she knew where to find him each night.

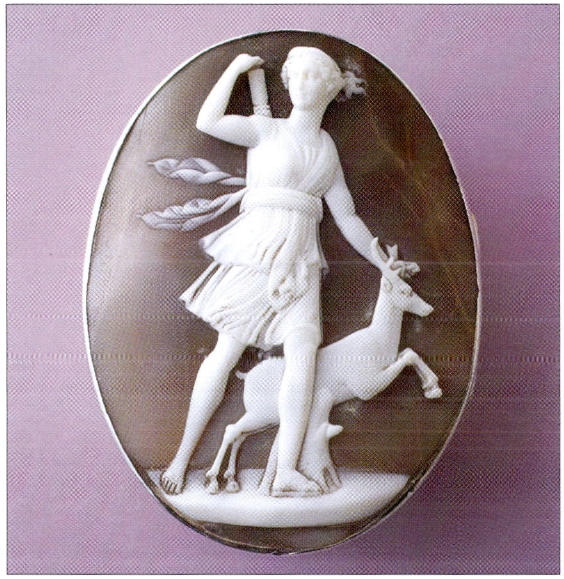

Plate 73. *Bull's Mouth shell, set in lid of a silver box, late 19th century. Artemis depicted as 'Diana Chasseresse', based on a 2nd century BC adaptation of a 4th century BC Greek original attributed to Leochares (Louvre, Paris). The athletic huntress, wearing a tunic, is in the act of drawing an arrow from her quiver, accompanied by a deer. 2½in. (6.5cm) x 2in. (5cm).* M. ROWAN AT www.rowanandrowan.com £450

Artemis as a Cameo Subject

Artemis the huntress – an athletic young girl in a chiton, carrying a bow and a quiver of arrows. Often a crescent moon above her head, deer or dogs may accompany her. See Plate 73.

Artemis and Actæon – the goddess with a youth or a fallen stag, representing Actæon

Artemis, Leto and Apollo – Artemis and Leto look similar, but Artemis is carrying a bow.

Artemis bathing, with attendant nymphs, crescent moon above her head identifying her as the moon goddess, not Aphrodite.

See also: Apollo.

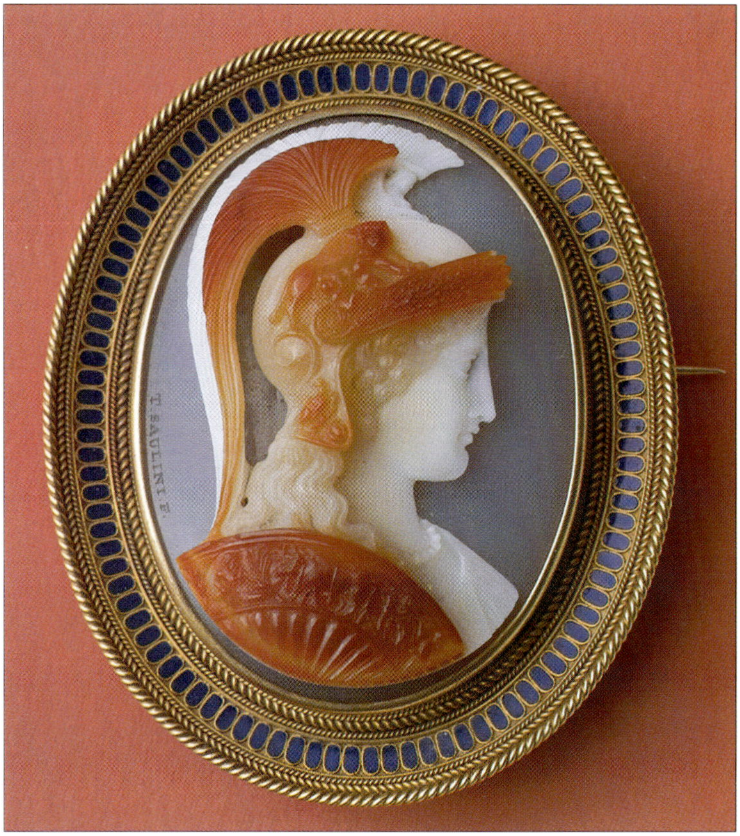

Plate 74. *Exceptional sardonyx, enamel and gold mount in the archaeological revival style. Cameo signed 'T. SAULINI F' for Tommaso Saulini (1793-1864), the prominent Roman gem-engraver. This cameo was exhibited at the International Exhibition, London, 1862. Athena is depicted as 'Roma' with the she-wolf suckling Romulus and Remus portrayed on her helmet, and Romulus, Remus and the Roman river god Tiber featured on her shield. 4in. (10cm) x 3⅛in. (8cm).*

S. J. PHILLIPS LTD., NEW BOND STREET, LONDON

ATHENA (Greek), **goddess of War**
MINERVA (Roman)
Cameo Key: Female in armour

ATHENA was goddess of War but also goddess of Wisdom, so unlike Ares she had no love of violence for its own sake. As a warrior goddess and protector of cities, she wore a helmet, war tunic, and the aegis (goatskin shield) of her father, Zeus. The aegis bore the head of the Gorgon Medusa to ward off evil. Her birth was unusual. Taking heed of a prophecy that his children would be greater than him, Zeus swallowed the pregnant Titaness Metis, Athena's mother. At her birth Hephaestus, the Smith god, split Zeus's forehead open with an axe and Athena emerged, fully grown and armed. Athena in battle costume presented an awesome figure:

'Now in turn Athene, daughter of Zeus of the aegis, beside the threshold of her father slipped off her elaborate dress which she herself had wrought with her hands' patience, and now assuming the war tunic of Zeus who gathers the clouds, she armed in her gear for the dismal fighting.
And across her shoulders she threw the betasselled, terrible aegis, all about which Terror hangs like a garland, and Hatred is there, and Battle Strength, and heart-freezing Onslaught and thereon is set the head of the grim gigantic Gorgon, a thing of fear and

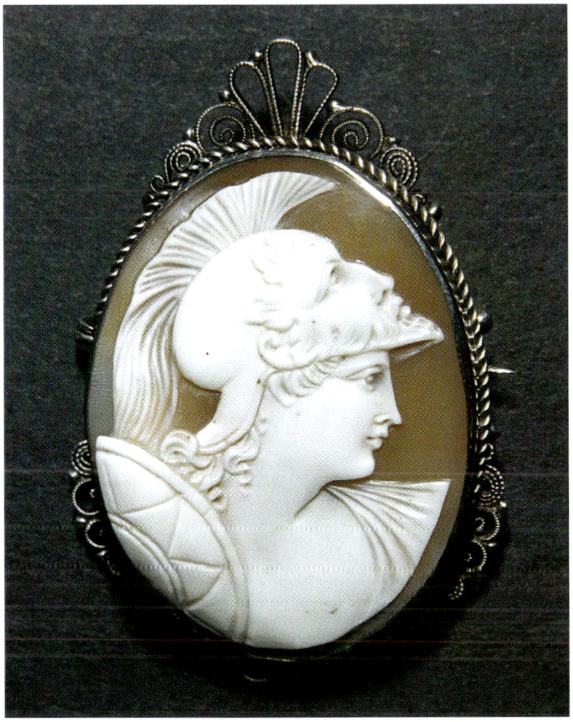

Plate 75. *Bull's Mouth shell, silver filigree mount, circa 1870-80. Athena assumes her armour – her helmet and the aegis. 1½in. (4cm) x 1⅛in. (3cm).*

M. ROWAN AT www.rowanandrowan.com £250

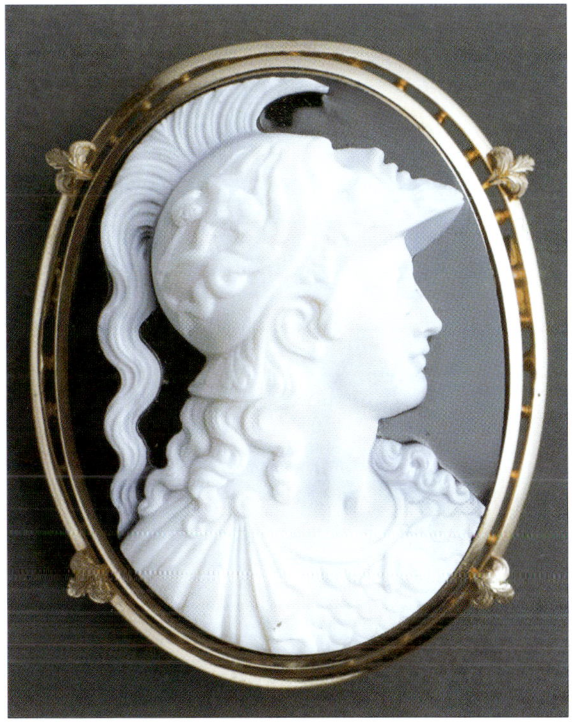

Plate 76. *Onyx, gold mount with leaf decoration. Scratch signed on reverse 'F. Zignani (?) engraver. Rome Via Condotti 9. 1875'. Athena in armour, wearing a crested helmet and the aegis, bearing the face of the Gorgon Medusa to ward off evil. 2¾in. (7cm) x 2in. (5cm).*

LANDSBERG AND SON (ANTIQUES LTD.), HATTON GARDEN, LONDON

horror, portent of Zeus of the aegis.'
Homer, the *Iliad*, V (lines 733-742, Lattimore translation)

Athena was a virgin goddess and her main temple was the Parthenon (Greek *parthenos*, virgin). She won the title of 'patron of Athens' by producing an olive branch, symbol of peace and prosperity and was patron of artisans, craftsmen and household activities such as spinning and weaving. Athena's attributes were the owl, which symbolised her wisdom, and the snake, representing her prudence.

Athena as a Cameo Subject

Athena – a regal woman in a draped robe wearing a helmet, holding a spear and the aegis (goatskin shield). An owl, snake or an olive branch may appear in the scene. See Plates 75, 76, 100.

Athena – in a biga (chariot drawn by two horses).

The Judgement of Paris – Athena stands before the seated Paris with Hera and Aphrodite. Hermes is in the scene. See Plate 29.

Roma – Athena the warrior goddess portrayed as 'Roma'. See Plate 74.

See also: Aphrodite, Medusa, The Trojan War.

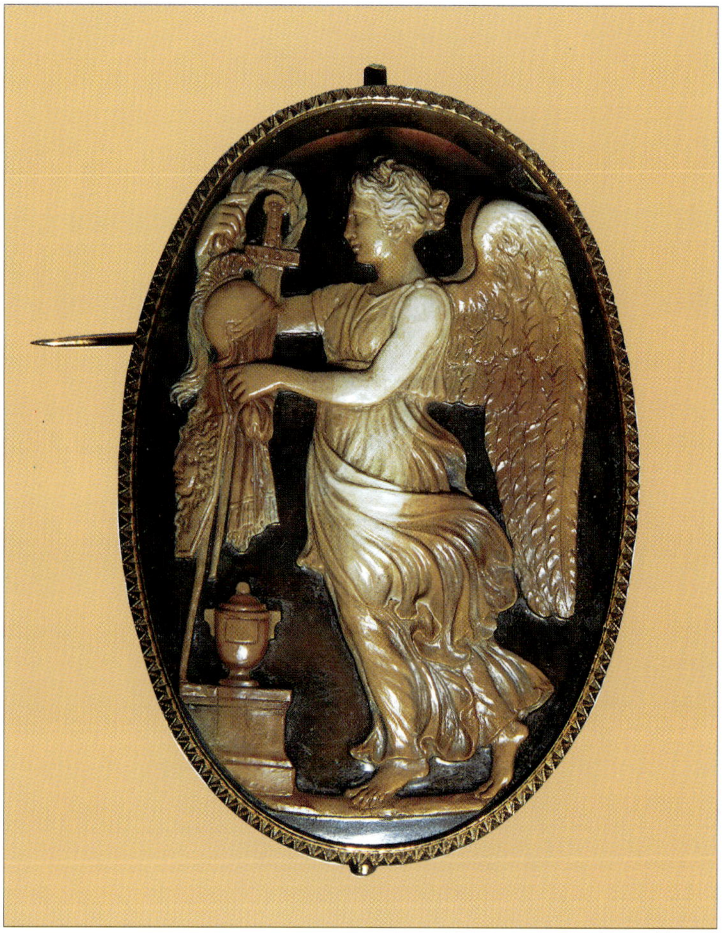

Plate 77. *Early 19th century sardonyx, gold mount. Nike erects a trophy consisting of a warrior's helmet, corselet, sheathed sword and shield. For 4th century BC models of Nike erecting a trophy, see plates 590 and 747 in* Greek Gems And Finger Rings *by John Boardman (2001 edition). 3⅛in. (8cm) x 2⅜in. (6cm).*

S. J. PHILLIPS LTD., NEW BOND STREET, LONDON

NIKE (Greek)
VICTORY (Roman)
Cameo Key: Winged female with laurel wreath or trophy

NIKE, goddess of Victory, honoured success in battle, in sporting and literary contests. Winged Nike descended from Olympus to bestow honours in the form of a laurel wreath or palm frond.

Nike as a Cameo Subject

A winged female in a draped robe with shield in a chariot. Holds a laurel wreath or palm frond.

Where the victory is in battle, Nike may have armour at her feet.

Nike erects a trophy to honour success. See Plate 77.

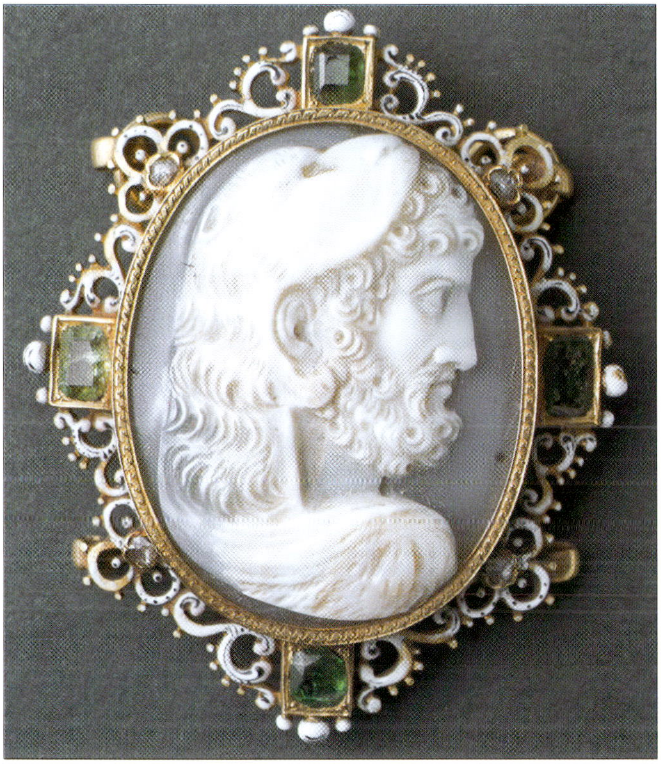

Plate 78. *Hardstone, 18th century, in a 19th century Holbeinesque enamel and gem frame. Heracles in profile, his head covered by the pelt of the Nemean lion, the first trophy of his mighty labours, which he wore for protection. 2¾in. (7cm) x 2in. (5cm).*

S. J. PHILLIPS LTD., NEW BOND STREET, LONDON

HERACLES (Greek)
HERCULES (Roman)
Cameo Key: Bearded warrior with bow, club and lionskin

Heroes were the mortal sons of gods who proved their worth by their courageous deeds. Heracles was the finest example of a hero. The son of Zeus and the mortal Alcmene, his name meant 'glory to Hera'. Zeus attempted to appease Hera after his infidelity with Alcmene, however Hera's wrath was unequalled and she drove Heracles to murder his family. As punishment he had to serve the Argive King Eurytheus who gave him twelve impossible tasks to perform. Pausanius in his *Guide to Greece* (2nd century AD), mentions these as 'the twelve labours of Hercules':

1. He strangled the Nemean lion with his bare hands, as no weapon would penetrate its hide.
2. He cut off, burnt and buried the nine heads of the Lernean hydra.
3. He struggled for a year to capture the elusive Arcadian stag.
4. He trapped the Erymanthian boar in a snowdrift.
5. He cleaned the stables of King Augeus, containing 1000 oxen, by diverting a river through them.
6. He shot the poisonous Stymphalian birds.
7. He captured the Cretan bull, sire of the Minotaur and took it back to Argos.
8. He slew the master of the man-eating mares of Diomedes, and tamed them.

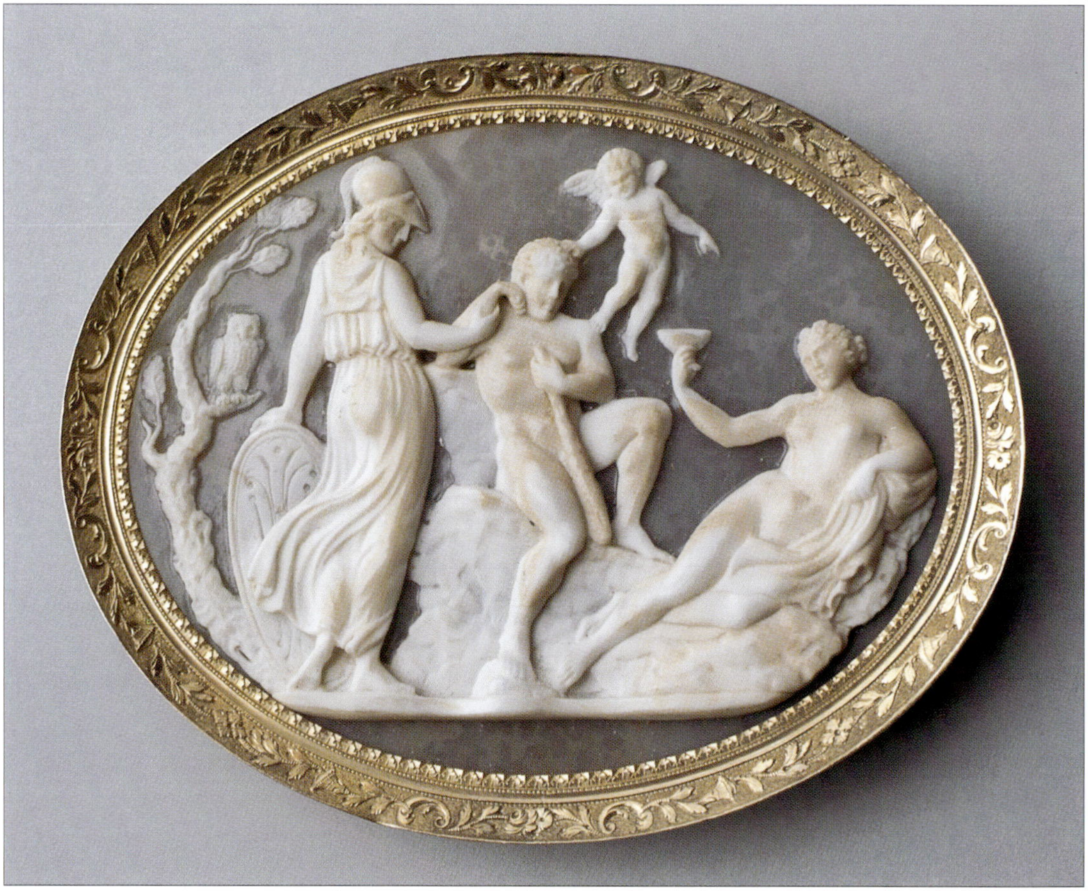

Hercules at the Crossroads / The Choice of Hercules

Plate 79. *Grey agate, late 18th century, engraved gold mount circa 1820. 3½in. (9cm) x 2¾in. (7cm). Depiction of a parable by the Sophist philosopher Prodicus, 'The Choice Of Hercules', reported by the 4th century BC Greek writer Xenophon in* Memorabilia II.

> *'Hercules, when he was advancing from boyhood to manhood (at which period, youths, becoming their own masters, indicate whether they will enter life by the paths of virtue or those of vice), retired to a quiet spot, and sat down to make up his mind as to the question of which of the two tracks he should follow...two females of imposing presence seemed to approach him, the one lovely of aspect and lady-like in demeanour...the other pampered to gross softness...clad in a robe by means of which her charms were conspicuously displayed.'*
>
> The Memoirs Of Socrates For English Readers, *E. Levien, 1872 (page 63)*

These two females were Virtue and Vice. Vice offered him a life of hedonistic idleness, while Virtue argued that true happiness came through labour and diligence. She scorned Vice for making her followers indolent, debauched and ultimately, miserable. Hercules chose Virtue and after a life of toil was received among the gods.

LANDSBERG AND SON (ANTIQUES LTD.), HATTON GARDEN, LONDON

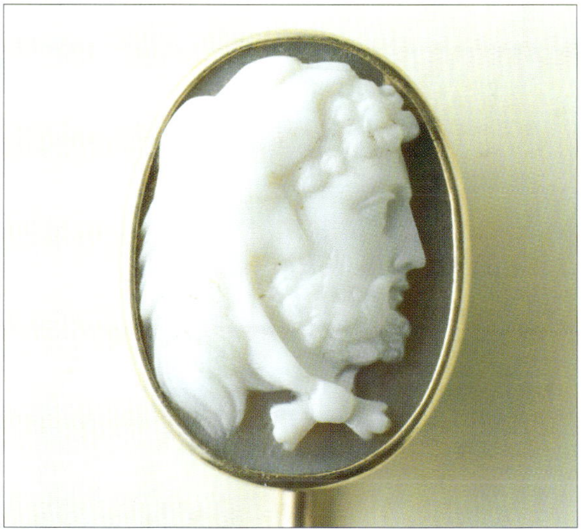

Plate 80. *Black Helmet shell, gold mount, circa 1850. An aged Hercules, his head covered by the pelt of the Nemean lion forming a fillet (ribbon) at the neck. 1⅛in. (3cm) x 1in. (2.5cm).* PRIVATE COLLECTION

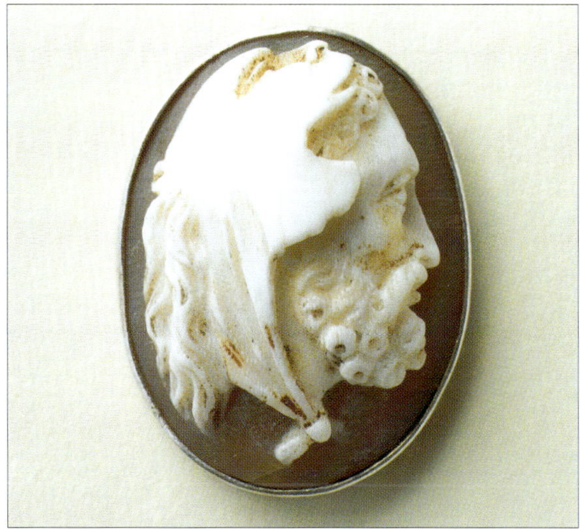

Plate 81. *Black Helmet shell, gold stickpin mount, circa 1850. Bearded Hercules with lion's skin. 1⅛in. (3cm) x 1in. (2.5cm).* PRIVATE COLLECTION

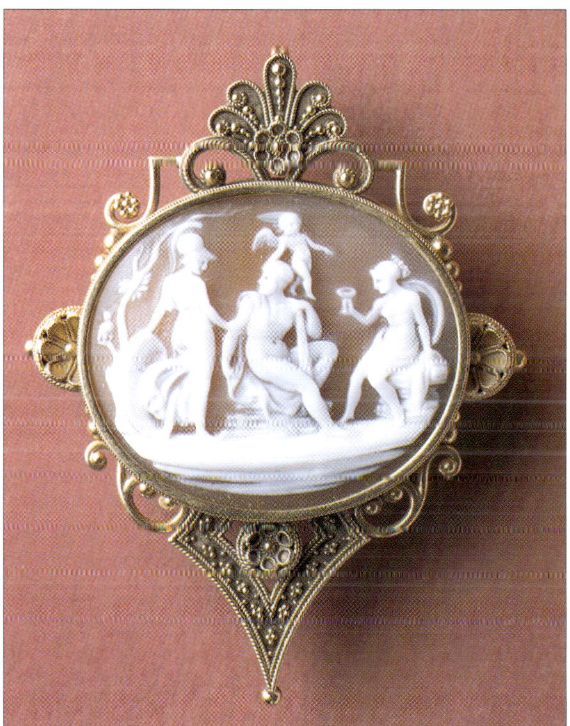

9. He killed the Amazon Queen, Hippolyta, in battle to obtain her girdle.
10. He tricked Atlas, bearer of the world, into telling him where Hera's golden apples were hidden, and stole them.
11. He battled with and killed the monster Geryon to obtain his cattle.
12. He dragged Cerberus, the three-headed dog which guarded the entrance to Hades, back to Argos.

Heracles continued to perform heroic deeds until Hera wreacked her vengeance upon him with a poisoned robe. Zeus deified Heracles and elevated him to Olympus, where he married the goddess of Youth, Hebe.

Plate 82. *Bull's Mouth shell, French archaeological revival mount, late 19th century. Hercules, seated centre, is tempted by Vice and Virtue. 2⅜in. (6cm) x 2in. (5cm).* MICHAEL G. LONGMORE, GRAYS, LONDON £1150

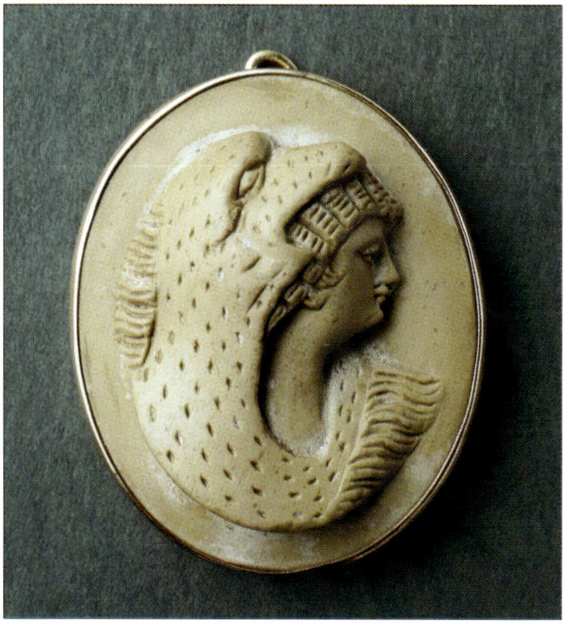

Plate 83. *Lava, gold mount, circa 1870. Omphale in profile, her head covered with the pelt of the Nemean lion. 2⅜in. (6cm) high x 2in. (5cm) wide.*

PRIVATE COLLECTION

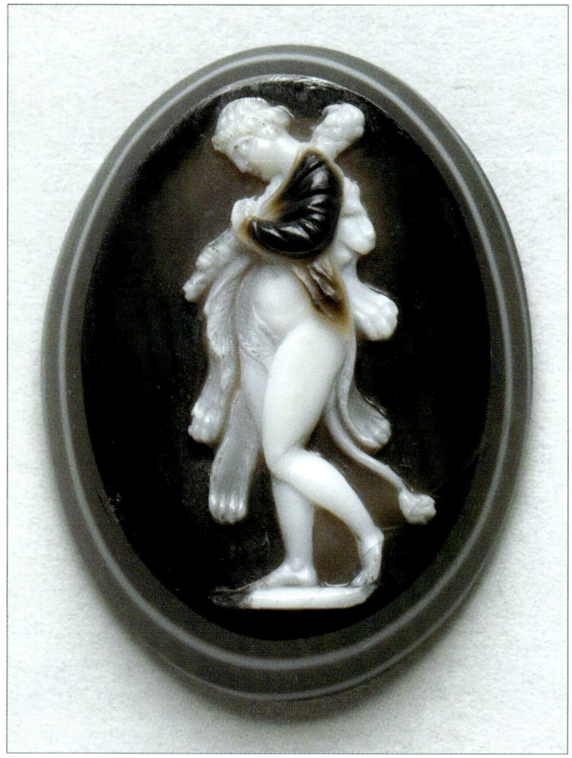

Plate 84. *Onyx cameo, circa 1800. Omphale parades in Heracles' lionskin, carrying his club. Zeus punished Heracles by making him a slave of the Lydian Queen, Omphale. During his enslavement he had to perform domestic tasks and Omphale, with whom he exchanged clothes, took him as her lover.*

PETER SZUHAY COLLECTION, GRAYS, LONDON

Heracles as a Cameo Subject

Usually portrayed covered with a lionskin, or with a lionskin in the scene, the hide of the Nemean lion which he wore for protection. See Plates 78, 80, 81.

Heracles with a club, or a bow and arrow.

The hero capturing Cerberus, the three-headed dog guarding the gates of Hades.

Heracles supporting a dying female warrior – the Amazon Queen, Hippolyta.

'The Choice of Hercules' – he must decide between a life of vice or virtue. See Plates 79, 82.

Omphale, lover of Heracles. see Plates 83, 84.

See also: Hebe, Hera, Zeus.

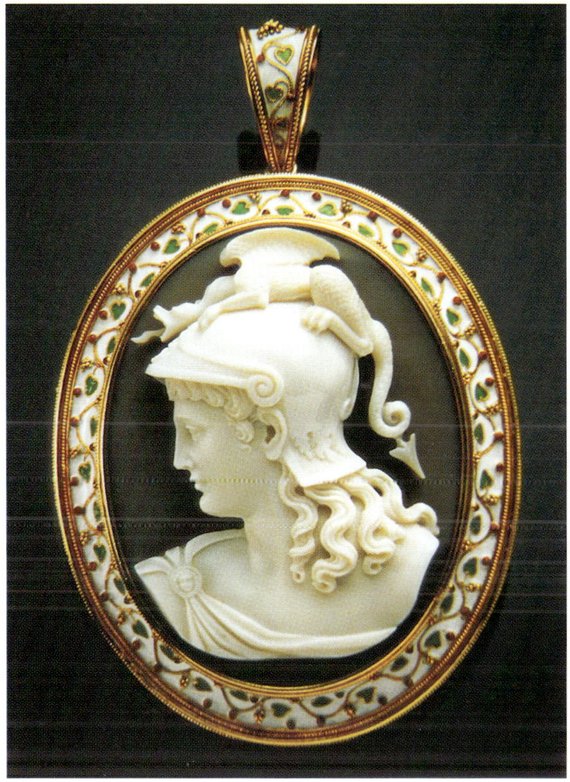

Plate 85. *Translucent chalcedony cameo by Luigi Isler, gold and enamel pendant mount in the Renaissance style by Giuliano. Isler, a Roman gem-engraver, worked in London in the 19th century. This cameo was exhibited in Paris in 1867 and is illustrated in* The Science Of Gems, Jewels, Coins, and Medals *by A. Billing (1867) (illustration 171). Achilles is depicted as a beautiful youth. At the time of the Trojan War his mother, Thetis, took him to the island of Scyros, knowing that if he took part in the war he was destined to die. On Scyros the King, Lycomedes, dressed Achilles in female attire and concealed him in his harem. So feminine was the nature of Achilles' beauty that he could have easily passed for one of the daughters of Lycomedes.*

COURTESY OF THE AKIBA MUSEUM OF ANTIQUE JEWELLERY, JAPAN

THE TROJAN WAR

Homer's epic poem the *Iliad*, believed to have been written in the 8th century BC, described events in the tenth and final year of the Trojan War. The war began with the Judgement of Paris and Paris's seduction of Helen, Queen of Sparta and ultimately resulted in the destruction of Troy. Many Greek myths were based on Homer's descriptions of the gods and heroes in this epic. Hera, Poseidon and Athena were the gods most hostile to Troy, while Ares, Apollo and Aphrodite supported the Trojans. During the nineteenth century, Homer was widely read, so scenes and heroes from the Trojan War were popular cameo subjects.

HEROES OF THE TROJAN WAR

Achilles/Achilleus: The tragic hero of the epic, the Greek warrior who brought disaster upon himself and Troy. Son of the sea nymph, Thetis, who tried to prevent his prophesied death by dipping him in the River Styx to make him immortal (she held him by his heel, which remained his vulnerable point). His mortal father, Peleus, entrusted him to the centaur Chiron, who schooled him in music and the use of the bow (see Plate 65). As a warrior, Achilles withdrew from battle in the Trojan War after quarrelling with the Greek commander Agamemnon. When the Trojan champion Hector killed Patroclus, Achilles felt compelled to re-

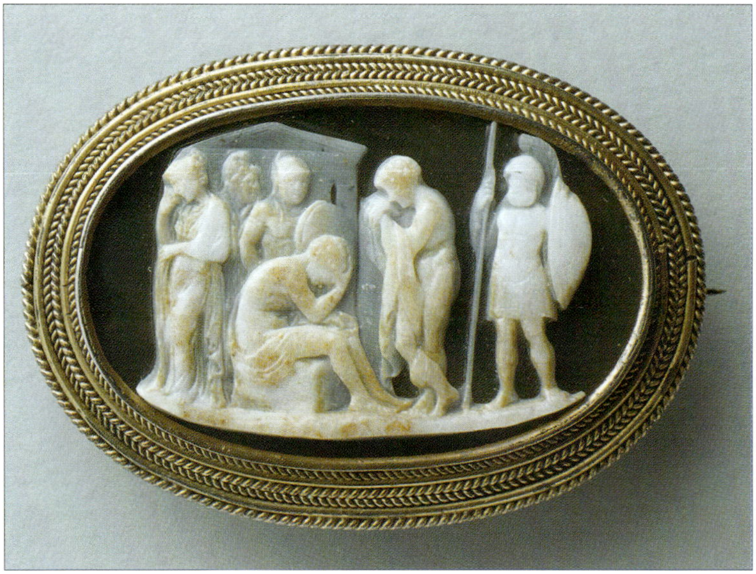

Plate 86. *Onyx, ropework mount, circa 1840. 1½in. (4cm) x 2⅜in. (6cm). Achilles, seated, mourns his friend Patroclus, who has been killed in battle by the Trojan, Hector. Based on an ancient fragment once owned by Cardinal Albani (with extra figures added). To the left of Achilles is his slave and concubine, Briseis and the Greek warrior Antilochus leans on a column. Other Greek warriors are in the scene. For similar, see Catalogue Entry 33 in* Geschnittene Steine des 18. bis. 20. Jahrhunderts *by Ingrid S. Weber.* PRIVATE COLLECTION

enter the fray to avenge his friend's death, killing Hector and dragging his body behind his chariot in triumph. Paris, Prince of Troy, used an arrow guided by Apollo to fatally wound Achilles (post-*Iliad*).

Achilles as a Cameo Subject

Achilles in helmet. See Plate 85.

Two warriors in combat – can be Achilles and Hector.

Achilles, lamenting the death of his friend Patroclus, sits pensively, mourning. See Plate 86.

Achilles drags Hector's body behind his chariot. Hector's father, the aged King Priam, begs for the return of his son's body.

A handsome youth in a helmet. See Plate 79.

'Andromache attempting to restrain Hector before his Encounter with Achilles'

Plate 87 (Opposite). *Superb 19th century agate cameo by Girometti in gold and enamel frame, 5⅞in. (15cm) x 4in. (10cm), after an 18th century intaglio by Luigi Pichler. The scene is from Homer's* Iliad*, Book VI. On the eve of battle with Achilles, Hector, commander of the Trojan forces and devoted husband and father, bids farewell to his wife Andromache, and their baby Astyanax. Andromache and others attempt to restrain him as he goes to face certain death in battle against Achilles.*

The cameo is in its original box. It was exhibited at the International Exhibition in London in 1862 by Phillips of Cockspur Street. J. B. Waring, in Masterpieces Of Industrial Art and Sculpture At The International Exhibition 1862*, described it as 'a gold plaque inlaid with a fine cameo by Girometti, surrounded with enamelled ornament in the Italian style.' (Vol. II, Plate 167.) The sheet in the lid of its fitted box cites the cameo as the work of Girometti, followed by a Greek quotation from Homer's* Iliad *describing the scene and an excerpt from Alexander Pope's verse translation of Homer's work.* S. J. PHILLIPS LTD., NEW BOND STREET, LONDON

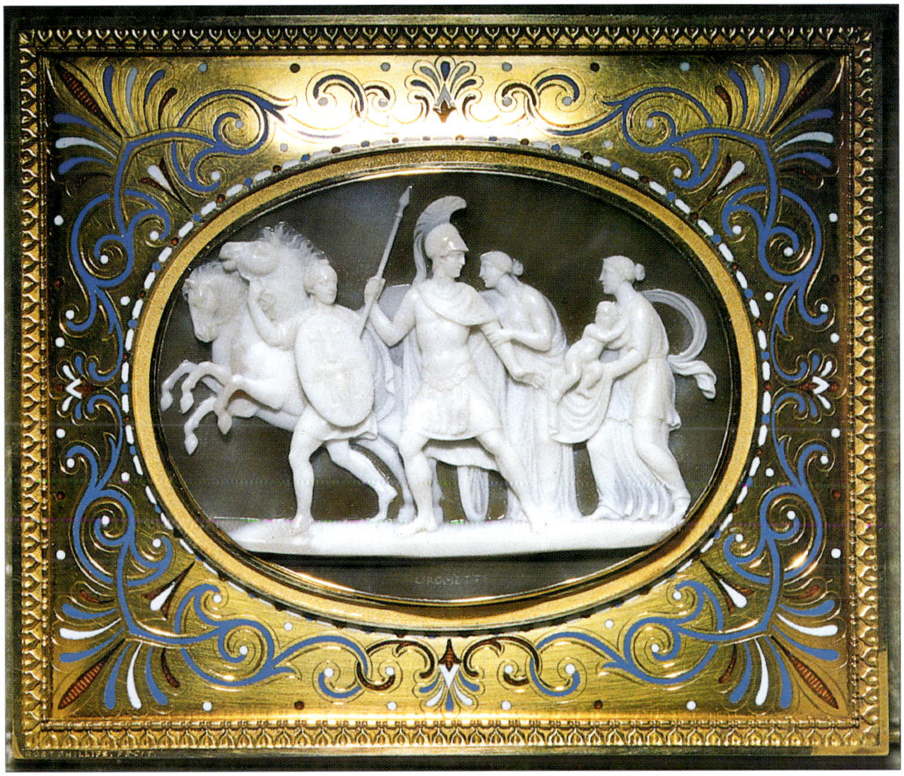

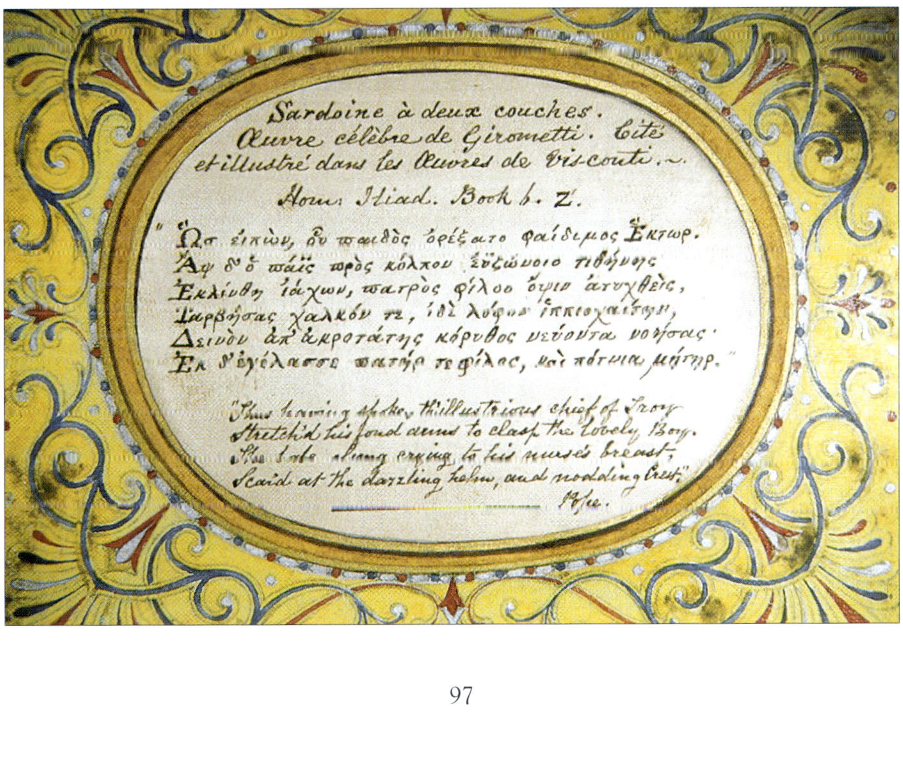
Sardoine à deux couches.
Œuvre célèbre de Girometti. Cité
et illustré dans les Œuvres de Vis-conti.~
Hom: Iliad. Book 6. Z.
"Thus having spoke, th'illustrious chief of Troy
Stretch'd his fond arms to clasp the lovely Boy.
Scar'd at the dazzling helm, and nodding crest."
Pope.

Plate 88. *Horned Helmet shell, set in a tortoiseshell necklace, circa 1860-70, portraying Menelaos or Pericles. For similar, see Entry 402 in* Geschnittene Steine Des 18. bis 20. Jahrhunderts *by Ingrid S. Weber. 2in. (5cm) x 1½in. (4cm).* JEAN A. BATEMAN, GRAYS, LONDON £295

Plate 89 (below). *Shell, late 19th century, modern gold ring mount. Paris wears the Phrygian cap of a Persian soldier. ⅜in. (1.5cm).*
M. ROWAN AT www.rowanandrowan.com £150

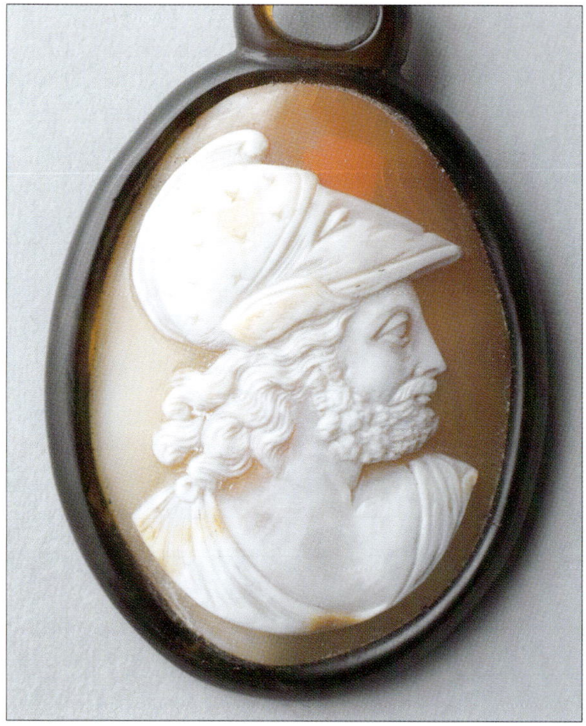

Agamemnon: King of Mycenæ, celebrated commander of the Greek forces who exhorted them to besiege Troy after Paris had seduced his brother's wife, Helen.

Menelaos: King of Sparta, husband of Helen. Single combat was arranged between Paris and Menelaos for Helen. Aphrodite intervened to save Paris and after this the conflict was inevitable.

Menelaos as a Cameo Subject
A regal, bearded man in a helmet. See Plate 88.

Paris: Son of King Priam of Troy and Hecuba, abandoned at birth as it was prophesised he would be the cause of the ruin of Troy. This Trojan prince had won Helen's love in the 'Judgement of Paris'. Paris played a minor role in battles. He was responsible for the death of Achilles and was himself killed by a poisoned arrow.

Paris as a Cameo Subject
The Judgement of Paris. See Plate 29.
A handsome young male wearing a Phrygian cap (folded, conical cap worn by Persian soldiers). See Plate 89.

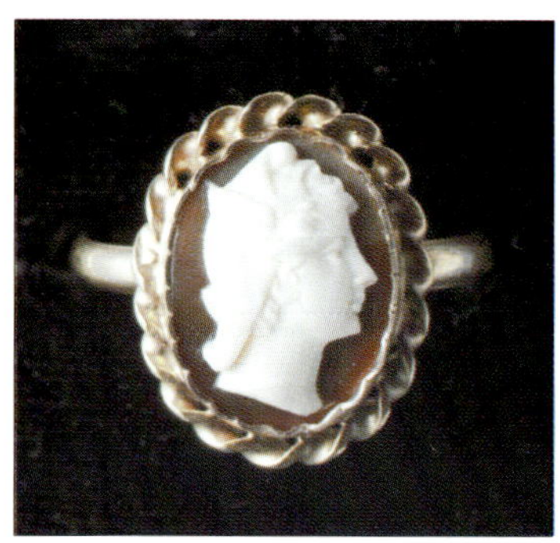

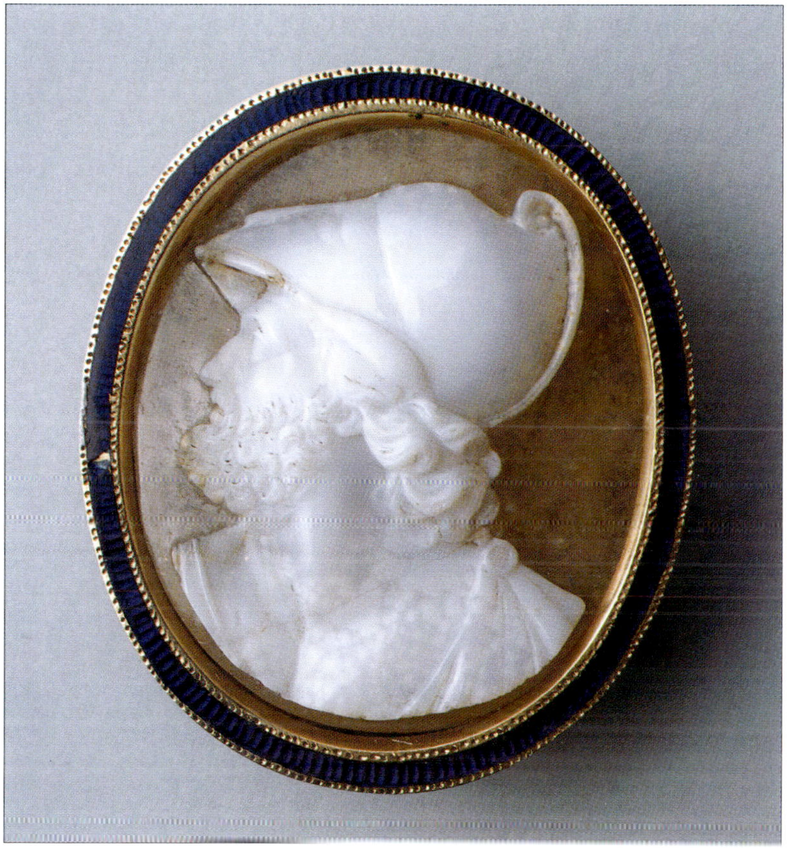

Plate 90. *Hardstone, enamel mount, early 19th century. The warrior Ajax in profile, wearing a helmet. 2¾in. (7cm) x 2in. (5cm).*

S. J. PHILLIPS LTD., NEW BOND STREET, LONDON

Hector: Prince of Troy, the noble Trojan champion. The brave, honourable Hector was preordained to be the loser in combat with Achilles. His wife Andromache tried in vain to prevent him going to his certain death. Hector's death determined the downfall of Troy.

Hector as a Cameo Subject

Hector in combat with Achilles/Patroclus/Ajax – a pair of warriors.

Hector's farewell to Andromache – his weeping wife and others attempt to restrain the warrior as he leaves to face Achilles. See Plate 87.

Ajax the Greater: Valiant Greek warrior, second in importance to Achilles. Ajax fought bravely against the Trojans but killed himself in despair when he felt dishonoured in not receiving the armour of Achilles.

Ajax as a Cameo Subject

A regal, bearded male in a masked helmet. See Plate 90.

Two warriors in combat – can be Ajax and Hector.

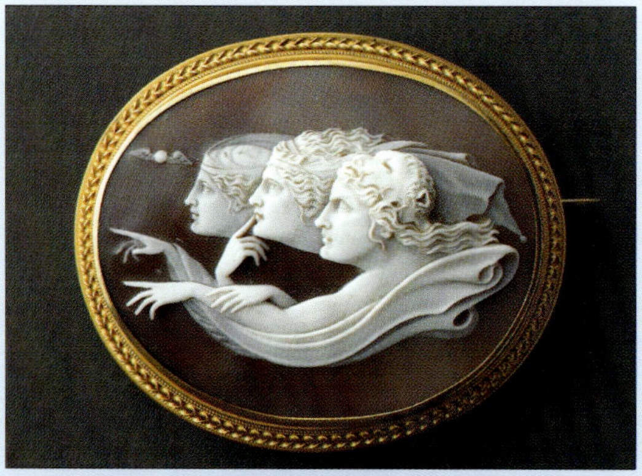

DARK FORCES AND MORAL TALES

Hades, god of the Dead

Medusa and the Gorgons, the Terrible Ones

Nemesis, Divine Justice

Chapter 8

DARK FORCES AND MORAL TALES

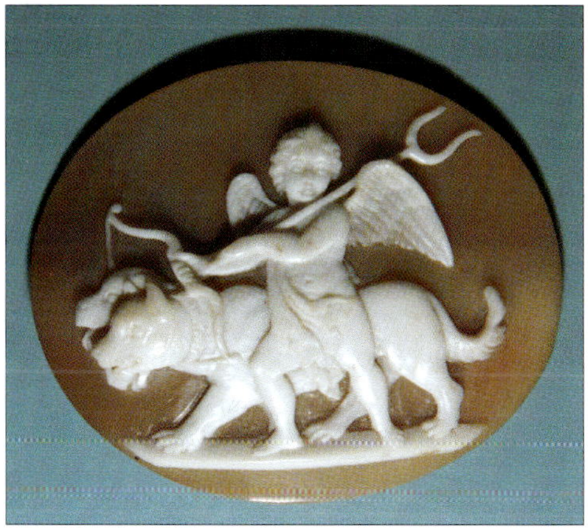

Myths that confronted man's fear of death and the unknown and warned of the consequences of disobeying the gods. Medusa was a popular cameo subject in both her beautiful and grotesque forms.

HADES (Greek), god of the Dead
PLUTO (Roman)

Hades, god of the Dead, ruled the Underworld, also called Hades. He was assigned this role when the Olympians defeated the Titans. Hades means 'the invisible' and although he was not an evil god, people were frightened to utter his name. Hesiod called him 'he who has many names', in reference to this. Hades

Plate 91. *Bull's Mouth shell, circa 1850, depicting Eros and Cerberus. 1½in. (4cm) x 2in. (5cm). After a bas-relief, 'The Four Elements' by Thorvaldsen (Rome 1828), described by Hawks Le Grice in 1841:*

> *'In allegorizing the four elements our author has considered Cupid as superior to all the gods…His power is recognised by earth and heaven, by sea and land; and hence we find that he is employed under various guises, by our author, to allegorize the four elements, Earth, Ocean, Fire and Air…*
> *'FIRE is allegorized by Cupid guiding Cerberus, the fierce guardian of the fiery regions by the string of his bow, while the captive sentinel willingly follows and obeys the god of love.'*
>
> *Count Hawks Le Grice,* Walks Through The Studii Of The Sculptors At Rome, *1841 (Vol. II, pages 83, 84)*

Pat Novissimo Collection, Central Gallery, Portobello Road, London

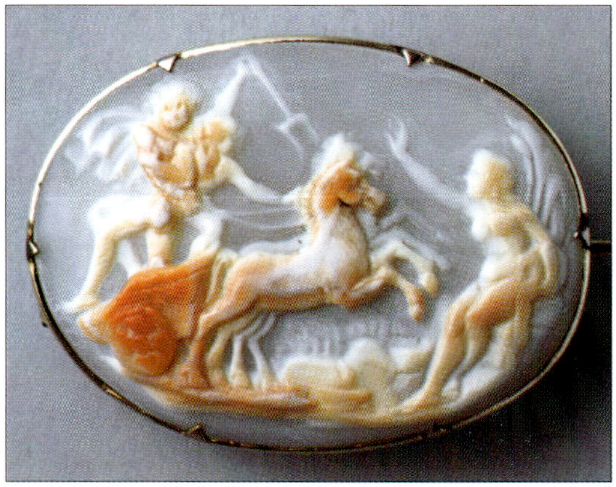

Plate 92. *Horned Helmet shell, gold mount, circa 1830. After the antique. 1½in. (4cm) x 2in. (5cm). See Catalogue Entry 90 in* Photographic Facsimiles Of The Antique Gems Formerly Possessed By The Late Prince Poniatowksi *(1857). Hades abducts Persephone and carries her off to the Underworld:*

> *'He caught her up reluctant on his golden car and*
> *bare her away lamenting. Then she cried out shrilly*
> *...But no one,*
> *either of the deathless gods or of mortal men, heard her voice.'*
> *Homeric Hymn II,* To Demeter *(page 291, Evelyn-White translation)*

PRIVATE COLLECTION

was a dark place reached by crossing the mythical River Styx, patrolled by Charon, the ferryman. A three-headed dog, Cerberus, prevented departure from the world of the dead. Hades owned a magical helmet which made the wearer invisible. He lent it to Perseus to help him defeat the Gorgon Medusa.

Hades as a Cameo Subject

Hades is a rare figure in art.

Hades, abducting Persephone, carries her off to the Underworld. See Plate 92.

Cerberus, the three-headed dog guarding the entrance to Hades, being captured by Heracles.

Eros leading Cerberus from Hades. See Plate 90.

See also: Demeter and Persephone, Heracles, Orpheus and Eurydice.

Plate 93 (opposite). *Sard cameo by Benedetto Pistrucci (1784-1855), white enamel and gold archaeological revival mount. 3½in. (9cm) x 5½in. (14cm). Pistrucci, celebrated Roman gem-engraver and pupil of Nicolo Morelli, came to England in 1814, and became Chief Engraver to the Royal Mint. This cameo is after the 'Rondanini Medusa', a Roman copy of a 5th century BC Greek sculpture by Phidias, named after the family and palace where the original sculpture existed before 1662. It depicts the Gorgon with the sad face of a beautiful woman.*

S. J. PHILLIPS LTD., NEW BOND STREET, LONDON

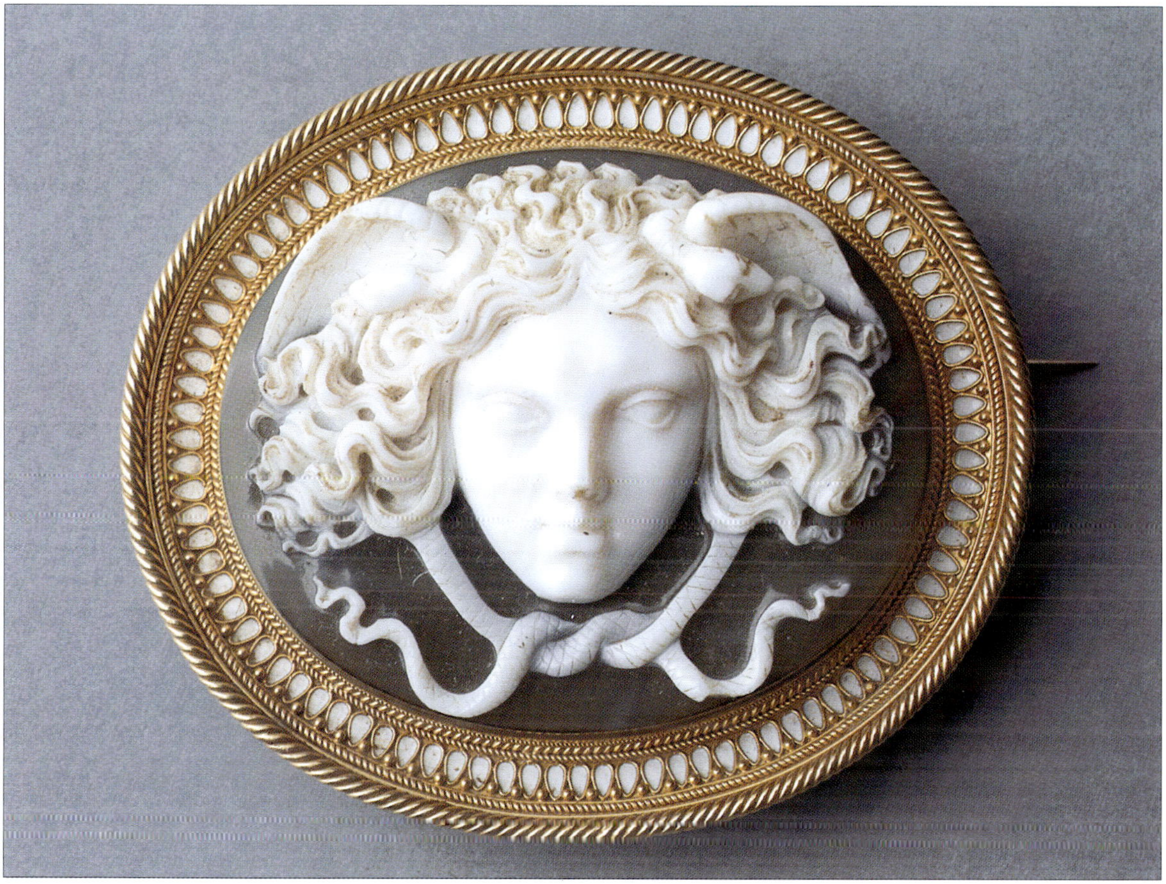

MEDUSA/THE GORGONS (Greek)
Cameo key: Female head, snakes in hair

MEDUSA, a mortal, and her two immortal sisters Stheno and Euryale, were known as 'The Gorgons' (the Terrible Ones). They lived in the far West in the land of darkness and were perceived as grotesque monsters with writhing snakes and often wings or tusks in their hair. According to Ovid, Medusa, once a beautiful woman, had been transformed into a gorgon by Athena for defiling her temple:

> 'Of all the beauties she [Medusa] possessed, none was more striking than her lovely hair. But, so they say, the lord of the sea robbed her of her virginity in the temple of Minerva. Jove's daughter turned her back, hiding her modest face behind her aegis: and to punish the Gorgon for her deed, she changed her hair into revolting snakes. To this day, in order to terrify her enemies and numb them with fear, the goddess wears as a breastplate the snakes that were her own creation.'
>
> Ovid, *Metamorphoses*, IV (page 115, Innes translation)

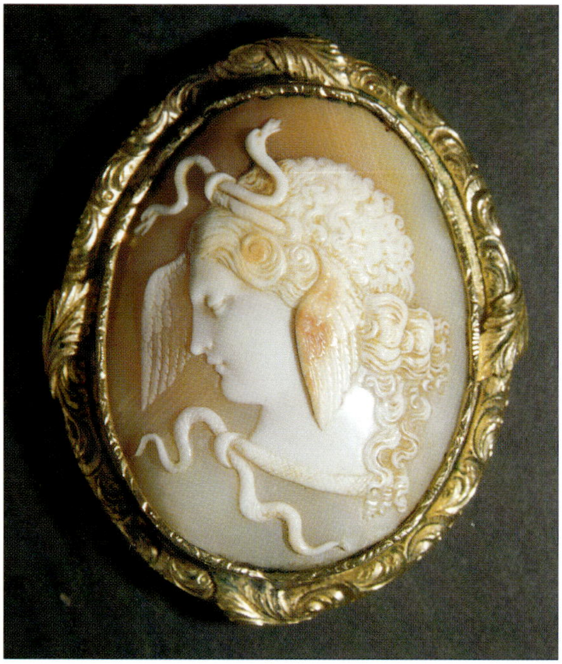

Plate 94. *Horned Helmet shell, ornate gold mount with scroll and leaf decoration, mid-19th century. 3⅛in. (8cm) x 2⅜in. (6cm). Head of Medusa in profile, a beautiful woman with snakes in her hair and forming a fillet (ribbon) around her neck, drooping wings on her head. After an ancient engraved gem signed 'Solonis' from the cabinet of Strozzi, see Plate LXIII in Stosch's* Gemmae Antiquae Caelatae. *There were many ancient representations of this type of Medusa, see for example Entry 9024 in Raspe/Tassie, Volume II, (1791).*

SILVER FOX GALLERY, PORTOBELLO ROAD, LONDON £350

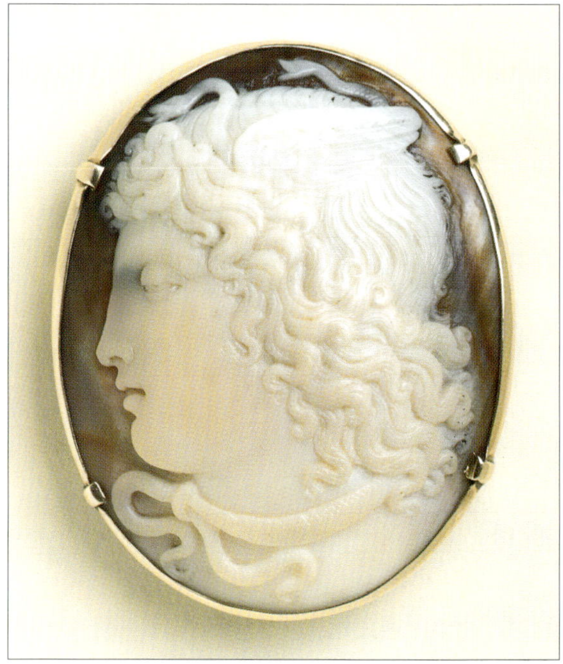

Plate 95. *Cowrie shell, gold cut-down setting, circa 1820. Medusa in profile to left with fillet under chin, after the antique. 2in. (5cm) x 1½in. (4cm).*

S. HARLOWE AT www.rowanandrowan.com £450

Medusa had the power to turn men to stone simply by looking at them. Perseus, the Greek hero, wearing Hades' helmet of invisibility, Hermes' winged sandals and using Athena's shield as a mirror, beheaded the Gorgon. From the blood of Medusa sprang the white winged horse, Pegasus. Perseus presented Athena with the Gorgon's head which thereafter formed the centrepiece of the aegis.

Medusa as a Cameo Subject

Medusa as a grotesque. See Plate 112.

Rondanini Medusa, front facing, the sad face of a beautiful woman. See Plate 93.

Medusa, profile to left, with snakes in her hair and forming a fillet (ribbon) around her neck, drooping wings on her head. See Plate 94.

'Strozzi-Medusa', profile to left, snakes in hair. See Plate 94.

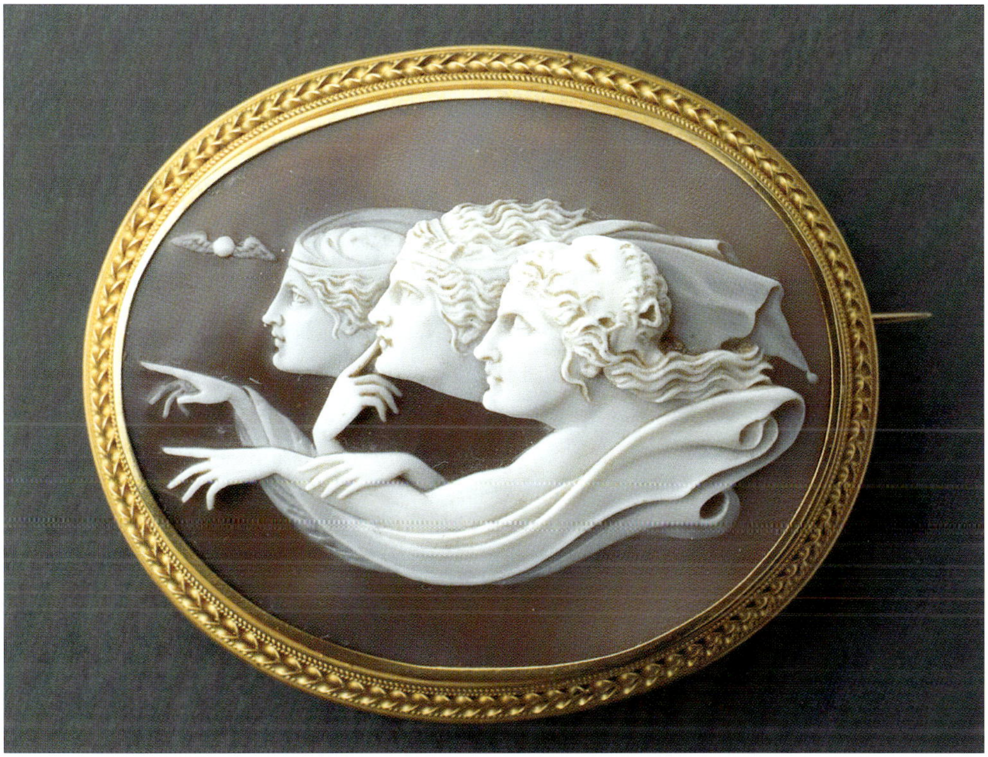

Plate 96. *Black Helmet shell, archaeological revival gold mount, circa 1870. 3½in. (9cm) x 2¾in. (7cm). Although this cameo is based on the H. Fuseli painting 'The Three Witches' (after 1783), depicting the three witches from* Macbeth, *it is stylised in a mythological form, possibly representing the goddess Nemesis (centre), accompanied by Themis, a personification of Justice, and the nymph Adrasteia.* PRIVATE COLLECTION

NEMESIS

'Nemesis, the specially implacable goddess to wicked and violent men.'

Pausanius, *Guide to Greece* I (page 33, Levi translation)

Daughter of Nyx (Night), Nemesis was the personification and goddess of vengeance and divine retribution, a merciless force quick to punish those guilty of crimes, especially the sin of 'hubris' – excessive pride. There existed a Nemesis of gods, men and the dead. Collignon describes Nemesis:

> 'The goddess is characterised by the headdress known as the polos and by her gesture; her right hand is held before her mouth, with one finger on her lips, as though to command silence.'
>
> M. Collignon, *Manual Of Mythology In Relation To Greek Art*, 1890 (page 303)

CAMEO IDENTIFICATION GUIDE: INDEX OF COMMON ATTRIBUTES

Listed are key attributes most often depicted on nineteenth century cameos.

Animals

Bat	Nyx (Night)
Butterfly	Psyche/Eros
Deer	Artemis, Apollo, Orpheus
Donkey	Silenus
Dove	Aphrodite
Eagle	Zeus, Hebe, Ganymede
Goat	Aphrodite, Dionysus and his Train, Eros, Pan
Horse	Apollo, Centaur, Poseidon
Lion	Dionysus and his Train, Heracles
Owl	Athena, Nyx
Panther	Dionysus and his Train
Sea Creatures	Poseidon
Snakes	Athena, Medusa
Stag	Artemis
Swan	Aphrodite, Eros, Leda

Arms/armour

Armed Male	Apollo, Ares, Heracles, Trojan War
Armed Female	Athena

Bow and arrow

Artemis, Apollo, Eros, Heracles

Chariots, drawn by:

Horses	Apollo, Eos, Nike, Poseidon
Sea horses	Poseidon
Swans	Aphrodite, Eros

Cosmos

Moon	Artemis, Selene
Stars	Eos, Nyx
Sun	Apollo, Eos

Crowns, made of:

Corn or wheat sheaves	Demeter, Persephone
Diadem	Hera
Flowers	Flora, Hemera, Muses, Nymphs
Ivy, or vine leaves	Dionysus and his Train
Laurel leaves	Apollo, Muses, Nike
Oak leaves	Zeus
Olive wreath	Zeus
Poppies	Nyx, Persephone
Turrets	Cybele
Veil	Hera, Nyx

Helmets

Ares, Athena, Trojan War heroes

Lovers

Aphrodite and Ares
Aphrodite and Adonis
Cephalus and Procris
Eros and Psyche
Flora and Zephyr
Orpheus and Eurydice
Paris and Helen
Zeus and one of his lovers

Mask

Dionysus, Muses

Musical Instruments

Flute	Muses
Lyre	Apollo, Muses, Orpheus
Pan pipes	Pan, Satyrs
Tambourine	Muses
Trumpet	Muses
Viol	Apollo

Plants/Fruit/Flowers

Cornucopia	Eros, Flora, Iris
Grapes	Dionysus and his Train
Ivy	Dionysus and his Train
Laurel	Apollo, Muses, Nike
Lily	Hera
Pine, pine cone	Dionysus and his Train, Pan
Poppy	Nyx (Night)
Vine leaves	Dionysus and his Train

Seated on Thrones

Cybele, Hera, Hades, Persephone, Zeus

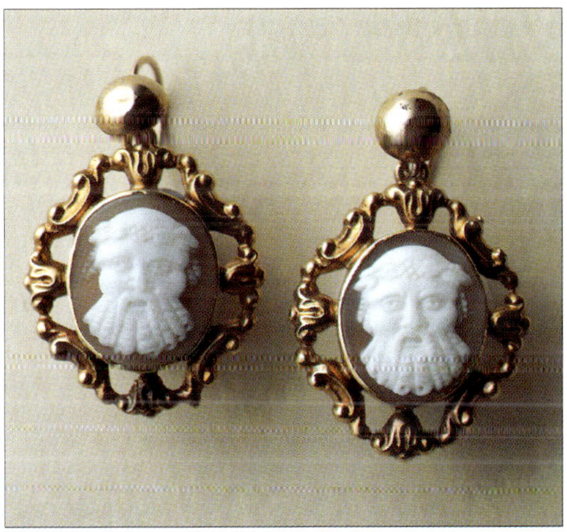

Plate 97. *Bull's Mouth shell, gold repoussé mounts, circa 1850, of Greek theatre masks, after the satyr Silenus. 1⅛in. (3cm) x ¾in. (2cm).*

PRIVATE COLLECTION

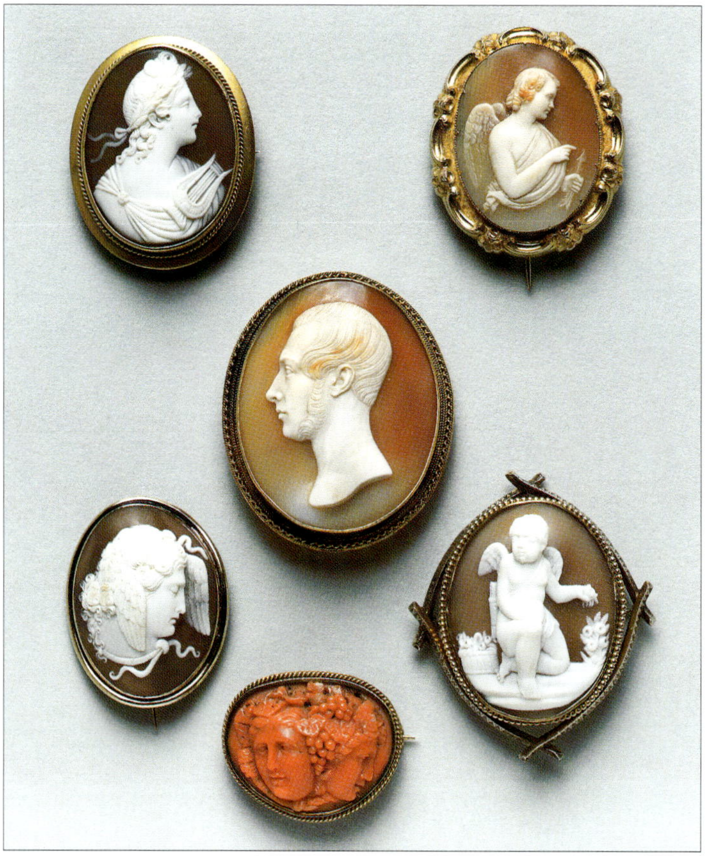

Plate 98.

Top left: Bull's Mouth shell, gold ropework mount, circa 1840. Apollo Musegete with lyre, wearing a laurel wreath, symbolic of poetic inspiration. 1¾in. (4.5cm) long x 1⅜in. (3.5cm) wide.

MONETA, HATTON GARDEN, LONDON £400

Top right: Horned Helmet shell, ornate William IV gold mount. Eros tests the sharpness of his arrow. 1¾in. (4.5cm) wide x 1½in (4cm) long. CHARLOTTE SAYERS, GRAY'S, LONDON £580

Centre: Horned Helmet shell, gold mount. A portrait of John Findlay from the Saulini workshop. Engraved on reverse of mount: 'John Findlay, Saulini, Sculpsit [sculptured by], Roma 1844'. 2⅛in. (5.5cm) long x 2in (4.8cm) wide. IAN STANLEY, PORTOBELLO ROAD, LONDON

Bottom left: Bull's Mouth shell, gold mount, circa 1840. High relief carving of Medusa after an ancient gem signed 'Socsocle'. See Plate LXV in Stosch's Gemmae Antiquae Caelatae. *1½in (4cm) long x 1⅜in (3.5cm) wide.* M. ROWAN AT www.rowanandrowan.com £650

Bottom centre: Coral cameo, gold mount, circa 1840. Bacchus, god of Wine, and his wife, Ariadne. 1⅛in. (3cm) long x 1½in (4cm) wide. PETER SZUHAY, GRAY'S, LONDON £650

Bottom right: Bull's Mouth shell, engraved gold mount, circa 1840. High relief carving of Eros surprised whilst picking flowers. 2⅛in (5.5cm) long x 1¾in (4.5cm) wide. JAYNE'S COLLECTION, OREGON, USA

NINETEENTH CENTURY CAMEO MATERIALS

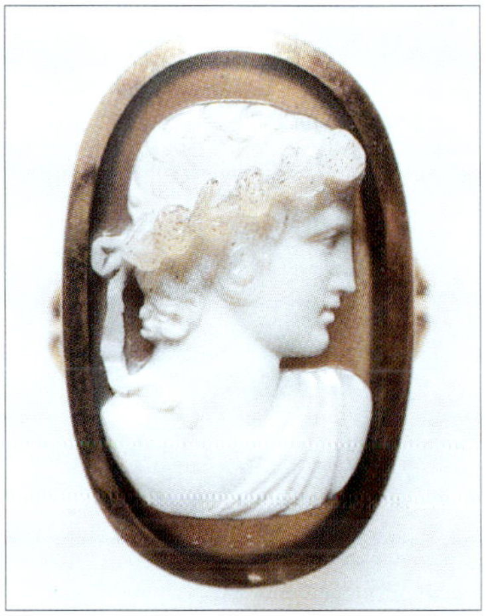

Plate 99. *Agate carved in white relief, translucent background, set in a gold ring, probably by Nicolo Morelli (1779-1836), Roman gem-engraver. 1½in. (4cm) x 1in. (2.5cm). Morelli's commissions included carvings for Napoleon I. The subject of Antinous is based on a relief found in Hadrian's Villa near Rome. For a similar ring, see Catalogue Entry 87 in* Geschnittene Steine des 18. bis 20. Jahrhunderts *by Ingrid S. Weber. For information on Antinous, see entry for 'Dionysus', page 70.* S. J. PHILLIPS LTD., NEW BOND STREET, LONDON

'HARDSTONE' CAMEOS

Nineteenth century 'hardstone' cameos were carved on forms of cryptocrystalline quartz of the group known as chalcedony, including the agates. The banded agates used for nineteenth century cameos can be described as onyx, most commonly black and white. Red and white banded agate is specifically referred to as sardonyx (with a ground the colour of sard). Other chalcedonies utilised by carvers included cornelian (carnelian), reddish-yellow in colour, and chrysophase, apple-green in colour. Jasper, an opaque multicrystalline quartz, occurring in mottled shades of brown, red, green and yellow, was also employed.

The Roman writer Pliny the Elder describes the curative power of agate:

> 'The agate ... was first discovered in Sicily near the river of the same name but was later found in many countries. Its size can be exceptional and its varieties are very numerous... it is thought to counteract the bites of spiders and scorpions... merely to look at the [agates] is good for the eyes. Moreover, if placed in the mouth, they allay thirst.'
>
> Pliny, *Natural History*, Book XXXVII (LIV 139-141)

The stones used for cameo carving in the nineteenth century came from Idar, Saxony, Scotland, Brazil, the East Indies and Ceylon. Often the natural colour of the stone bore little resemblance to the colour of the finished cameo, as stones used by gem-engravers have been colour-enhanced since ancient times. To create a brown and white contrast between the background and the foreground, the stone was soaked in honey or olive oil, then heated to release carbon. A true black and white contrast could only be achieved with the use of acids. To achieve a more intense red colour base, iron was the key ingredient – iron oxide was added and the stone was heated in an iron nitrate solution.

Rome, the centre of art, was also the centre of gem-engraving during the early nineteenth century. When carving a cameo, the gem-engraver first made a large-

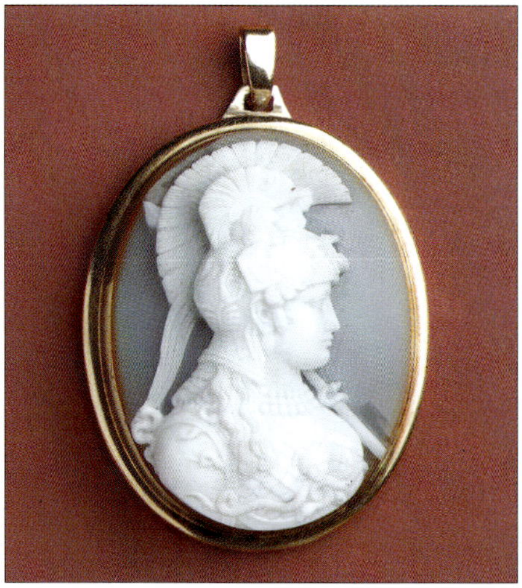

Plate 100 (left). *Agate, gold mount, circa 1860-70. Athena, in helmet, wearing the aegis (goat skin shield), bearing the head of the Gorgon Medusa. Her attribute, the snake (prudence) is entwined around her spear.* MICHAEL G. LONGMORE, GRAYS, LONDON £1450

Plate 101 (below left). *Agate, gold mount, circa 1870. A classical woman depicted as Flora. 2⅛in. (5.5cm) x 1½in. (4cm).* ALEXANDRA BOLLA, ANTIQUARIUS, LONDON £1800

Plate 102 (below). *Agate, gold Etruscan Revival mount, circa 1870. A classical head.* M. ROWAN AT www.rowanandrowan.com £1250

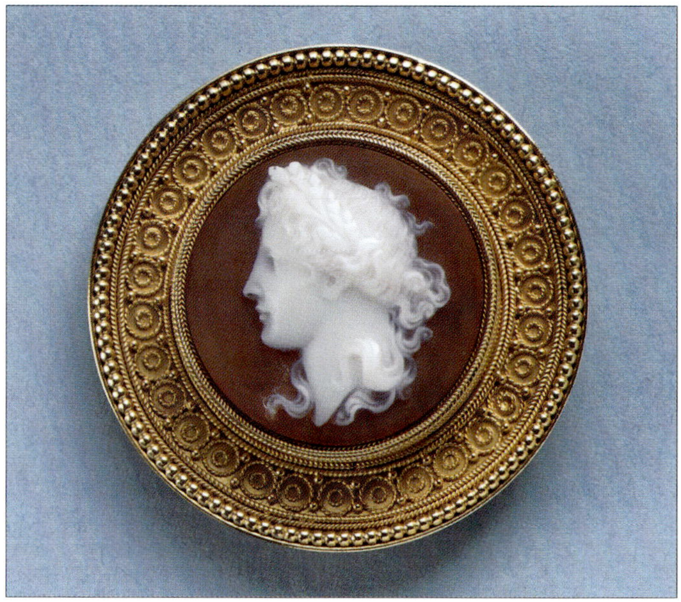

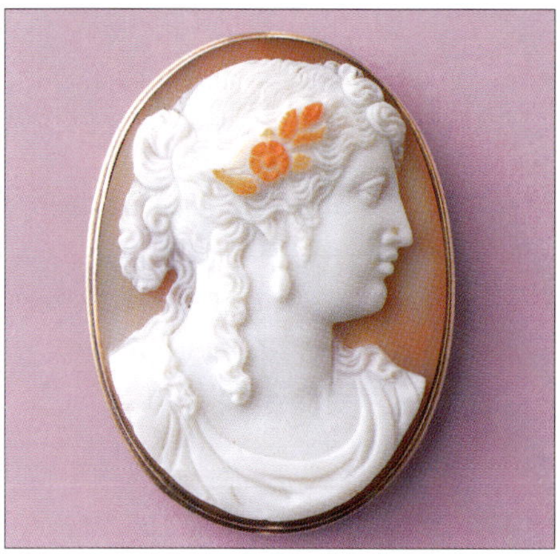

scale sketch and then a wax model the same size as the stone he intended to use. Next, he drew an outline on the stone and cut it down with a circular saw to remove superfluous upper layers. This was called 'roughing out'. Then, using a treadle-driven lathe with abrasive-impregnated soft iron spinning tool attachments, he created the design by applying the stone to a cutting point, using water or olive oil as a lubricant. Detail was achieved using a fine powder, embedded in the tools. The final carving was oiled and polished. The process required a high degree of skill and patience and the results achieved were remarkable, given the size of the stones engravers utilised and the primitive conditions of the nineteenth century workshop, as Hawks Le Grice noted in 1841:

> 'Nay the mechanical part of gem-engraving is more difficult than that of sculpture... Not unfrequently (*sic*) [the engraver] has to take advantage of every accidental vein that presents itself on the surface of the gem.'
>
> Count Hawks Le Grice, *Walks Through The Studii Of The Sculptors At Rome* 1841, Vol. II (pages 163-4)

Many eminent gem-engravers were short-sighted and could therefore see close-up in great detail. As a result, they often went blind later in life.

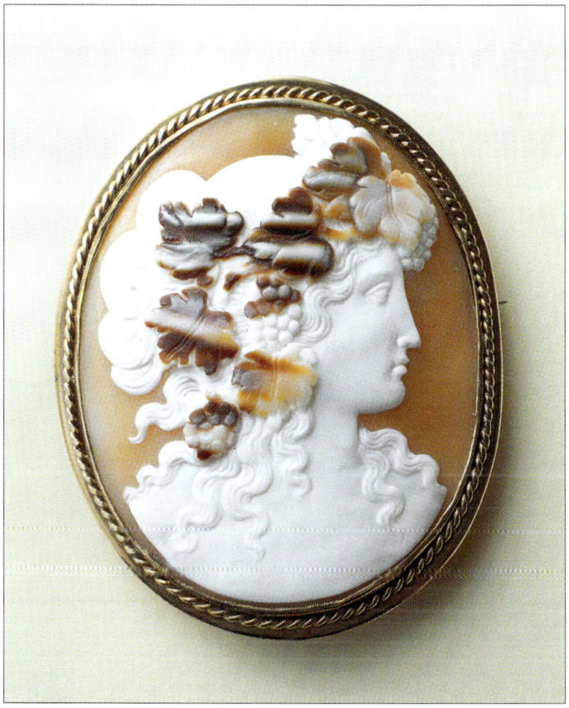

Plate 103. *Bull's Mouth shell, carved in three layers, gold rope-twist mount, circa 1870. A maenad (bacchante), with vine leaves highlighted. 2⅜in. (6cm) x 2in. (5cm).* PRIVATE COLLECTION

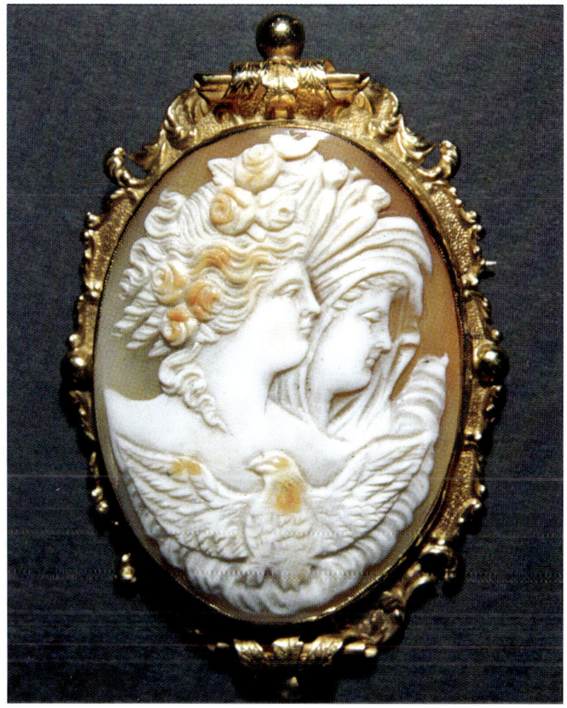

Plate 104. *Horned Helmet shell, ornate gold mount, circa 1870. The goddesses 'Day and Night'. 2½in. (6.5cm) x 2in. (5cm).*
H & J PALMER, ANTIQUARIUS, LONDON £950

SHELL

The later Georgians and Victorians were largely responsible for the resurgence of the shell cameo. After the fall of Napoleon, more and more prosperous travellers visited Europe and as a result the affordable souvenir became an essential item. The Sicilians had revived the Renaissance craft of carving on shells around 1805, and the increased demand saw the trade flourish. Various visitors to Rome noted the importance of the shell cameo industry:

> '...in the elegant manufacture of cameos out of oriental shell, they [the Romans] are very industrious. The demand for articles of this kind is constant, and...foreigners are the principal customers.'
>
> Henry Matthews, Esq. *The Diary of an Invalid Being a Tour In Pursuit Of Health in Portugal Italy Switzerland And France In the Years 1817 1818 1819*, Vol. I, 4th edition, MDCCCXXIV (page 164)

'Genoa and Rome are the seats of the best work, although many common ones are cut in France. In Rome there are about eighty shell-cameo cutters, and in Genoa thirty, some of whom also carve on coral... The value of the

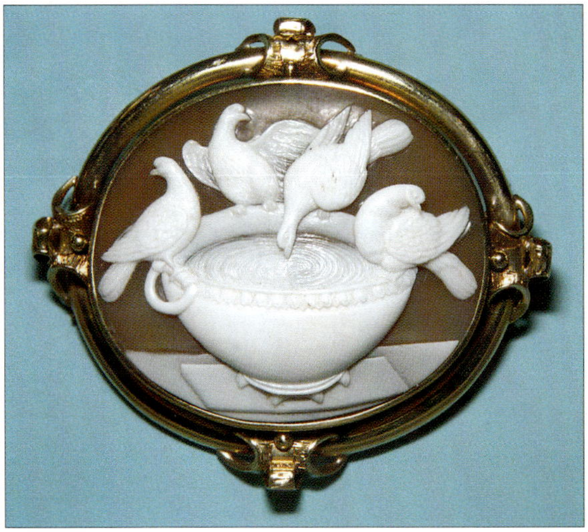

Plate 105. *Bull's Mouth shell, ornate gold mount, circa 1860, the Doves of Pliny. 2¾in. (7cm) x 2in. (5cm).* LOOKOUT TRADING CO. LTD., SILVER FOX GALLERY, PORTOBELLO ROAD, LONDON £1050

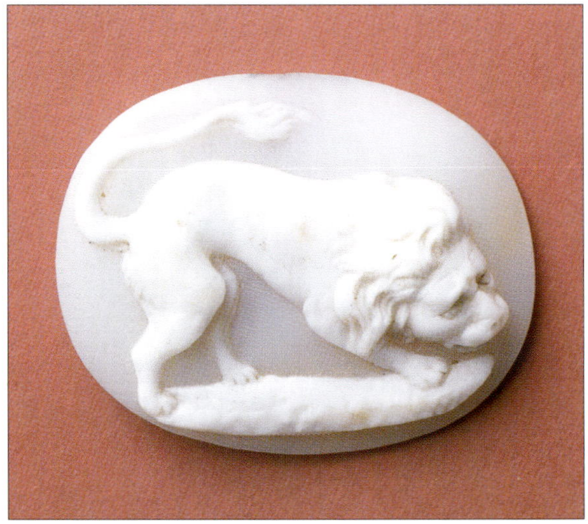

Plate 106. *White shell carving of a lion passant, circa 1800, after the antique. 1½in. (4cm) x 2in. (5cm).* S. HARLOWE AT www.rowanandrowan.com

shell-cameos cut in Rome is estimated at about £8000 a year.'

P.L. Simmonds, 'Marine Contributions to Art', in the *Art Journal*, 1874, Vol. I (page 53)

Other visitors praised the beauty of these cameos:

'Oriental shells are made at Rome into beautiful cameos, by the white outer surface being cut away upon the deeper-coloured internal part, forming figures in minute bassirilevi... These shell cameos make beautiful ornaments.'

Charlotte A. Eaton, *Rome in the Nineteenth Century*, Vol. II, 5th edition, 1860 (page 312)

Shell cameo-carving in the south was centred in the Naples region (notably Torre del Greco). Shell cameos were also carved in Florence and Venice, and carving centres were established in France (Paris and Marseilles) by the middle of the century.

The shells most widely used were varieties of conch, mainly imported from the West Indies, Ceylon and Madagascar:

Black Helmet, *Cassis (L.) Madagascariensis*, which has a dark brown to black ground (inner layer) called onyx.
Bull's Mouth, *Cassis (L.) Rufa*, which has an orange, reddish-brown ground called sardonyx.
Horned Helmet, *Cassis (L.) Cornuta*, which has a yellow/orange ground.
Queen Conch, *Strombus (L.) Gigas*, which has a pink ground.
Tiger Cowrie, *Cypraea tigris*, which has a mottled ground with purple.
Brown Cowrie, *Cypraea cervus*, which has a mottled brownish ground.

Shell was softer than hardstone and could be worked with hardened steel engraving tools, therefore it was much easier to work with. The

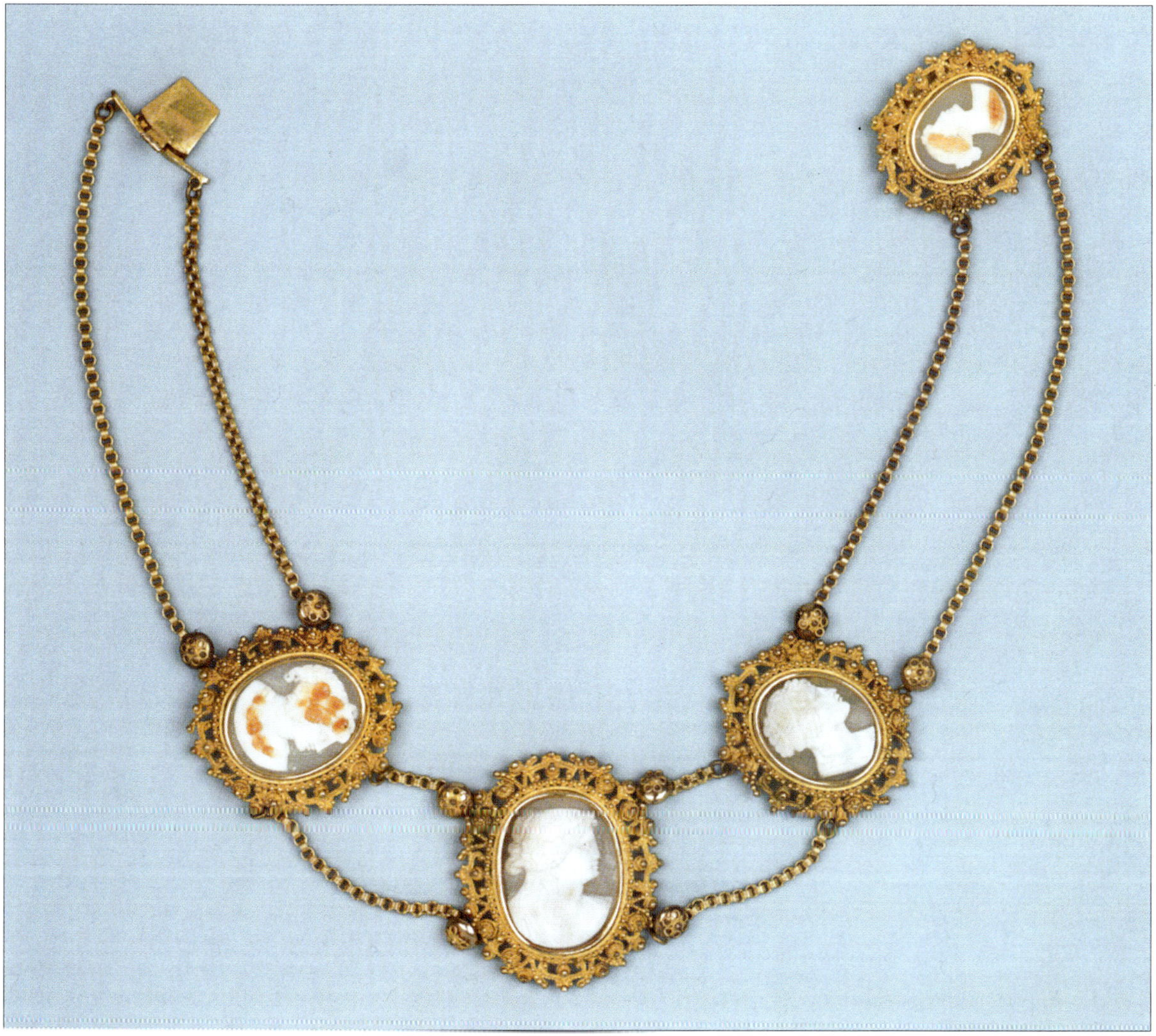

Plate 107. *Bull's Mouth cameos set in a pinchbeck necklace, featuring classical heads, circa 1840.*

M. Rowan at www.rowanandrowan.com £750

engraver's art lay in exploiting the natural contours of each shell. Carvers selected shells which had three layers – an inner layer to form the ground, a central layer to form the relief and an outer layer of superficial colour which could be used to vary the surface appearance of the figure. The selected area was first cut with a saw or mill, then shaped into an oval. Next, the blank cameo was mounted on a piece of wood and the design pencilled and etched in. The surround was removed using files and small chisels called 'gravers' and finally the figure was carved. Colour contrasts on the hair, dress or face of the figure were achieved by leaving the outer layer of shell in those areas.

CORAL

In ancient times, coral was regarded as a talisman that could ward off evil spirits, as it was reputed to have been formed from the severed head of the Gorgon, Medusa, after the hero Perseus had slain her:

> 'The victor [Perseus] himself washed his hands in water drawn from the sea, and in case Medusa's head, with its growth of snakes, should be injured by the harsh sand, he made a soft bed of leaves on the ground, covered it with seaweed; and there laid down the head of Phorcy's daughter [Medusa]. The freshly gathered weed, still living and absorbent, drew into itself the power of the monster; hardening at the touch of the head, it acquired a strange new rigidity in its leaves and branches. The sea nymphs tested this miracle, trying it on several twigs, and were delighted to find the same thing happening again... Even today coral retains this same nature, hardening at the touch of air: that which was a plant when under the water becomes rock when brought above the surface.'
>
> Ovid, *Metamorphoses*, IV (page 114, Innes translation)

Coral is a product of the sea, a hard, calcerous organic substance formed from marine invertebrates, described by P.L. Simmonds in 1873: 'coral has the hardness and brilliancy of agate; it polishes like gems and shines like garnet, with tints of the ruby.'[1]

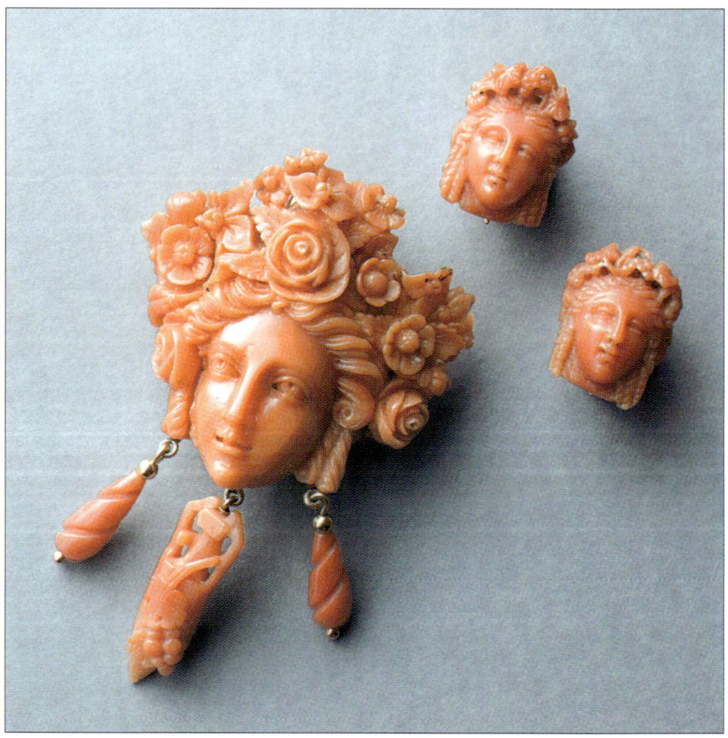

Plate 108. *Coral suite, circa 1840, bacchante-nymph heads bedecked with garlands of flowers. Brooch, 1¾in. (4.5cm) x 1½in. (4cm).*

PRIVATE COLLECTION

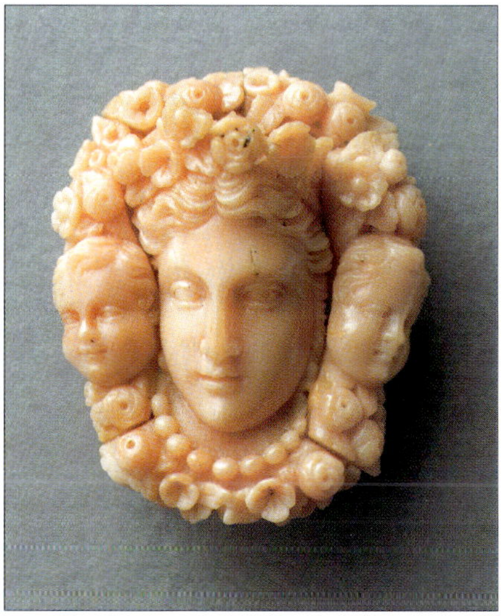

Plate 109. *Salmon pink coral carving, circa 1840. Nymph attended by two cherubic heads, framed with flowers. 1½in. (4cm) x 1½in. (4cm).*

PRIVATE COLLECTION

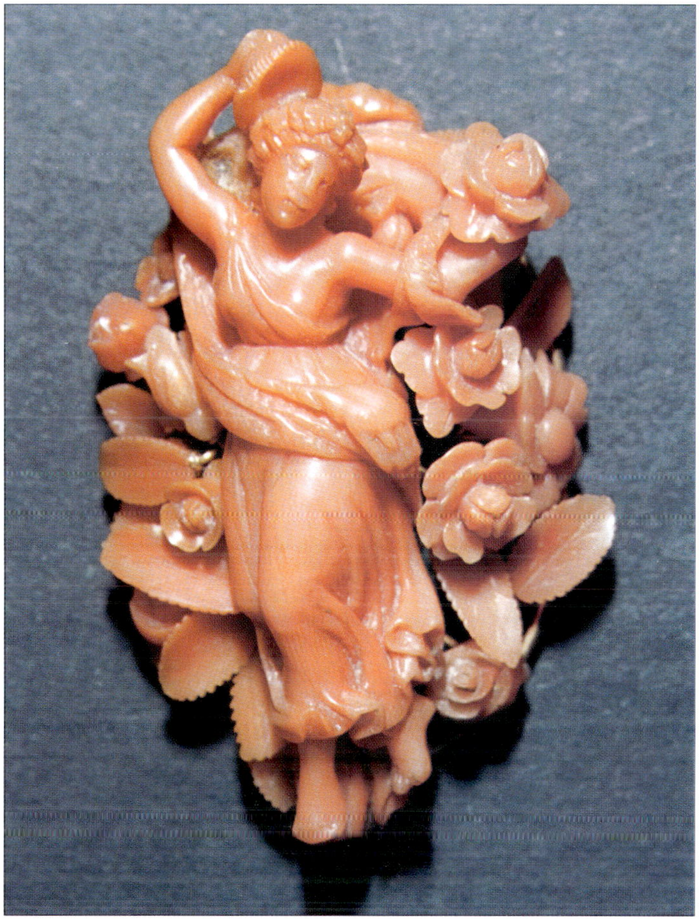

Plate 110. *Coral carving, circa 1840. A maenad (bacchante) holding a tambourine with a pelt wrapped around her waist. 2⅛in. (5.5cm) x 1in. (2.5cm).*

BEAUTY AND THE BEAST, ANTIQUARIUS, LONDON £950

The type of coral used for jewellery was *Corallium Noble*, ranging in colour from deep crimson, through pale red and vermillion to black and white. The principle Italian coral centres in the nineteenth century were the Naples area (Portici and Torre del Greco), Trapani in Sicily and Genoa and Livorno. A royal coral factory was established at Portici, and Frenkel[2] cites the establishment of a 'School of Incision' in Torre del Greco, devoted to the development of carving skills utilising coral, shell, ivory, tortoiseshell, lava and agates. He refers to eighty-two coral-carving establishments in Torre del Greco, providing employment for four thousand people.

Coral cameos were carved with incising tools called 'bulini', then polished to a high lustre. The artisan was often confined by the natural form of the coral branch. Although large coral cameos exist, many carvings follow a style more sculptural than relief. Acanthus scrolls reminiscent of the Rococo period often appear on such branch carvings.

Footnotes

1. P.L. Simmonds, 'Marine Contributions to Art No. IV – Coral And The Coral Fisheries', *The Art Journal*, 1873, page 229.

2. W. Frenkel, *Pompei, Pompei Scari, Valle di Pompei, Vesuvio, Ercolano, Torre del Greco, Castellammare di Stabia. Nuova Guida*, 1924, pages 172, 173.

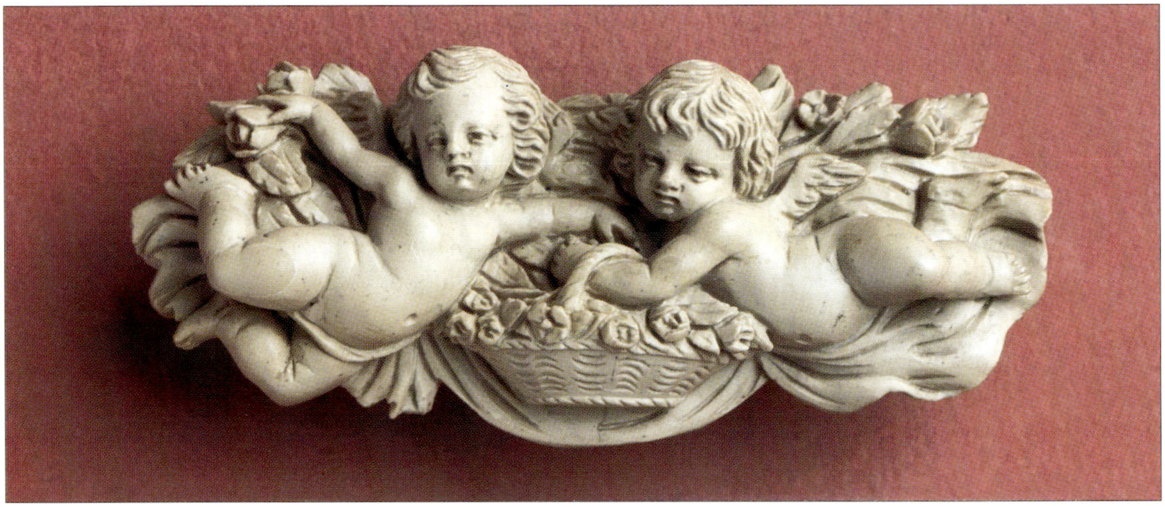

Plate 111. *Lava carving, circa 1860. Winged cherubs in flight scatter flowers from a basket.*

S. HARLOWE AT www.rowanandrowan.com £850

LAVA

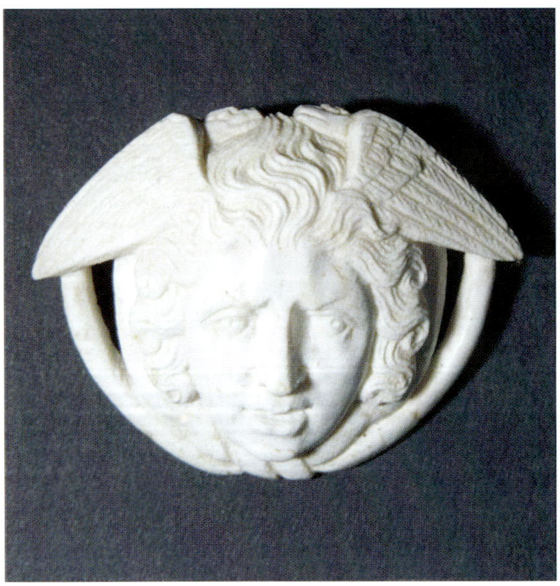

Cameos carved on lava (limestone and other mined rocks from the volcanic Mount Vesuvius region in Italy) were popular souvenirs from about 1840, commemorating the excavations at Pompeii and Herculaneum. The softness of lava made it relatively easy to carve, especially in high relief, and many cameos were sold as attractive and portable tourist souvenirs. Lava cameos were mainly carved in the area south of Naples, especially Torre del Greco, described by John Murray on page 208 of *A Handbook For Travellers To Southern Italy* (1874) as 'a flourishing town… built of and upon lava'. The colours of lava range from cream and sand to the putty shades of olive and grey and less commonly black, white, terracotta and burgundy. Lava stone has a dull, matt finish, is highly absorbent and easily damaged.

Plate 112. *Lava, Italian, circa 1840. Medusa with wings in her hair and snakes forming a fillet (ribbon) under her chin. 1⅛in. (3cm) x 1½in. (4cm).*

M. ROWAN AT www.rowanandrowan.com £300

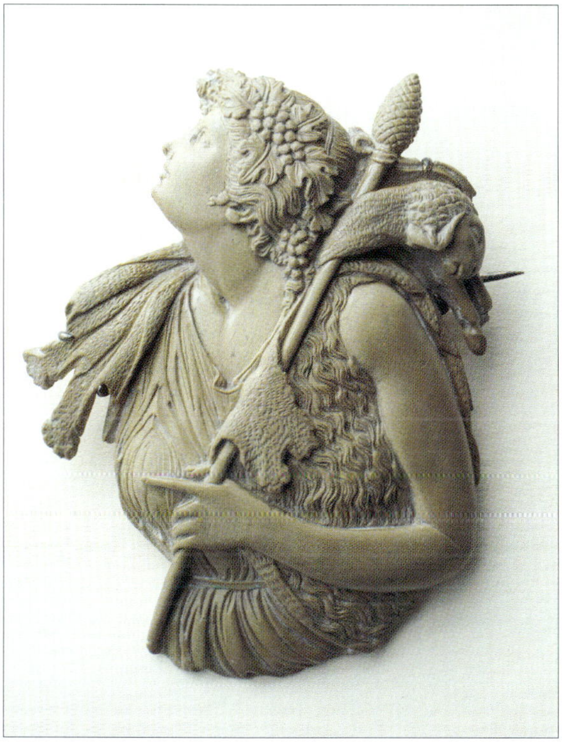

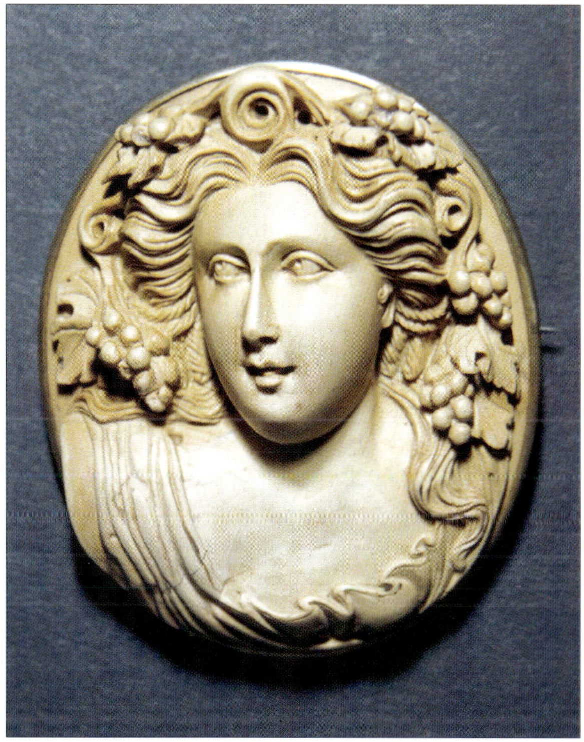

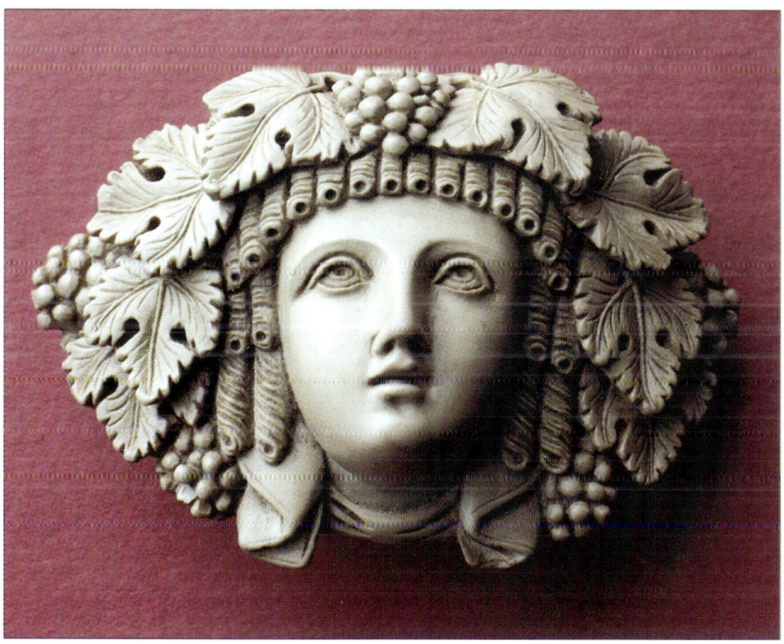

Plate 113 (above left). *Lava carving, circa 1840. A classical maenad (bacchante) holding a thyrsus. Inspired by Dionysiac libations, she looks upwards. 2¾in. (7cm) x 2⅜in. (6cm).*

PRIVATE COLLECTION

Plate 114 (above right). *High relief lava, silver mount, circa 1860. A maenad (bacchante). 2⅜in. (6cm) x 2in. (5cm).*

M. ROWAN AT www.rowanandrowan.com £750

Plate 115 (left) *Lava carving, circa 1840, a richly decorated head of a maenad (bacchante) with a fringe of tight ringlets. 1½in. (4cm) x 2⅜in. (6cm).*

PRIVATE COLLECTION

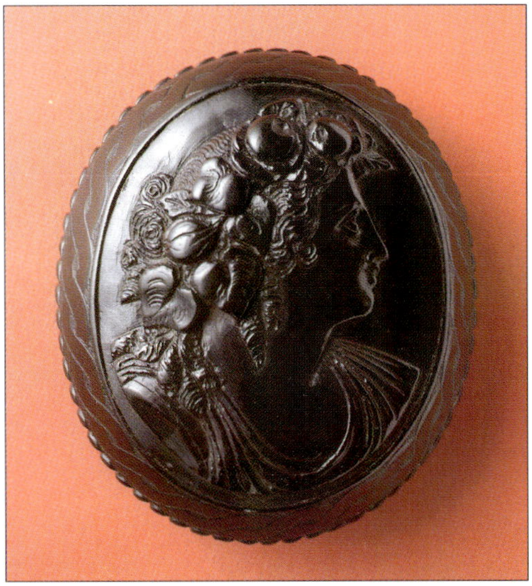

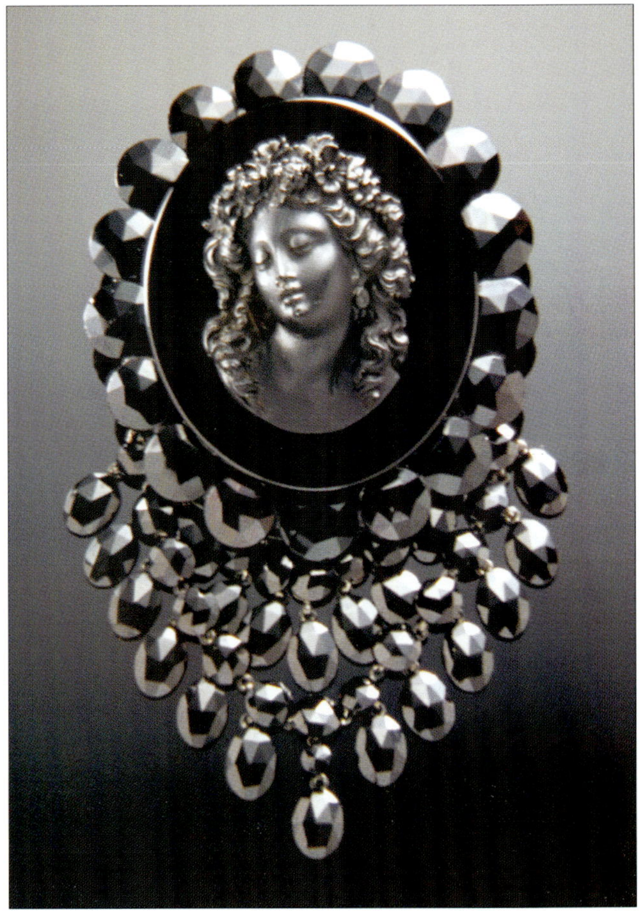

Plate 116. *Whitby jet brooch, English, circa 1870. A maenad (bacchante). 2⅜in. (6cm) x 2in. (5cm).* KIKUCHI TRADING CO. LTD., GRAYS, LONDON £365

Plate 117. *Glass and French jet brooch, circa 1870, depicting a maenad (bacchante). 3⅛in. (8cm) x 2⅜in. (6cm).*
COURTESY OF THE AKIBA MUSEUM OF ANTIQUE JEWELLERY, JAPAN

JET

The Whitby jet jewellery trade flourished during the nineteenth century. Jet is a mined, hard, bituminous coal-like substance, deep black in colour, with a chemical composition of lignite. The Great Exhibition of 1851 had helped to promote its popularity and after Prince Albert's death in 1861 Queen Victoria's elaborate and extended period of mourning caused a surge in the popularity of all things black and the jet trade prospered.

The raw material was worked on a lathe, carved and highly polished and often fashioned into outsized necklaces, brooches and earrings that were deceptively light in weight. Jet's counterpart existed in Ireland in the form of bog oak – old wood preserved in peat bog marshes.

Such was jet's popularity that imitations existed, especially 'French jet', a black glass mounted on metal. Gutta-percha, the hardened sap of the Isonandra Gutta tree from Malaysia, was heated and moulded into mass-produced 'vulcanite' cameos. All forms of black jewellery remained popular until the late nineteenth century.

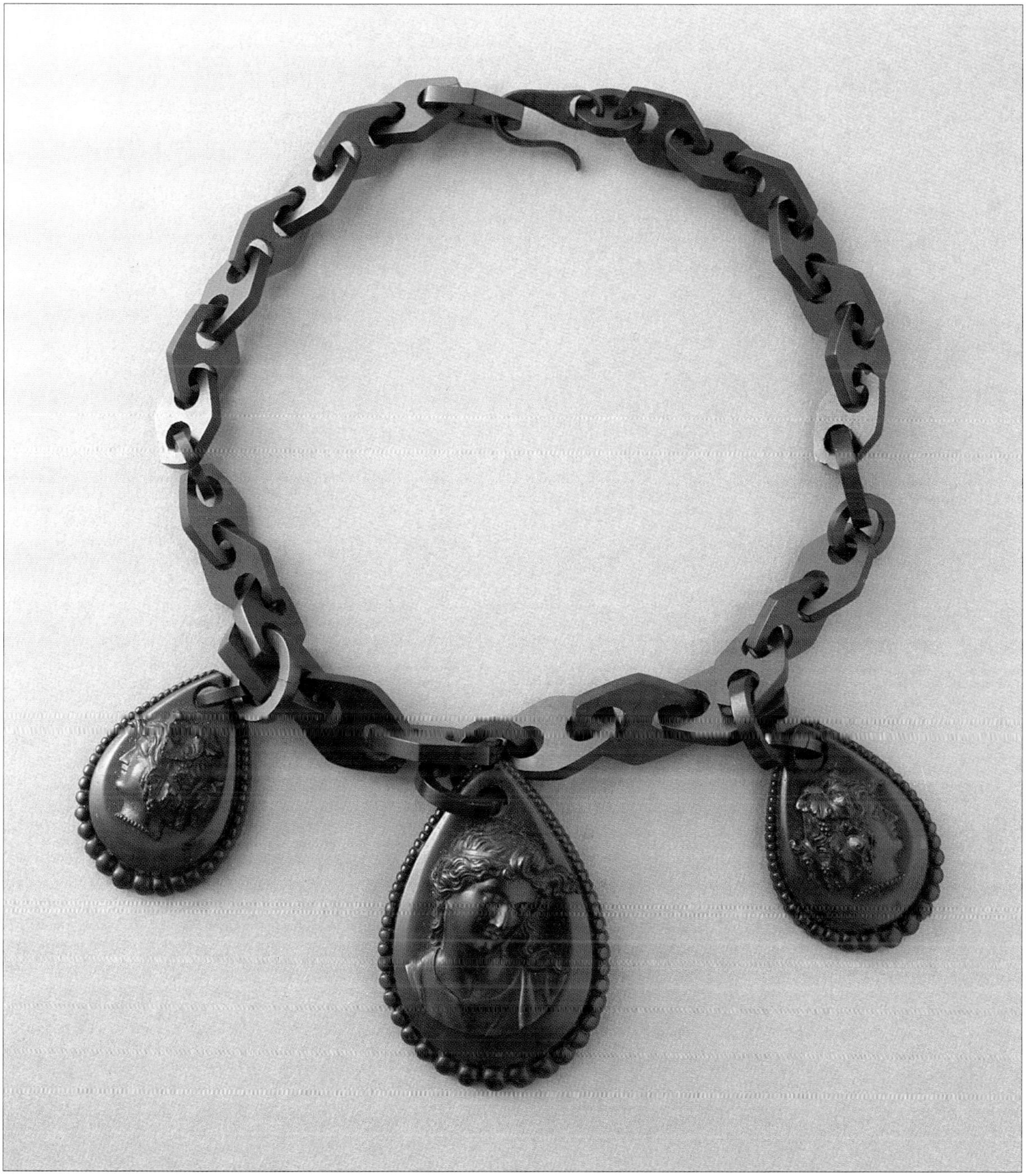

Plate 118. *Pendulous vulcanite necklace, late 19th century, featuring maenads and a classical maiden.*

HEATHER SAYER COLLECTION £550

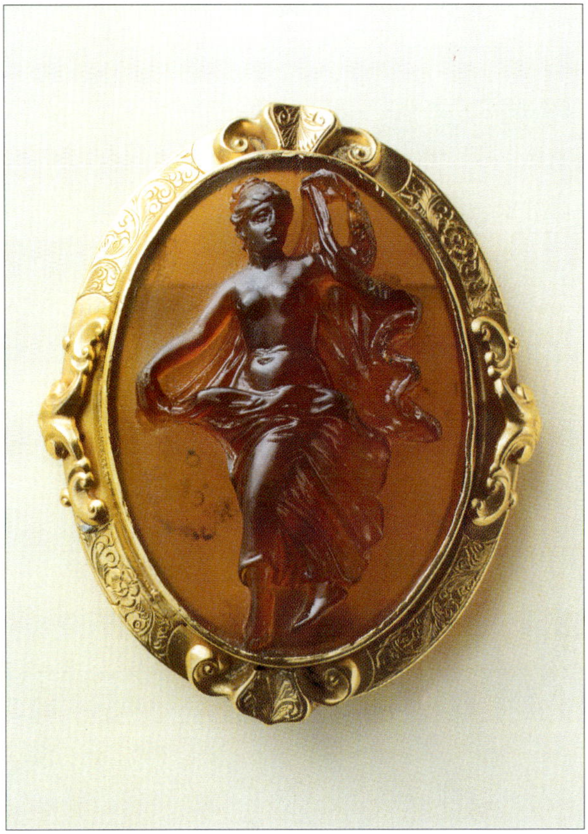

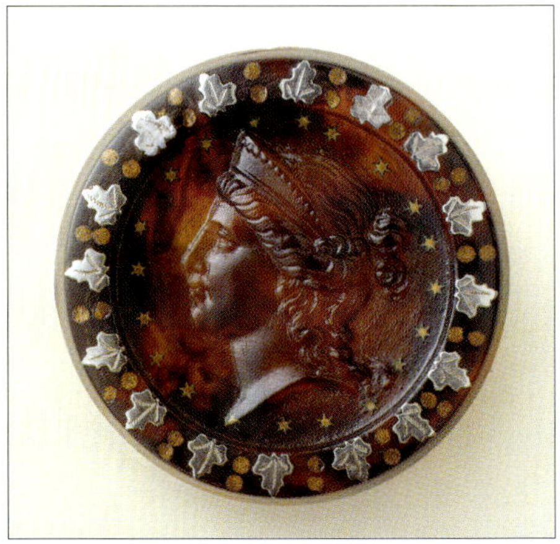

Plate 119. *Moulded tortoiseshell cameo with applied silver and gold pique decoration, circa 1870. An idealised classsical head. 1½in. (4cm) diameter.*

PRIVATE COLLECTION

Plate 120. *Tortoiseshell, engraved and scrolled gold mount, circa 1860. 2⅛in. (5.5cm) x 1¾in. (4.5cm). A dancing figure, swathed in diaphanous drapery, after an intaglio by Pichler based on a Pompeian mural. For similar, see Catalogue Entry 327 in* Geschnittene Steine des 18. bis 20. Jahrhunderts *by Ingrid S. Weber.*

PRIVATE COLLECTION

TORTOISESHELL

The term 'tortoiseshell' actually refers to the horny plate of the Hawksbill turtle, imported to Europe in the nineteenth century from the West Indies, Asia and Africa. Its colour ranges from black to dark brown, mottled with red or yellow. When used to create items of jewellery, it was softened in boiling water to which salt was added and pressed into moulds, or carved on a lathe. 'Pique' jewellery incorporated gold and silver floral and geometric decoration applied during the heating process. 'Pique' was manufactured principally in France and Italy. Sculptural carvings of maenads and Medusas were produced in the Neapolitan manner. Simmonds describes the rising popularity of tortoiseshell jewellery during the Victorian era (its colour making it suitable for items of mourning jewellery):

> 'At the first London Exhibition in 1851, tortoiseshell bracelets, brooches, ornaments, circlets and rings were shown by M. Philip, a Parisian manufacturer; but it is only lately that this species of ornament has come much into vogue here. This tortoiseshell jewellery, however, is neat, tasteful, and moderate priced, and is taking the place of the vulcanite and jet ornaments which have been so long worn.'
>
> P.L. Simmonds, 'Marine Contributions to Art', *Art Journal*, 1873 (page 6)

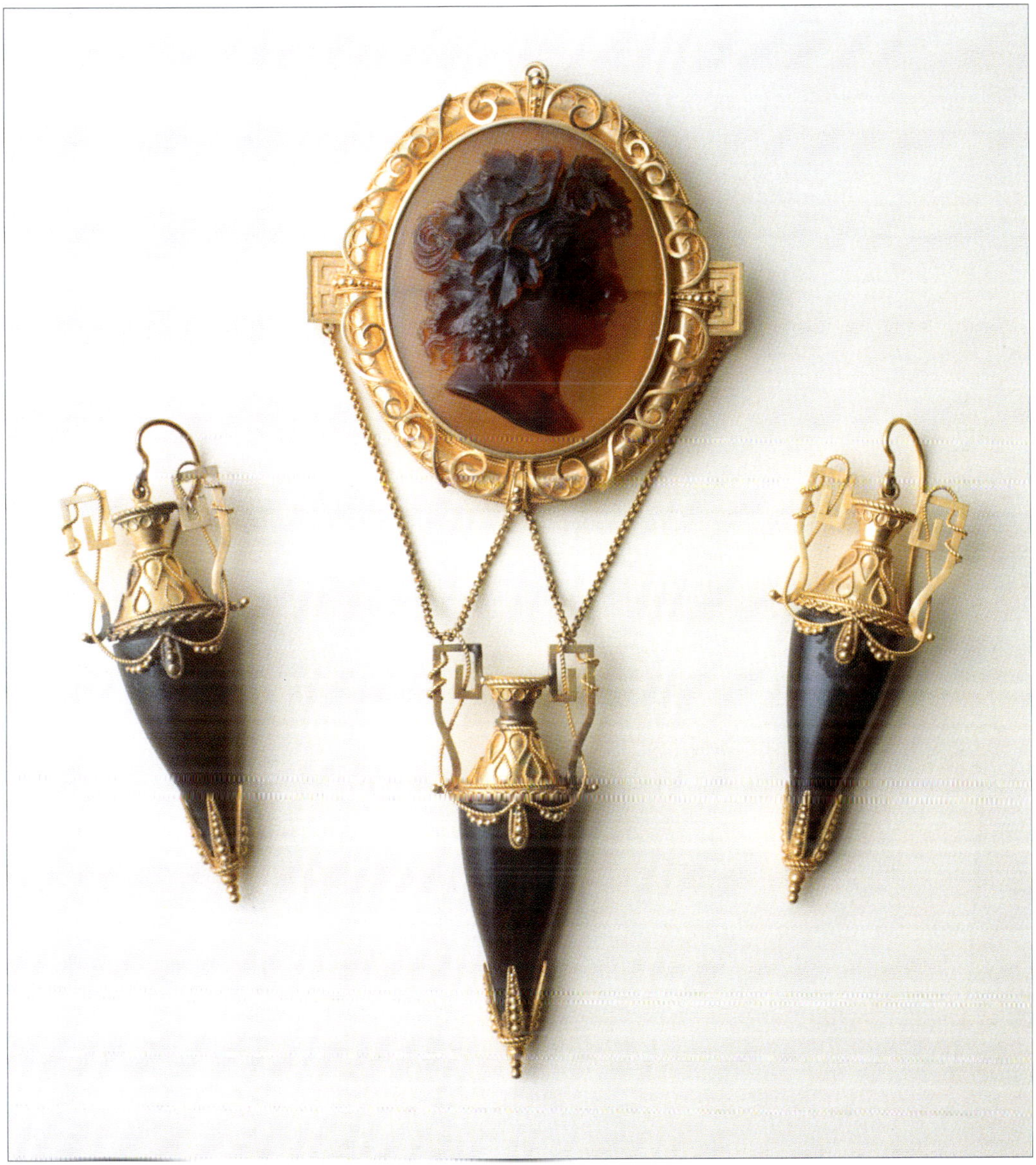

Plate 121. *Tortoiseshell suite, gold mounts with applied decoration, in the archaeological revival style using Greek amphorae, circa 1860-70. The subject is Ariadne, wife of the god of Wine. Brooch, 2¾in. (7cm) x 2in. (5cm).* S. J. PHILLIPS LTD., NEW BOND STREET, LONDON

IVORY

Ivory, in jewellery, describes the hard, creamy opaque dentine from the tusks of African and Indian elephants, the canine teeth of the hippopotamus (seahorse ivory) and the tusks of the walrus. From about 1840 to 1870 high-relief work ivory cameos were fashionable, depicting stylised Floras, bacchante-nymphs and winged cherub heads. The female heads were commonly 'Victorianised' to incorporate a contemporary hairstyle, necklace and earrings.

Ivory was worked with chisels, scalpels and files, whitened and highly polished. The principle carving centres were in France (Paris, Dieppe and Chamonix), Germany (Erbach im Odenwald) and Italy (Naples). French carvers were the chief sources of ivory cameos and cherubs, while German carvers specialised in fretwork and floral composition. For a comprehensive study of ivory carving in Europe see *Elfenbein Kunst* by P.W. Hartmann (Wien, 1999).

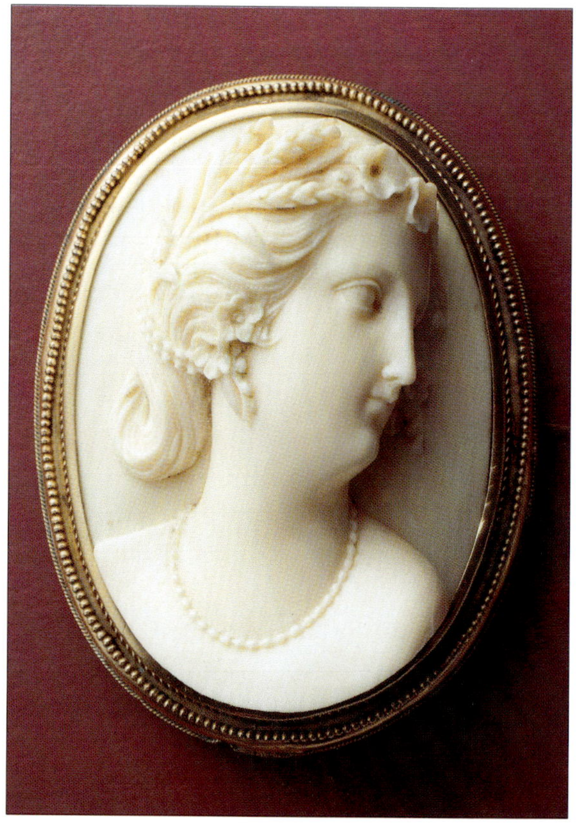

Plate 122. *Ivory, beaded gold mount, circa 1870. A 'Victorianised' portrayal of Demeter (Ceres) with ears of wheat and flowers as a headdress. As with many ivory cameos of this era, she wears fashionable jewellery. 3⅛in. (8cm) x 2⅜in. (6cm).* PRIVATE COLLECTION

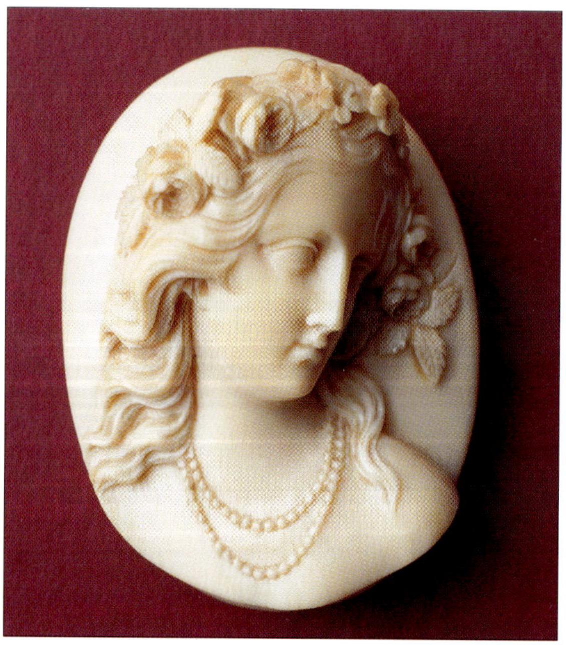

Plate 123. *Ivory, circa 1870. A 'Victorianised' depiction of a nymph wearing a crown of flowers, with contemporary coiffure and jewellery. 2⅛in. (5.5cm) x 2in. (5cm).* S. HARLOWE AT www.rowanandrowan.com £450

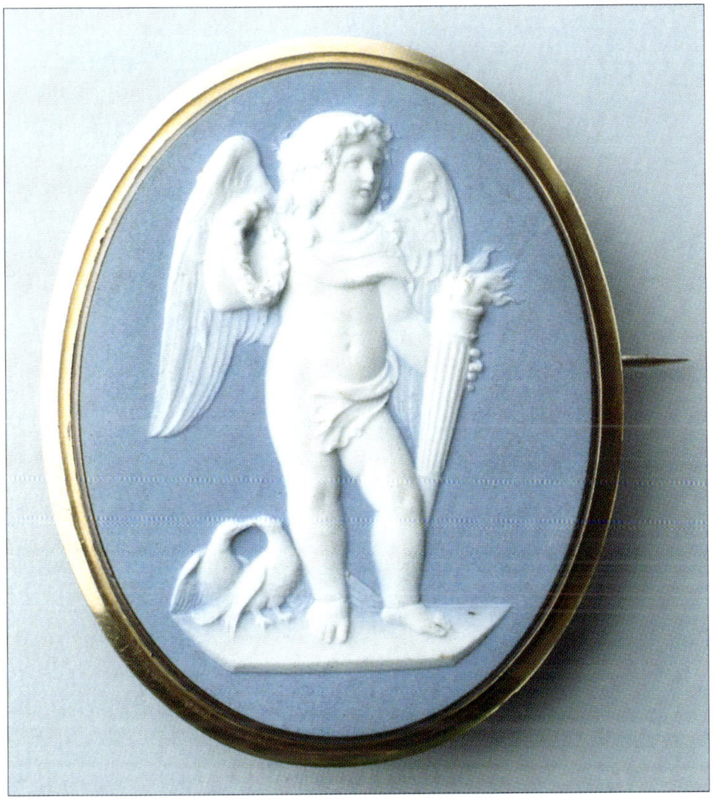

Plate 124. *Blue Wedgwood plaque, gilt metal mount, late 19th century. The Genius of Life, holding the torch of Life. 3⅛in. (8cm) x 2⅜in. (6cm).* S. HARLOWE AT www.rowanandrowan.com £350

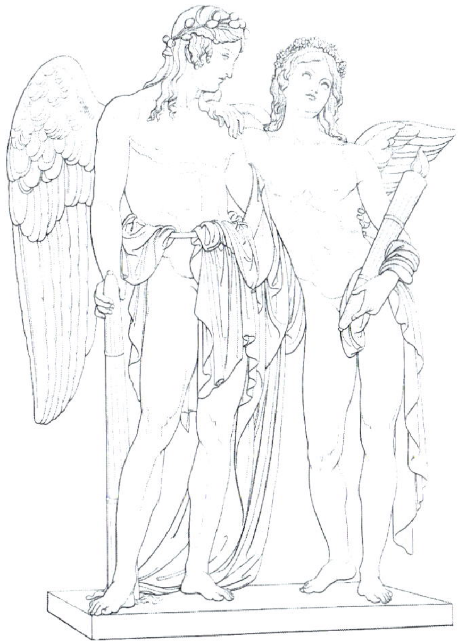

A marble sculpture executed by Bertel Thorvaldsen in 1829. The head of the Genius of Life, who holds a burning torch, is adorned with a wreath of immortelles, whilst poppies are entwined in the hair of the Genius of Death, whose torch is inverted and extinguished.

WEDGWOOD CAMEOS

The potter Josiah Wedgwood (1730–1795) invented 'jasper ware' ceramics and was quick to see the commercial potential of producing miniature reliefs in the Neo-classical style. Imitating cameos, the relief section was moulded separately, then fixed to the coloured base. In the late eighteenth century Wedgwood collaborated with Matthew Boulton of Birmingham who set the 'cameos' in cut steel mounts. In the nineteenth century the Wedgwood factory continued to produce items of jewellery, always in the same particular palette of colours, ranging from the typical powder blue, through lilac and dusty pink, to buff, olive green and black. During the nineteenth century Wedgwood's classical subjects and portraits were complemented by Victorian romantic and sentimental scenes. For a study of Josiah Wedgwood's life and work, see *The Genius of Wedgwood*, editor H. Young, V & A, 1995.

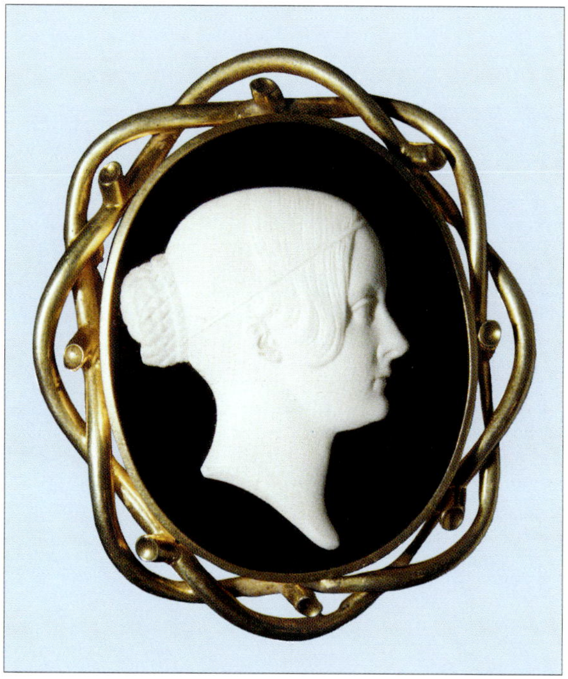

Plate 125. *Glass, tubular gold mount, circa 1850. A female portrait (Queen Victoria?). 2¾in. (7cm) x 2in. (5cm).* BELLUM ANTIQUES, ANTIQUARIUS, LONDON £695

Opposite page:

Plate 126 (left). *Onyx, gold mount, circa 1870. Veiled Demeter with a crown of wheat-sheaves. Signed by* Georges Bissinger, *a gem-engraver renowned for his virtuoso work and fine detail.*

S. HARLOWE AT www.rowanandrowan.com £1250

Plate 127 (centre). *Onyx, French gold mount in Greek key design with enamel and diamond decoration, mid-19th century, 2⅜ in. (6cm) long, 2in. (5cm) wide. A female classical head, signed on the obverse 'Michelini' in Greek characters, for L. Michelini, a 19th century sculptor and gem-engraver born in Rome but naturalised as a French citizen.*

KIERON REILLY COLLECTION, ANTIQUARIUS, LONDON

Plate 128 (right). *Lemon and white chalcedony cameo in a blue enamel tubular frame with quatrefoil decoration, 1⅜in. (3.5cm) long x 1in. (2.5cm) wide. The subject is Sappho, the poetess, with lyre. Signed M.E. Pistrucci for Maria Elisa Pistrucci, gem-engraver and daughter of Benedetto Pistrucci.* PRIVATE COLLECTION

PASTE 'CAMEOS'

Paste, glass made from powdered flint rock or pure flint sand, has been used to make cameos since ancient times. During the eighteenth century James Tassie (1735-1799) produced an enormous range of intaglios and cameos in moulded glass based on subjects from antiquity, copying almost all of the celebrated gems extant. He took sulphur moulds of gems, mixed sulphur and white wax and made casts in a clay paste. 'Tassies' were extremely popular and Catherine the Great of Russia purchased many for her collection. A descriptive catalogue of Tassie's work was published by Raspe in 1791.

Other paste cameos featured relief sections cast in opaque glass, attached to glass or stone backgrounds. 'Sulphides' (crystallo-ceramie), invented by the glassmaker Apsley Pellatt and patented in 1819, were cameo incrustations in a white paste formed of china clay and supersilicate of potash moulded into portraits, copying earlier intaglios and engravings. They were praised by Simmonds in 1854:

> 'The beautiful opaque cameos, incrusted in transparent glass by Mr. Apsley Pellatt, form another and very interesting variety of glass cameos.'
>
> P.L. Simmonds, *The Art Journal*, 1854 (page 222)

SIGNED CAMEOS

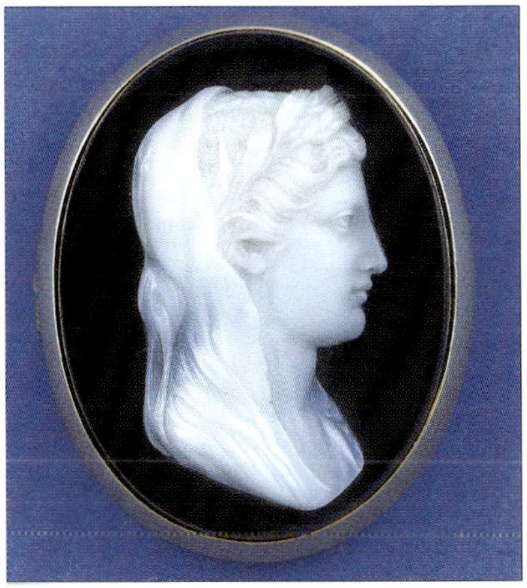

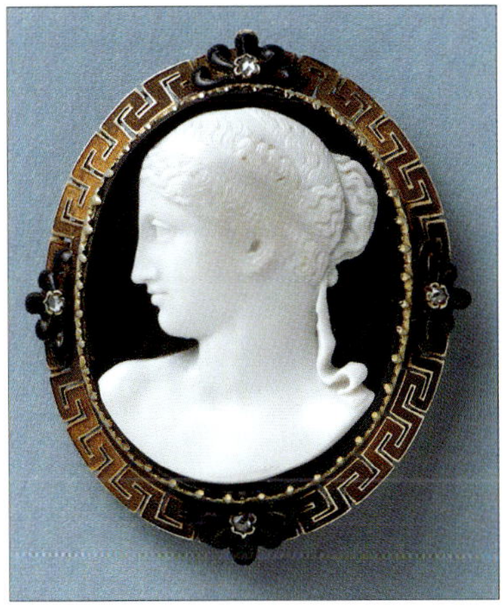

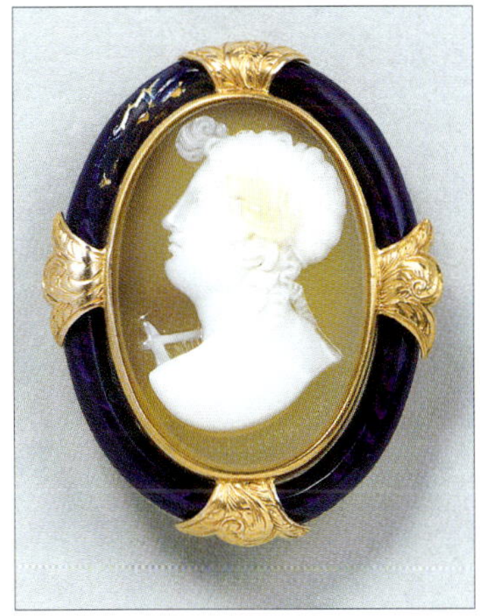

Many eminent late eighteenth and nineteenth century gem-engravers signed their work, following the introduction of the custom by Anton Pichler (1697-1779), in an attempt to prevent the unscrupulous passing off of contemporary gems as true antiquities. Examine a cameo carefully for evidence of a signature – it will usually be signed on the obverse, or more rarely, may have a carver's mark hidden in the hair or costume. Listed are examples of gem-engravers' signatures appearing on cameos illustrated in this book:

Bissinger, Georges
Nineteenth century gem-engraver of German origin who worked in Paris. Exhibited in Paris in 1867 where he was awarded a silver medal. Examples of his work were loaned to the South Kensington Museum in 1872, he also exhibited in Vienna in 1873 and Paris in 1878. See Plate 126.

Girometti, Guiseppe (1779-1851)
Girometti, Pietro (1811-1859)
These eminent Roman gem-engravers, father and son, both used the same signature, 'GIROMETTI', sometimes written in Greek characters. The 1856 *Artistical Directory* mentions Pietro:

> 'VIA DEL QUIRINALE
> N. 49, 2nd floor
>
> GIROMETTI PIETRO (Roman), Gem-engraver. ...This artist, being exclusively a Cameo engraver, has no Engravings on Shell for sale. He takes likenesses on Cameo, and receives commissions for other works coming within his department of art.' (page 82-83)

Examples of carvings by the Giromettis are illustrated in Plates 5, 14 and 87.

Morelli, Nicolo (1771-1838)
Leading Roman gem-engraver whose commissions included cameos for Napoleon I. He signed his cameos 'MORELLI' or 'N. MORELLI'.
An example of a cameo carved by Nicolo Morelli is shown in Plate 99.

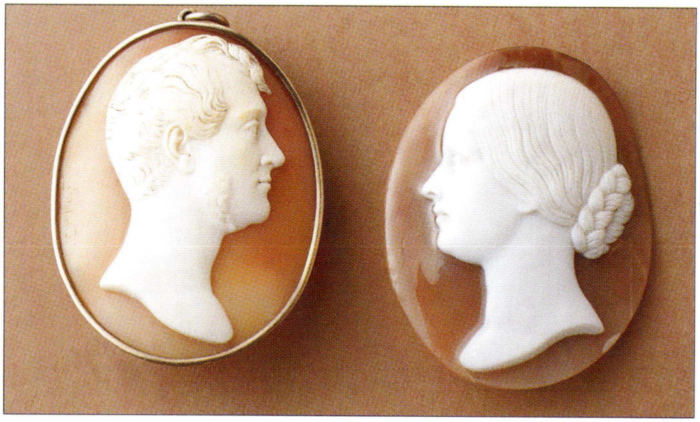

Plate 129. *Two shell portrait cameos from the Saulini workshop. Left, Horned Helmet shell, gold mount, a portrait of a gentleman, signed Saulini. Right, Bull's Mouth shell, a portrait of a lady, signed Saulini. 2⅜in. (6cm) x 2in. (5cm).*

M. ROWAN AT www.rowanandrowan.com

Pistrucci, Benedetto (1784-1855)
Pistrucci, Elena (1822-1886)
Pistrucci, Maria Elisa (1842-1881)
Pistrucci, a celebrated Roman gem-engraver, came to work in London in 1814. He was Chief Engraver to the Royal Mint from 1817-49. He signed his name 'PISTRUCCI' and often hid an extra mark, the Greek letter 'lambda' in the hair or folds of the costume to prevent the sale of his cameos as ancient works. His daughters signed their cameos 'E. PISTRUCCI' and 'M.E. PISTRUCCI'.
Examples of carvings by the Pistruccis are in Plates 53, 93.

Saulini, Tommaso (1793-1864)
Saulini, Luigi (1819-1883)
Outstanding Roman cameo-carvers of the nineteenth century, this father and son worked in both stone and shell, as noted in a guide book to Rome in 1856:

> 'VIA DELLA CROCE
> N. 8 A.
> SAULINI TOMMASO (Roman), a Shell and Gem-engraver. He takes likenesses on Shell or Cameo. He also engraves subjects either from ancient Originals or of his composition. He was HONOURABLY mentioned at the Exhibition of London.'
> *The Artistical Directory Or Guide To The Studios Of The Italian And Foreign Painters and Sculptors Resident in Rome*, 1856 (page 79)

Tommaso Saulini exhibited cameos at the Great Exhibitions of London in 1851 and 1862. Many Saulini cameos were portraits of noted contemporaries, and in 1856 Queen Victoria commissioned their work. Their carvings were signed:

> T SAULINI F.
> L. SAULINI F.
> SAULINI F. (carved by the Saulini workshop)
> F. refers to *fecit* (by the hand of)

Examples of their carvings are illustrated in Plates 2, 20, 41, 68, 74, 98, 128.

Hawks Le Grice praised the work of Tommaso Saulini in 1841:

> 'Saulini has drawn and modelled in the Studio of Thorwaldsen, and has executed for that eminent artist many of his works in pietra-dura, as well as in shell. The classic productions from the chisel of Thorwaldsen, Gibson and other distinguished sculptors, are also copied by Saulini in cameo, with more care than subjects merely intended as an accessory to a Lady's toilet, and in fact their artistic execution and high finish entitle them to a place in the cabinet of a dilettante.'
> *Walks Through The Studii Of The Sculptors At Rome*, 1841 (pages 225-6)

For a comprehensive list of gem-engravers and examples of their signatures, see *The Art of the Jeweller. A Catalogue Of The Hull Grundy Bequest To The British Museum*, Editor: Hugh Tait, 1984.

PORTRAIT CAMEOS

Portrait cameos had long been commissioned by royalty, the aristocracy and those who had amassed fortune enough to leave their mark on society. In nineteenth century Victorian society the newly-wealthy commissioned their own portrait cameos, often carved after photographs sent to Rome. A popular trend also existed in collecting cameo representations of historical figures such as Shakespeare, Mary, Queen of Scots and Dante; and images of contemporary notables, including the Romantic poets, novelists and politicians.

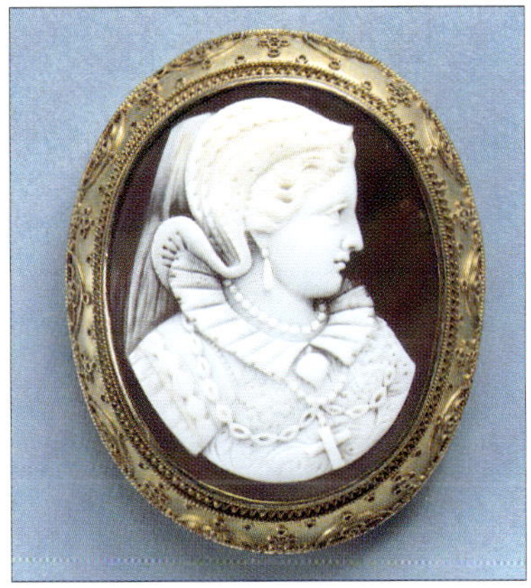

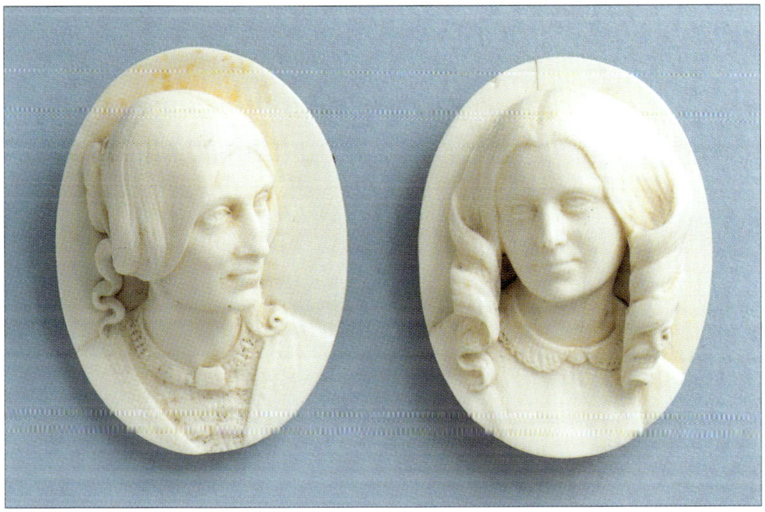

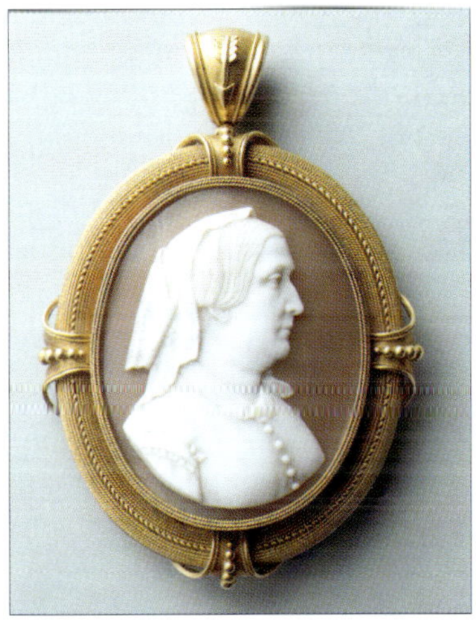

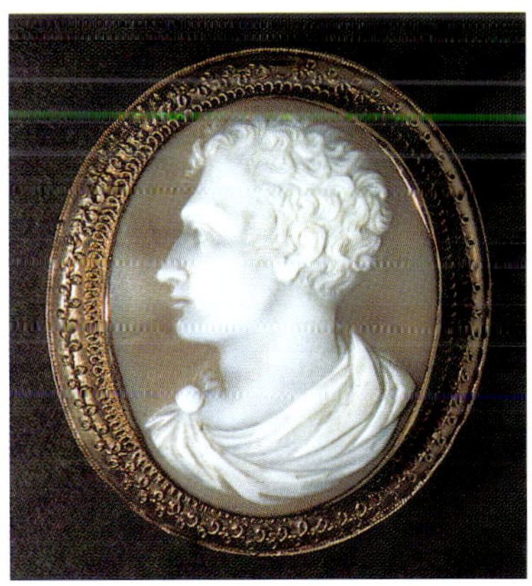

Plate 130 (above). *Two ivory carvings in high relief by Jacques-Pierre-Theodore Blard, 3in. (7.6cm) long x 2in. (5cm) wide, of left, Elizabeth Barrett (Mrs Browning), and right, Mrs Elizabeth Gaskell, signed Blard on the front of the carvings.* HISTORICAL PORTRAITS LTD

Plate 131 (above right). *Black Helmet shell portrait cameo of Mary, Queen of Scots. Gold with applied decoration, circa 1870.*

M. ROWAN AT www.rowanandrowan.com £650

Plate 132 (centre right). *Bull's Mouth shell, fine bloomed gold archaeological revival style mount, circa 1870. A female portrait, Florence Nightingale(?). 2¾in. (7cm) x 2⅛in. (5.5cm).* S. HARLOWE AT www.rowanandrowan.com £750

Plate 133 (below right). *Bull's Mouth shell, gilt archaeological revival mount, circa 1860-70, portraying the Romantic poet Lord Byron. 1½in. (4cm) x 1⅛in. (3cm).* FOX COLLECTION

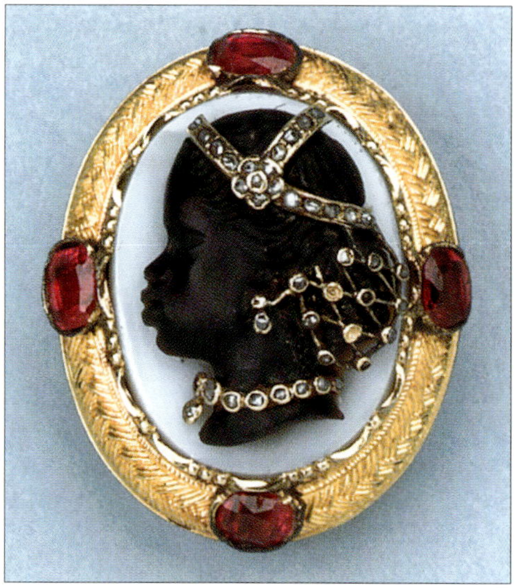

Plate 134. *Cameo* habillé, *gold and ruby mount, circa 1870, of a Nubian woman with diamond hair ornamentation and necklace, in the manner of Dafrique.*

KIERON REILLY COLLECTION, ANTIQUARIUS, LONDON

PURCHASING AND CARING FOR CAMEOS

A cameo collection can be based on a theme, material, period or a particular engraver. It may include all of these areas. The quality of the carving is of paramount importance. The best nineteenth century cameo compositions depict almost photo-realistic subjects, minutely detailed, comparable to fine sculpture. Condition is a major consideration, greatly affecting the value of the piece. However a beautiful carving should not be dismissed because of minor flaws. A jeweller's loupe is a useful tool to detect cracks, chips, stress and wear; typical areas to check on cameos are those in highest relief (noses, chins, headdresses, tips of wings etc.). Restoration will reduce the value of a piece and a loose antique cameo set in a modern mount obviously will be less valuable than an untouched original. For commercial reasons, pieces may also have been adapted, typically a stickpin converted to a ring, a single earring to a pendant, a cameo buckle to a brooch. These adaptations make the items wearable yet less favoured by the 'purist' collector. Important engravers signed their work, predominately on the obverse. Such signed pieces would be the jewels in any collection.

All cameos should be stored in protective containers. Shell, tortoiseshell, coral and ivory are particularly fragile, prone to stress and can become brittle if exposed to extreme changes in temperature. A small amount of almond oil gently rubbed into the shell will prolong its life and revive its lustre. A light detergent and a soft toothbrush may be used to clean the cameo but over-cleaning, bleaching and soaking are not recommended.

For any prospective purchaser of cameos, the study of museum collections is invaluable. In London we would recommend viewing the Hull Grundy Bequest at the British Museum and the Victoria & Albert Museum's Jewellery Gallery. Fine cameos can also be found at the Ashmolean in Oxford, the Fitzwilliam in Cambridge and at Windsor Castle and the Wedgwood Museum, Barlaston, Stoke-on-Trent. It is also helpful to consult and view the stock of reputable antique dealers in shops, antique centres and markets.

BIBLIOGRAPHY

Aghion, I., Barbillon, C., Lissarrague, F., *Gods and Heroes of Classical Antiquity*. Flammarion, Paris, 1996.

Anderson, B.W., *Gem Testing*. Butterworth & Co., London, 1980.

The Art Journal. George Virtue Publishers, London, 1854-1874.

Apuleius, Lucius, *The Golden Ass*, translated by Robert Graves. Penguin, London, 1990.

Artistical Directory to Rome, 1856. The Artistical Directory or Guide to the Studios of Italian and Foreign Painters.

Avery, C.B. (editor), *The New Century Classical Handbook*. Harrap & Co., London.

Bailey, Colin B., *The Loves of the Gods, Mythological Painting from Watteau to David*. Rizzoli, New York, 1992.

Becker, Vivienne, *Antique and Twentieth Century Jewellery*. Nag Press, Colchester, 1987.

Bennett, David and Mascetti, Daniela, *Understanding Jewellery*. Antique Collectors' Club, Woodbridge, 1989, to be reprinted 2004.

Biederman, Hans, *The Wordsworth Dictionary of Symbolism*. Wordsworth Reference, 1992.

Billing, Archibald, *The Science of Gems, Jewels, Coins and Medals*. Bell & Daldy, London, 1867.

Bremmer, J. (editor), *Interpretations of Greek Mythology*. Routledge, 1988.

Brewer, Rev. E. Cobham, *Dictionary of Phrase and Fable*. Cassell & Co. Ltd., London.

Bullfinch, Thomas, *Myths of Greece and Rome*. Complied by Bryan Holme with an Introduction by Joseph Campbell. Penguin, London, 1979.

Bury, Shirley, *Jewellery 1789-1910*, Vols. I and II. Antique Collectors' Club, Woodbridge, 1991.

Carr, Malcolm Stuart, 'Tommaso and Luigi Saulini'. *The Connoisseur*, Nov. 1975.

Clark, Kenneth, Introduction to *Hall's Dictionary of Subjects and Symbols in Art*. John Murray, London, 1996.

Collignon, Maxime, *Manual of Mythology in Relation to Greek Art*. H. Grevel & Co., London, 1890.

Davenport, Cyril, *Cameos*. Seeley & Co., London, 1900.

Eaton, Charlotte A., *Rome in the Nineteenth Century*, Vols. I and II, 5th edition, Henry H. Bohn, York St., Covent Garden, 1860.

Eichler, F. and Kris, E., *Die Kameen im Kunsthistorischen Museum*. Vienna, 1927.

Eicholz, D.E., *Pliny Natural History*. William Heinemann Ltd., Harvard U.P., 1962.

Folkard, Richard Junior, *Plant Lore, Legends and Lyric*. Sampson Low Marston Searl & Rivington, London, 1884.

Forrer, L., *Biographical Dictionary of Medallists*. Spink & Son, London, 1909.

Frenkel, W., *Pompei, Pompei Scavi, Valle de Pompei, Vesuvio, Ercolano, Torre del Greco, Castellammare de Stabia, Nuova Guida*. Torre del Greco, Italy, 1924.

Graves, Robert, *Greek Myths*. Cassell Ltd., London, 1981.

Gray, J.E., *Transactions of the Society for the Encouragement of Arts Manufactures and Commerce*, Supplemental Volume 'On the Manufacture of Shell Cameos'. London, 1852.

Grimal, Pierre, *Penguin Dictionary of Classical Mythology*. Penguin Books, London, 1991.

Hallam, Elizabeth, *Gods and Goddesses*. Blandford, London, 1997.

Haskell, F. and Penny, N., *Taste and the Antique. The Lure of Classical Sculpture, 1500-1900*. Yale University Press, New Haven and London, 1981.

Hawks Le Grice, Count, *Walks Through the Studii of the Sculptors at Rome, with a Brief Historical and Critical Sketch of Sculpture*. Rome, 1841.

Hesiod, The Homeric Hymns and Homerica, with an English translation by Hugh G. Evelyn-White. William Heinemann Ltd., London, MCMLXXVII.

Hesiod, *Theogony and Works and Days*. Translated with an Introduction and Notes by M.L. West. Oxford University Press, Oxford, 1988.

Higham, T.F., and Bowra, C.M. (editors), *The Oxford Book of Greek Verse in Translation*. Oxford University Press, London, 1953.

Hinks, Peter, *Nineteenth Century Jewellery*. Faber & Faber, London, 1975.

Hodge, Jessica, *Who's Who in Classical Mythology*. Smithmark, London, 1995.

Homer, The Iliad, translated by Robert Fagles, Penguin, New York, 1991.

The Iliad of Homer, translated and with an Introduction by Richard Lattimore. University of Chicago Press Ltd., London, 1976.

Hornblower, S. and Spawforth, A. (editors), *The Oxford Classical Dictionary* 3rd Edition. Oxford University Press, Oxford, New York, 1996.

Hunt, R., *Handbook to the Industrial Department of the International Exhibition 1862*, Vol. I. Edward Stanford, London, 1862.

Jenkyns, Richard, *The Victorians and Ancient Greece*. Basil Blackwell, Oxford, 1980.

Journal des Dames et des Modes. Francfort sur le Man. 1805.

King, Rev. C.W., *Antique Gems … Their Origin, Uses and Value as Interpreters of Ancient History; and as Illustrative of Ancient Art with Hints to Gem Collectors*. 1860.

King, Rev. C.W., *Handbook of Engraved Gems*. George Bell and Sons, London, 1885.

Levien, Edward, *Memoirs of Socrates for English Readers, A New Translation from Xenophon's 'Memorabilia'*. Sampson Low, Marston, Low & Searle, London, 1872.

Matthews, Henry, *The Diary of an Invalid being a Journal of a Tour in Pursuit of Health in Portugal, Italy, Switzerland and France in the Years 1817, 1818 and 1819*. Vol. 1, John Murray, London, MDCCCXXIV.

Meleèyard, Eliza, *Museum Etruriae*. Printed for James Boardman, Liverpool, 1817.

Murray, A.S., *A Catalogue of Engraved Gems in the British Museum*. British Museum, London, 1888.

Murray, J., *A Handbook for Travellers to Southern Italy*, 7th edition. John Murray, London, 1874.

Murray, J., *A Handbook of Rome and its Environs*. John Murray, London, 1881.

Newman, Harold, *An Illustrated Dictionary of Jewelry*. Thames & Hudson, London, 1981.

Osborne, Duffield, *Engraved Gems*. Henry Holt & Co., New York, 1912.

Ovid, *Metamorphoses*. Translated with an introduction by Mary M. Innes. Penguin, London, 1955.

Pausanius, *Guide to Greece*, Vols. I and II, translated with an Introduction by Peter Levi. Penguin, Harmandsworth, 1971.

Le Pitture Antiche D'Ercolano Esposte Napoli MDCCLXV. Nella Regia Stamperia, 1762.

Prendeville, J., *Photographic Facsimiles of the Antique Gems Formerly Possessed by the Late Prince Poniatowski*. Longman, Brown, Green, Longman & Roberts, 1857.

Raspe, R.E., *A Descriptive Catalogue of a General Collection of Ancient and Modern Engraved Gems, Cameos as well as Intaglios… by James Tassie*, Vols. I and II. Printed and sold for James Tassie, London, 1791.

Richter, G.M.A., *Catalogue of Engraved Gems*. Published for Metropolitan Museum of Art, New York by L'Erma di Bretschneider, Rome, 1956.

Righetti, Romolo, *Incisori di Gemme e Cammei in Roma dal Rinascimento all'Ottocento*. Fratelli Palombi, 1950.

Stosch, M. Philippe, *Gemmae Antiquae Caelatae*. MDCCXXIV Amsterdam (1724). Apud Bernardum Picartum.

Tait, Hugh (editor), *The Art of the Jeweller: A Catalogue of the Hull Grundy Gift to the British Museum*, Vols. I and II. British Museum, London, 1984.

Thiele, J.M., *Thorwaldsen and his Works*, Vols. I and II. John C. Unnevehr, New York, 1869.

Walters, H.B., *Catalogue of the Engraved Gems and Cameos Greek Etruscan and Roman in the British Museum*. British Museum, London, 1926.

Waring, J.B., *Masterpieces of Industrial Art and Sculpture at the International Exhibition 1862*. Day & Son, London, 1863.

Weber, Ingrid S., *Geschnittene Steine des 18. bis 20. Jahrhunderts*. Deutscher Kunstverlag, Germany, 1995.

West, M.L. (translator), *Greek Lyric Poetry*. Oxford University Press, Oxford, New York, 1994.

INDEX

Numbers in bold type refer to plate numbers

THE ANTIQUE COLLECTORS' CLUB

Formed in 1966, the Antique Collectors' Club is now a world-renowned publisher of top quality books for the collector. It also publishes the only independently-run monthly antiques magazine, *Antique Collecting*, which rose quickly from humble beginnings to a network of worldwide subscribers.

The magazine, whose motto is *For Collectors-By Collectors-About Collecting*, is aimed at collectors interested in widening their knowledge of antiques both by increasing their awareness of quality and by discussion of the factors influencing prices.

Subscription to Antique Collecting is open to anyone interested in antiques and subscribers receive ten issues a year. Well-illustrated articles deal with practical aspects of collecting and provide numerous tips on prices, features of value, investment potential, fakes and forgeries. Offers of related books at special reduced prices are also available only to subscribers.

In response to the enormous demand for information on 'what to pay', ACC introduced in 1968 the famous price guide series. The first title, *The Price Guide to Antique Furniture* (since renamed *British Antique Furniture: Price Guide and Reasons for Values*), is still in constant demand. Since those pioneering days, ACC has gone from strength to strength, publishing many of today's standard works of reference on all things antique and collectable, from *Tiaras* to *20th Century Ceramic Designers in Britain*.

Not only has ACC continued to cater strongly for its original audience, it has also branched out to produce excellent titles on many subjects including art reference, architecture, garden design, gardens, and textiles. All ACC's publications are available through bookshops worldwide and a catalogue is available free of charge from the addresses below.

For further information please contact:

ANTIQUE COLLECTORS' CLUB

www.antique-acc.com

Sandy Lane, Old Martlesham
Woodbridge, Suffolk IP12 4SD, UK
Tel: 01394 389950 Fax: 01394 389999
Email: info@antique-acc.com
or
Market Street Industrial Park
Wappingers' Falls, NY 12590, USA
Tel: 845 297 0003 Fax: 845 297 0068
Email: info@antiquecc.com

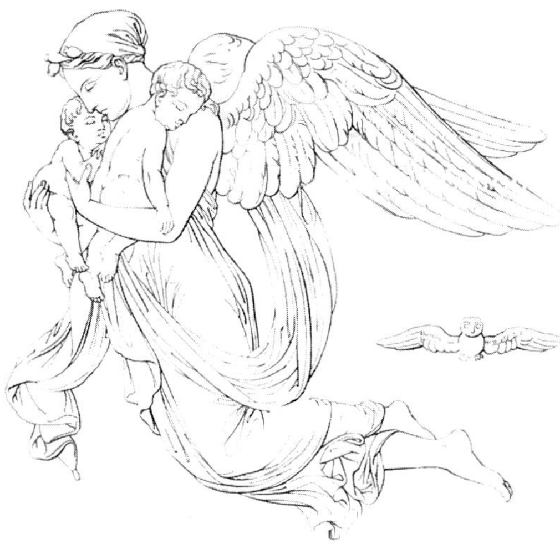

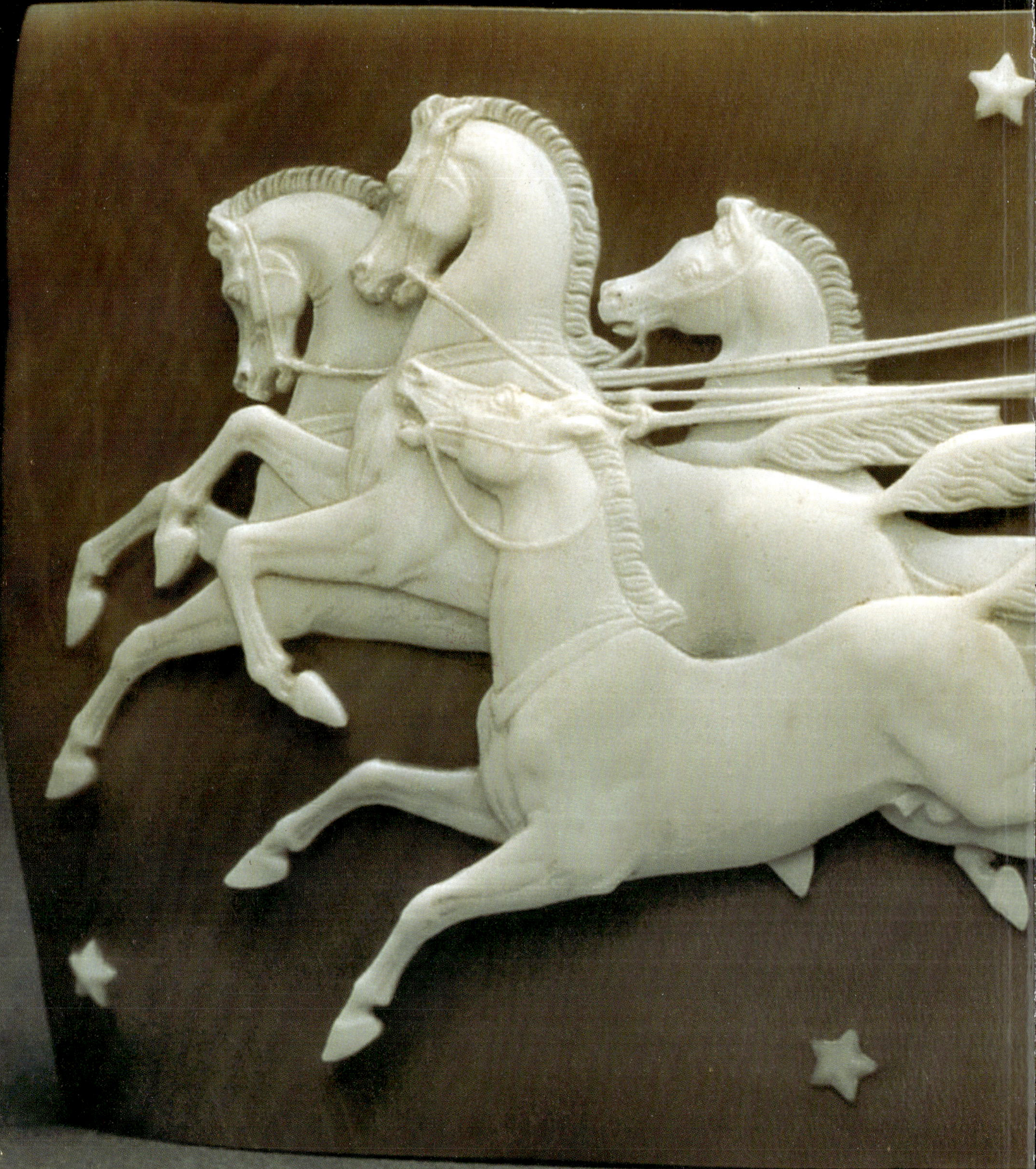